FROM FJORD TO FREEWAY

FROM FJORD TO FREEWAY

100 YEARS · AUGSBURG COLLEGE
By Carl H. Chrislock

AUGSBURG COLLEGE · MINNEAPOLIS

TABLE OF CONTENTS

FOREWORD

Augsburg's Centennial history, *From Fjord to Freeway*, is the first attempt in the past five decades to record in detail the development of the institution from its genesis to the present, and the only complete chronicle of the college in the English language.

A centennial history of a college is likely to be viewed by many, especially in this generation, as a sentimental journey, pursued by the romantic for the purpose of recalling old faces and remote events and for sorting out a few dubiously valuable souvenirs of information considered by some to be worth preserving. Had this been the aim of this Centennial history, I doubt whether Dr. Chrislock would have considered its writing worthy of his professional talent.

It is a fact, however, that when confronting the one hundred years of Augsburg's history, the historian is faced with a more formidable task than merely collecting and connecting data regarding the college. The object had to be to clarify for the uninformed reader why Augsburg did not more quickly develop into the college it had every opportunity to become, given its earliest direction, its favorable location, and its rich cultural and religious contexts. The uniqueness of this institutional history is not merely its description of an unmitigated struggle to remain alive, but its treatment of the equally intense and prolonged struggle actually to bring forth a modern liberal arts college as recently as 1954. All this the author has treated with accuracy, sensitivity, candor and a wry sense of humor.

In telling this college story without undue involvement in the history of Augsburg Seminary, no longer a part of Augsburg College, or of the Lutheran Free Church which surrounded Augsburg for seventy years, Dr. Chrislock has performed a necessary and vital service for the college at this Centennial juncture. For the long-time friend of Augsburg, he has shown that the modern evolution of the college has not been a departure from what was genuinely valid in the past. For the many members of the college's new sponsor, The American Lutheran Church, who have had no occasion to become acquainted with Augsburg, he has provided in readable fashion essential information about this newest member in a distinguished synodical family of colleges.

For the vast numbers of those who may be interested in yet are ignorant of Augsburg's history and academic effort, to say nothing of its whereabouts, but who may have been puzzled by the college's seemingly late emergence on the higher educational scene, he has supplied honest answers.

For the present and future Augsburg community, he has presented a splendid opportunity to recognize with gratitude what is valuable from the past, while setting a course which hopefully will avoid repeating its mistakes.

The scholarly and attention-holding character of this volume will provide ample support for the decision by the Centennial Committee in requesting Dr. Chrislock to undertake this history of Augsburg College. He was admirably fitted by experience and competence to assume the task. He is able to explore the vast amount of essential material in the Norwegian language. He has known, been a student of, or served on the faculty with five Augsburg presidents and thereby combines personal association and experience with careful research, especially in recording the important developments which have taken place in the last three and a half decades. His mark as an historian, teacher, author and academic leader has been made and recognized. In 1957 and 1958 he was awarded the Solon J. Buck Award by the Minnesota Historical Society for his contributions to *Minnesota History*. On leave from his duties as chairman of the department of history at Augsburg College for the past two years, he has given himself with characteristic concentration and thoroughness to the preparation of this Centennial opus. His students, colleagues and friends will gratefully acknowledge this solid piece of research and writing as a tribute to his skill as an historian and as a valuable contribution to Augsburg and its future. For Dr. Chrislock has made it abundantly clear to all of us that the Augsburg of the next one hundred years must be shaped more by the ready acceptance of dynamic change than by any deadly enslavement to continuity.

The importance of this book lies in its grasp of truth which can mean greater freedom for Augsburg in its second century of education for service.

Oscar A. Anderson
President

Augsburg College
Minneapolis, Minnesota
August, 1969

PREFACE

My involvement with the centennial history of Augsburg began as a limited commitment — I had originally agreed to edit a volume of essays dealing with selected aspects of the school's development. When this approach failed to develop the publications committee of the Augsburg College Centennial Commission authorized the present work. The arrangement included a stipulation giving me complete freedom to interpret Augsburg's history in accordance with the findings of my research, a condition that was fully met. At the same time I assume full responsibility for all judgments pronounced and whatever errors may mar the text.

Several other acknowledgments also are due. Without the able help of Mrs. Theresa Gervais Haynes the volume could never have been produced. In addition to researching English-language sources, Mrs. Haynes edited the text; typed successive drafts of the manuscript; conducted negotiations with the printer; arranged the picture layout; supervised publicity; and assumed major responsibility for proofreading and indexing.

Conversations with the late Dr. Theodore C. Blegen yielded valuable insights with respect to Augsburg and Norwegian-American history generally. Miss Gerda Mortensen arranged interviews with individuals possessing knowledge of Augsburg's past, and always was available for consultation. Martin Quanbeck, chairman of the publication committee, read the entire manuscript and offered suggestions to improve it. Oscar A. Anderson, Kenneth C. Bailey, and Merrill E. Jarchow also read the work; Bernhard M. Christensen, Eugene M. Fevold, and Paul G. Sonnack perused the opening chapters. Discussions with Einar O. Johnson clarified the similarities and differences between the original academic programs of Augsburg and Luther College. John B. Mosand capably supervised the book's unique graphic design.

A generous contribution from Marvin F. Borgelt, member of the Augsburg College board of regents, helped finance the project. A donation by the Augsburg College Women's Craft Shop was applied to photo processing expenses. Miss Agnes B. Tangjerd, Augsburg College archivist until her retirement in June, 1968 rendered valuable assistance in locating sources. I am indebted to my colleagues in the history department for assuming some of my duties, thereby releasing time for work on the book. I also thank the many individuals who provided both encouragement and information while research and writing was in progress.

Finally, a special acknowledgement is due Miss Marilyn Petersen of our placement office, who suggested the book's appropriate title: "From Fjord to Freeway."

Carl H. Chrislock
July, 1969

IN THE BEGINNING

IN THE EARLY decades of its existence, Augsburg College was one of the three departments constituting Augsburg Seminary, a training school for Lutheran ministers founded in 1869 by a group of Norwegian immigrants to the United States. The other two were a preparatory department which later became Augsburg Academy — a high school — and a three-year theological department that in time came to be called Augsburg Theological Seminary.

Augsburg Seminary's claim to uniqueness rested largely on the theoretical unity of its three departments. As a 1908 catalog statement put it, "The three departments of the Seminary are . . . one in purpose and not distinct schools." [1] Together they made up what Augsburg spokesmen called a *"Presteskole,"* a ministerial training school. Before the turn of the century the preparatory department "as a rule" limited admission to applicants who had "some thoughts of entering the service of the Church." The program of the college department was "specially designed for those who [had] the ministry in view." And the theological department, which completed the ministerial candidate's formal education, claimed to offer "a thorough and scientific course of three years in Theology." [2]

After 1900 the college and preparatory departments came under increasing pressure to serve needs other than theological preparation. Before long this pressure began to erode the tripartite *"Presteskole"* concept, and gradually the college emerged in fact, though not immediately in theory, as an entity in its own right. Up to 1916 the catalog name of the institution had been Augsburg Seminary; thereafter it became Augsburg College and Theological Seminary, a change that was belatedly formalized in 1942. The 1917 catalog altered the time-honored preparatory department, college department, and theological department designations to read Augsburg Academy, Augsburg College, and Augsburg Theological Seminary. More important, in the period from 1916 to 1922 the institution replaced its essentially non-elective classical college course — which primarily emphasized languages — with a modern college pro-

1

gram based on general education requirements and elective majors. It also sought to win accreditation as a liberal arts college — a goal that was achieved by stages — adopted coeducation, made an effort to upgrade the faculty, and entered intercollegiate athletic competition.

This transformation profoundly affected the relationship of the college both to the academy and theological seminary. In the 1920s the college became less dependent on the academy as a feeder, and a declining proportion of its graduates enrolled in the theological seminary.[3] The college, in other words, was becoming the vital center of the institution. In 1933 the academy went out of existence. The theological seminary continued operation on the campus until 1963, when it merged with Luther Theological Seminary in St. Paul as part of the merger agreement between the Lutheran Free Church, Augsburg's synodical sponsor, and the American Lutheran Church. At the same time, the official name of the institution was changed from Augsburg College and Theological Seminary to Augsburg College.

SOON AFTER its first contingents arrived in the United States in the 1830s and 1840s, Norwegian Lutheranism split into several factions. By 1860 three distinct camps had formed. The Evangelical Lutheran Church in America — founded in 1846, and commonly called the Elling Eielsen Synod after its founder — represented the American followers of Hans Nielsen Hauge, the late 18th and early 19th century lay preacher who helped transform the religious life of Norway. In line with the Haugean tradition, the Eielsen Synod placed strong stress on personal conversion, tended to distrust a learned clergy, and favored a low church form of worship. After a schism in the 1870s that separated Eielsen from most of his followers, the Eielsen Synod became Hauge's Norwegian Evangelical Lutheran Synod in America (Hauge Synod) which in 1879 established Red Wing Seminary at Red Wing, Minnesota, as its chief educational institution.[4]

Meanwhile, in 1853 the confessional wing of Norwegian Lutheranism in America had organized the Norwegian Synod (The Norwegian Evangelical Lutheran Synod in America), a church body that in 1861 founded Luther College at Decorah, Iowa. The Norwegian Synod emphasized doctrinal purity, defended the prerogatives of ordained clergy, held to traditional forms of Lutheran worship, and took a dim view of lay preaching. It maintained a close relationship with the German Lutheran Missouri Synod, with which it had an arrangement for the training of Norwegian Synod clergy in Concordia Seminary at St. Louis.[5]

The founders of Augsburg Seminary belonged to a third group that

2

prized both the Haugean legacy and fidelity to the Lutheran confessions, but disliked the extreme positions taken by the Haugeans and the Norwegian Synod. After a brief attempt at cooperation with the Eielsen Synod, pioneer members of this middle group in 1851 joined with other Swedish and English-speaking Lutherans to found the Northern Illinois Synod. At this synod's school, misleadingly named Illinois State University, the prominent Swedish-American clergyman and educator, L. P. Esbjörn, represented Scandinavian interests. The Norwegian-Swedish element maintained the Northern Illinois affiliation until 1860 when it separated from the English-speaking group to form the Scandinavian Augustana Synod, a step dictated both by theological differences and language complications. In the same year, founders of the new synod established Augustana College and Theological Seminary, located in Chicago. Three years later this institution moved to Paxton, Illinois, where it remained until 1875 when it relocated at Rock Island, Illinois, its permanent home.[6]

Basically Norse-Swedish relations within the Scandinavian Augustana Synod were harmonious. But a dissimilar cultural outlook and, above all, language differences frustrated the Norwegians, who were junior partners in the enterprise. As a Norse clergyman put it, Norwegian-American ministers trained at Augustana spoke a mongrel tongue that failed to qualify as either Norwegian or Swedish.[7] To ease the problem, Augustana Seminary in 1868 called the Reverend August Weenaas from Norway to serve as Norwegian theological professor. Weenaas accepted the post, taking up his duties in the fall of 1868.[8]

The Weenaas expedient may have allayed Norwegian discontent to some extent, but Norse spokesmen believed their problem remained unresolved. At the 1869 Annual Conference of the Scandinavian Augustana Synod, held at Moline, Illinois in June, a meeting of delegates representing the Augustana Norse-speaking congregations proposed the establishment of a separate seminary, a proposition adopted by the Annual Conference at a plenary session. Thereupon, a Norse division of the synod reassembled and, among other things, elected Weenaas president of the embryonic institution, selected a board of trustees and a board of directors (*Skoledirektionen*, a body having responsibility for matters relating to the curricular program and on which President Weenaas served *ex officio*). It also authorized the trustees to purchase an available school building at Marshall, Wisconsin, as a site for the projected seminary, providing suitable terms could be negotiated.[9] The new school was known by a variety of names, including Marshall College, Marshall Seminary and Academy, or simply the Theological Seminary at Marshall, until a reconvened meeting of the Scandinavian Augustana Synod Norse delegates, held at Racine, Wisconsin, in late October, 1869, resolved that the institution be called Augsburg Seminarium.[10]

As may be inferred, this name commemorated the German Free City of Augsburg where in 1530 the Augsburg Confession (*Confessio Augustana*), generally regarded as the foundation creed of the Lutheran church, was officially presented to Emperor Charles V. Weenaas recognized that a name like Augsburg may not have sufficiently underscored the Norse origins of the institution.[11] But it did clearly identify the new seminary as Lutheran, and it recognized the descent from Augustana College and Theological Seminary — Augustana being the Latin equivalent of Augsburg.

The Moline convention of June, 1869, established the new seminary on paper. To put it into operation by September required a summer of busy activity. Shortly after adjournment of the Moline meeting, the trustees negotiated an agreement to purchase the Marshall Academy property, an agreement obligating the seminary administration to operate the academy as a private American secondary school. Money also was an urgent consideration, and the multiplicity of routine preparations necessary to set an educational machine into motion had to be made. Time did not permit completion of all these preliminaries; nevertheless, on September 1, 1869, classes opened as scheduled.[12]

IN A MEMOIR published twenty years after the founding of Augsburg Seminary, August Weenaas affirmed: "There were . . . many difficulties which we as founders had to overcome at Marshall." [13] This remark understated the case. During the three years that Augsburg remained at Marshall, it faced the usual problems confronting 19th century denominational schools — inadequate financial resources, unavailability of competent faculty, and lack of even minimal academic preparation on the part of entering students.

In addition, Weenaas found the task of administering a Lutheran theological seminary in conjunction with an essentially non-sectarian American academy extremely distasteful. As he put it, "We had . . . only unpleasantness and loss from this American institution." Academy enrollment fell far short of furnishing the tuition money required to finance its operation, and Weenaas found the academy students, both men and women, "difficult to control. . . . I was," he added, "committed to an entirely different goal than conducting school for Americans." [14] Moreover, controversy concerning the role of Marshall Academy in the educational program of the church accentuated dissension within the Norwegian division of the Scandinavian Augustana Synod.[15]

This dissension reached the breaking point in the summer of 1870. In that year the Annual Conference of the Scandinavian Augustana Synod approved a step that had been discussed for several years and had been foreshadowed by the founding of Augsburg Seminary: the amicable division of the synod into two independent church groups, the one Swedish and the other basically Norwegian with a small Danish contingent. Before formal completion of arrangements for the separation, the Norwegian division split into two irreconcilable factions which presently organized two synods, the Conference (officially the Conference of the Norwegian-Danish Evangelical Lutheran Church in America), and the Norwegian Augustana Synod. A scramble for synodical assets followed. Thanks largely to Weenaas and the students' loyalty to him, Augsburg Seminary affiliated with the Conference. The academy proper which, after several moves and consolidations with other institutions ultimately became Augustana College at Sioux Falls, South Dakota, was placed under the control of the Norwegian Augustana Synod.[16]

This schism and its accompaniments freed Weenaas of the disagreeable responsibility of managing Marshall Academy. But Augsburg Seminary experienced considerably more loss than gain from the turn of events. It lost a substantial part of a precariously narrow supporting base. Worst of all, the Weenaas flock found itself without a home. On October 17, 1870, the Marshall Academy Principal, J. J. Anderson, appeared in Weenaas' office with a letter from the president of the Norwegian Augustana Synod ordering Weenaas to deliver the building's key to Anderson and to vacate the seminary operation forthwith. Weenaas' refusal of this demand no doubt would have resulted in a legal suit. However, he chose to comply. He later explained that he found it both wise and consistent with the Christian spirit to leave the building in the possession of the Norwegian Augustana Synod and permit the academy's continuance.[17]

Lack of available structures in Marshall, a sleepy village near Madison with few prospects of becoming an urban center, complicated the problem of finding a new seminary site. Weenaas lodged from ten to twelve of the twenty students in his own home for the remainder of the school year; the others obtained rooms wherever they could. A small attic, measuring ten by eighteen feet and eight feet high was leased from a farmer named Cooper, to serve as combined classroom, chapel, and student center.[18]

In later years the Cooper attic phase of Augsburg's history provided material for a heroic legend. Both Weenaas and his students nostalgically recalled the period as a time of creative hardship that tested their own religious commitment and the will of their institution to survive.[19] The challenge they faced went beyond temporary endurance of physical limitations; the broader question was whether the school could continue. Obtaining new quarters was impossible so long as available resources failed to meet even basic operating needs. At the close of the 1870–71 academic year, the greater part of Weenaas' salary remained unpaid, other financial obligations were accumulating, and the supporting congregations seemed unable or unwilling to honor pledges of monetary support.[20]

Among the forces that worked to overcome the 1871 crisis, the leadership of President Weenaas deserves considerable credit. It may be that Augsburg tradition has failed to do justice to the school's founder. The massive reputation of the Georg Sverdrup-Sven Oftedal team, Weenaas' immediate successors in Augsburg leadership, has to a large extent obscured the pioneer president. Equally important, disagreement between Weenaas on the one hand and Sverdrup and Oftedal on the other clouded the Weenaas departure from Augsburg in 1876, and later interpretations of this episode have, on the whole, favored the Sverdrup-Oftedal point of view.[21]

The particular Weenaas trait that commanded the admiration of both friend and adversary was an immense capacity for work. While the seminary remained at Marshall, he taught all the theological courses offered, participated in the preparatory instruction, managed the institution's administrative routine, and served as pastor of six widely scattered congregations. From Monday through Saturday he labored at teaching and administration duties; on Sunday he preached morning and evening to outlying congregations, often taking his night's rest either aboard a returning train or on a railway station bench. He also found time to write regularly for the church press, and to participate actively in Conference affairs.[22]

This staggering work load no doubt reduced the efficiency of Weenaas' pedagogical and administrative performance. Nevertheless, he managed to communicate to his students a basic enthusiasm for the seminary and its mission that in turn sustained him. At the close of the 1870–71 school year Weenaas, yielding momentarily to ultimate discouragement, called the students together to inform them that the school would have to discontinue operation. They refused to accept this decision, however, and their attitude persuaded the president to change his mind.[23]

Notwithstanding its delinquency in extending financial support — a weakness that would persist into the future — the Conference was no more willing than the students to consider the liquidation of Augsburg. The tide of immigration was bringing to the United States thousands of Norwegians who needed spiritual ministration; and the hostility of the powerful Norwegian Synod to rival church bodies stimulated Conference élan. The second annual convention of the Conference, which assembled at Minneapolis in early June, 1871, did not debate the issue of whether or not the school should continue, but where it should relocate. The convention chose Minneapolis over Madison, Wisconsin, with the understanding that Minneapolis citizens stood ready to provide a building site and a fund of $4,000, a contribution that supposedly would cover the entire cost of the projected campus.[24]

The initiative taken by Pastor Ole Paulson of Trinity Lutheran Congregation at Minneapolis largely predetermined this decision. Two years earlier Charles E. Vanderburgh, a Minnesota district court judge, had suggested to Paulson, his friend and neighbor, that Scandinavian-Americans should adopt Minneapolis as their cultural center and, among other things, establish an educational institution in the city.[25] Following a special meeting of Conference leaders at Madison in March, 1871, which recommended that a new location be sought for Augsburg, Paulson, remembering past conversations with Vanderburgh, turned to the judge for help. Vanderburgh responded by inviting a number of prominent Minneapolis citizens to a meeting in his office on April 13, 1871. The participants endorsed a city-wide fund drive to finance the relocation of Augsburg at Minneapolis, and they commissioned Paulson to organize the campaign.[26]

Paulson went to work immediately and quickly obtained substantial promises of land, building materials, and cash. The larger pledges included six town lots, the nucleus of the Augsburg campus, four of them donated by Edward Murphy, one by Judge Vanderburgh, and one by Eugene M. Wilson. Cash commitments of $250 each were pledged by three well-known Minneapolis leaders, William D. Washburn, William S. King, and Dorilus Morrison. Promises of building material came from a number of firms. With these commitments in hand, Paulson easily persuaded the June convention to choose Minneapolis rather than Madison. The convention selected Paulson to head a building committee vested with virtually full authority over the details of the venture.[27]

Augsburg's first development program soon encountered rough going. The Minneapolis economic outlook was temporarily clouded in 1871. For some time the base sustaining St. Anthony Falls had threatened to give way, a situation that not only required a costly engineering effort, but also cast a shadow over the city's future. Paulson found additional building fund contributions difficult to obtain, and pledges already given hard to collect. His report to the 1872 Conference convention estimated that a total of $4,708 had been contributed of which only $1,493 was in cash. The remainder included the market value of the six lots, donated building material, and scattered land tracts some distance from the projected campus.[28]

Nevertheless, the Paulson committee proceeded to fulfill its mandate. By the autumn of 1871 the Trinity pastor had assembled enough brick, mortar, and wood to begin construction. He ignored the grim reality that not one penny was on deposit in the building fund and borrowed $60 on his own credit from Karen Danielson, a young servant girl. This sum financed laying the foundation of what later became the west wing of the first Old Main, a structure located at what would become the corner of 7th Street and 21st Avenue South.[29]

Although the onset of winter precluded further work in 1871, a visible foundation encouraged delinquent pledgers to honor their commitments. The 1872 Conference convention also promised monetary help.[30] While the financial situation remained stringent, enough funds dribbled in to permit the resumption of construction in the spring. By late summer the building, a three-story structure with combined classroom, dormitory, and dining facilities was ready for occupancy, and the first academic year in Minneapolis opened on September 15, 1872.[31]

MINNEAPOLIS opened fresh opportunities for Augsburg Seminary, offering several advantages over the Marshall location. The school now operated closer to the center of Norwegian-American settlement. Vast areas of western and northwestern Minnesota were being preempted by Scandinavian farmers in the 1870s. One Norwegian-American writer asserts — with some exaggeration — that by the middle 1880s a traveler could walk from Fergus Falls, Minnesota, to the Canadian border without stepping off land under Norwegian-American ownership. To a greater extent than the older Norse-American communities in Wisconsin, Iowa, and southeast Minnesota, where the Norwegian Synod had an established dominance, the region north and west of the Twin Cities lay open to the influence of the Conference, Augsburg's synodical sponsor. The Norwegian Synod, to be sure, also organized congregations in the Red River Valley, and the Conference maintained several strongholds in Iowa and southern Minnesota, but the center of Conference gravity lay farther west than that of the Norwegian Synod.

The growth potential of Minneapolis also augured well for Augsburg. Although a number of difficulties, including the danger to the falls, conspired to make the 1870s a troubled decade in the history of Minneapolis and St. Anthony (which in 1872 merged to form a greater Minneapolis), a potent combination of waterpower, lumber, railroads, wheat, immigration, a vast hinterland, Yankee enterprise, and the University of Minnesota promised the rise of a substantial city.[32]

In addition, Minneapolis showed an interest in Augsburg. Without the help of Minneapolis citizens the institution scarcely could have relocated. Mayor Eugene M. Wilson accepted an invitation to speak at the ceremony dedicating the new campus on October 31, 1872. He thanked the leaders of the school for their pioneering enterprise: "you of the Scandinavian race have taken the lead in giving us a Theological Institution." He also remarked that "Any class of emigrants [sic] can be better trusted who are accompanied by their ministers. . . ."[33]

Although the move to Minneapolis would mark a major turning point for Augsburg, the immediate break in the continuity of its development was not drastic. The new campus was more commodious than the cramped facilities at Marshall, but the setting was equally rural. Neither residential nor commercial expansion had yet reached the future Cedar-Riverside area of Minneapolis, then a city of approximately 20,000. To the north and west a large open space, part prairie and part swamp, separated the campus from the settled section of the city, a cluster of modest structures in the vicinity of St. Anthony Falls. A scant three blocks to the east, the Mississippi River flowed southward. Professor John H. Blegen, a member of the Augsburg faculty from 1885 to 1916, who arrived as a student in 1875, recalls that "On the south side there was not a single house so far as the eye could see, except a decrepit uninhabited cabin" which, according to rumor, was haunted.[34]

Vital statistics for 1872–73 reinforce the impression of continuity between Marshall and Minneapolis. The faculty still consisted of Weenaas and an assistant. Enrollment that year was 24, the same as for the previous year. And both preparatory and theological courses of study remained substantially unchanged.[35]

Nevertheless, a more optimistic spirit became evident in 1872–73. Faculty expansion, a need that had worried supporters of the school since its founding, now seemed attainable. The 1873 Conference convention commissioned President Weenaas and M. Falk Gjertsen, the future pastor of Trinity Congregation at Minneapolis, to search Norway for additional professorial talent during the summer of that year.[36] They

9

recruited Sven Oftedal, who joined the faculty shortly after his arrival at Minneapolis in October, 1873.[37]

Oftedal was born at Stavanger, Norway, in 1844. Following completion of his secondary education at the Stavanger Latin School, where his father taught, he studied languages, philosophy, and theology at several European universities. In 1871 he graduated from the theological school at the University of Christiania (Oslo). By this time his basic values and commitments had taken shape. Like many young Norwegians of his generation, he was profoundly critical of his country's ecclesiastical and political *status quo*. He strongly identified with reformers who were working for renovation of the Norwegian state church and democratization of Norway's political life.[38]

Soon after unpacking his bags, Oftedal made his presence felt, not only at Augsburg, but also within the Lutheran church and the Norwegian-American community. Four months after his arrival, he and Weenaas published in *Skandinaven*, a Norwegian-language newspaper with a wide circulation, a manifesto known as *"Aapen Erklaering"* (Public Declaration) that, among other things, charged the Norwegian Synod with representing an "anti-Christian tendency." Although this polemic — which ironically was issued to refute rumors that Oftedal secretly sympathized with the Norwegian Synod — explicitly foreswore animosity toward "individual persons, either ministers or congregational members," its appearance aggravated hostility between the Conference and the Norwegian Synod. Since several Conference leaders disliked the tone of the Public Declaration and questioned some of the argument, it also planted dissension within Augsburg's supporting church. Weenaas subsequently withdrew his endorsement of the document, thereby adding to a growing rift between the founder on the one hand and Oftedal and Georg Sverdrup on the other.[39]

Five weeks after the Public Declaration appeared, *Skandinaven* carried another Oftedal blast. This time the new Augsburg professor sharply disputed claims that Norwegian-Americans had reached a high level of cultural sophistication. The opposite was true, wrote Oftedal. Norwegian-Americans were blessed with great potential, he argued, but the blighting influence of the Norwegian Synod clergy and the Norwegian-language press was blocking any visible Norse contribution to the development of the Middle West.[40]

While establishing himself as a controversialist, Oftedal also became involved in a multitude of other activities outside of the classroom. Following his ordination in early 1874 he assumed the pastorate of Trinity Congregation which he held until 1877. He became president of the

Augsburg Board of Trustees in June, 1874, a post he continued to fill, with the exception of a single year, until his death in 1911. In addition, he soon emerged as a local civic leader. In 1878, only five years after his arrival in the United States and shortly before he received his final citizenship papers, he won election to the Minneapolis Board of Education.

According to Professor Andreas Helland, historian of Augsburg's first fifty years, Oftedal's presence at Augsburg "brought not only additional help but also new impulses." [41] During the 1873–74 academic year, Weenaas and his board of directors formulated for presentation to the 1874 Conference convention a plan for institutional expansion in three areas: faculty, plant, and instruction. The extent of Oftedal's involvement in the development of the new design cannot be determined; at the very least it is probable that the exuberance of the new professor helped foster a climate favoring innovation and expansion. In any case, the 1874 Conference convention enthusiastically accepted the plan. [42]

The first point of the plan proposed that Sven Rud Gunnersen and Georg Sverdrup, two close friends of Oftedal whom he highly recommended, be invited to join the faculty. Both men accepted. They arrived at Minneapolis on August 17, in time to begin classes when the 1874–75 school year opened in September. [43]

Gunnersen and Sverdrup had much in common with each other, and with Oftedal. Their academic backgrounds were similar — theological training at Christiania, together with brief periods at Continental universities — and all three supported the ecclesiastical reform movement in their homeland. Weenaas later characterized them as a "new triumvirate in which Sverdrup was the mind, Gunnersen the heart, and Oftedal the spirit." [44] Although this remark was not meant to commend the three professors, it conveys a convincing interpretation. Oftedal certainly personified "spirit" in the sense that this term is usually understood. Gunnersen is more obscure. Unfortunately, misunderstanding between him and the Oftedal-Sverdrup team soon dissolved the triumvirate, and after several years of uneasy coexistence with his colleagues, Gunnersen left Augsburg in 1883. While he remained at the school, he became known as an effective teacher, but his temperament apparently shrank from the continuous combat that marred — or enlivened — Norwegian-American church politics in the 1870s and 1880s. Helland writes that Gunnersen readily descended "from sunny heights into dark valleys." [45]

Sverdrup, who had spent one year at Erlangen University in Germany and one year at Paris, was five years younger than Oftedal and Gunnersen. Although he preferred the seclusion of a study to the disorder of the market place, Sverdrup's zest for controversy equaled Oftedal's. In his later years he often said that he "enjoyed nothing better than to walk against a snowstorm."[46] But Sverdrup was scarcely a rebel without a cause. He brought to the New World a set of clearcut commitments which were rooted in a distinguished family tradition, and reinforced by association with the Church reform party in Norway.

The first Georg Sverdrup, great uncle of the Augsburg professor, presided over the 1814 Eidsvold assembly, which produced Norway's modern constitution. His father, Harald Ulrich Sverdrup, was a prominent clergyman who combined service to the church with a political career; he served for many years as a member of the *Storthing*, Norway's parliament. Johan Sverdrup, brother of Harald Ulrich, held a position in Norwegian politics somewhat comparable to that of William E. Gladstone in Great Britain. A lawyer by profession, a passionate civil libertarian, and the acknowledged leader of Norway's Liberal party, Johan was moving to the summit of his career during his nephew's first decade at Augsburg, becoming Norwegian Prime Minister in 1884. His cabinet included another member of the family, Georg's older brother, Jakob Liv Rosted Sverdrup, who served as Minister of Church and Education.[47]

The reform program championed by the Sverdrups in Norway touched education and church affairs as well as politics. In broad terms it advocated the extension of "practical" education, revitalization of the Norwegian state church, strengthening of parliamentary institutions, and extension of the suffrage. Early in life, Johan developed an intense enthusiasm for the French Revolutionary tradition. Along with other members of the family, he believed that the establishment of social and political equality would not subvert Christianity — as many 19th century Lutheran clergymen feared — but that democracy could, and probably would, revitalize the nation's religious life.[48] Georg frequently developed this thesis after he reached the United States.[49]

Thanks to the second part of the 1874 school plan, Gunnersen and Sverdrup were able to move their families into new quarters shortly after arriving at Minneapolis. Their home was a three-family residence — Oftedal occupied the third apartment — facing what became 21st Avenue, immediately south of the main building where Weenaas lived. The plan also called for the addition to the main building of a five-story center section and a three-story east wing with a full basement. Completion of this project in the spring of 1875 added substantial classroom, dormitory, and other facilities.

The third section of the school plan dealt with curriculum and instruction. Its most important provision converted the pre-theological division of the seminary into a full-fledged preparatory school offering courses on two levels, one of which became Augsburg Academy and the other Augsburg College. The adoption of this part of the 1874 plan, rather than the action of the 1869 Scandinavian Augustana Conference, marked the founding of Augsburg College.

THE SEARCH FOR A
COLLEGE PROGRAM

IMMIGRANT ADAPTATION to American life involved, among other things, the problem of identity. Permanent migration from a European homeland may have been a declaration of intent to change nationality, but the values and ways of the old country could not be discarded by a mere act of will. In addition, arriving immigrants held divergent views on the issue of how rapidly and completely they should enter the mainstream of American culture. A confessional religious commitment, for example, worked for the preservation of Old World identity. Adherents of church groups that insisted on the importance of understanding and accepting specific theological formulations avoided association with other denominations, and also tended to believe that continued fidelity to the creeds depended in large measure on the maintenance of the old language and culture.

This, in turn, had significant implications for education. The founders of the highly confessional Norwegian Synod made an effort to model Luther College on the Norwegian Latin School (or *Gymnasium*), an institution whose course of study heavily stressed classical languages and literature.[1] The Norwegian Synod also promoted the establishment of a system of Lutheran elementary education designed to preserve the young in the "true" faith. Neither attempt completely succeeded. For many years the Luther College curriculum continued to give the classics an important place, but in other respects Luther yielded to American norms and standards.[2] The elementary school project failed even to get underway; by and large, Norwegian-Americans preferred to educate their children in the public schools.[3]

The Haugeans did not share Norwegian Synod hostility to the public schools. Elling Eielsen, their first leader, counseled his followers to give their children English instruction "in such a way that the district school is not neglected." [4] However, higher education, whether private or public, theological, pre-theological, or non-theological, was of little concern

14

to the first Haugean generation. Personal religious experience and strong commitment were the essential attributes of a Haugean spiritual leader — in fact, a number of pioneer Hauge Synod ministers were ordained without formal theological training.[5] Before long a more positive appreciation of higher education began to develop within the flock, but not until 1879, when Red Wing Seminary was founded, did the Haugeans succeed in permanently establishing their own institution of higher learning.

As on other issues, the educational policy of the Scandinavian Augustana Synod followed a course approximately midway between that of the Haugeans and the Norwegian Synod. Like the Haugeans, the Augustana group regarded the public elementary school as an agency that would help their children adapt to American life, and worthy of support. On the other hand, the establishment both of a seminary and an institution offering pre-theological instruction commanded high priority in Augustana thinking. It will be recalled that the Scandinavian Augustana Synod and Augustana College and Theological Seminary were founded simultaneously in 1860.

Operation of Augustana College in conjunction with the seminary, an arrangement regarded by some Augustana spokesmen as a perpetuation of the Old World university plan, was in a sense more European than the Luther College pattern which involved no direct seminary connection. However, Augustana College did not use the European Latin school as a guiding model. From its early days it offered a modern American college program, which in the 1860s and 1870s meant more courses in natural science and modern literature than the curriculum of the classically oriented Latin school permitted.[6]

SHORTLY AFTER arriving at Augustana in 1868 to take up his duties as Norwegian theological professor, August Weenaas registered emphatic objection to the institution's college program. His memoir recalls "unpleasant arguments" between himself and Professor Sidney L. Harkey, a strong proponent of the school's modern curriculum. "In [Harkey's] presence," writes Weenaas, "I expressed my contempt for this humbug." According to Weenaas, the "Yankee" retorted by asking if his colleague desired the seminary "to be merely a 'Mission School,' " to which Weenaas replied that "a good mission school was exactly what our circumstances required."[7]

Weenaas' view of pre-theological education was less rigid and dogmatic than his exchange with Harkey might indicate.[8] His dislike of the institution's college program, to be sure, was one reason for the separation from Augustana that brought Augsburg into existence.[9] But Weenaas objected to the program on practical rather than ideological — or theological — grounds. A wish to prepare clergy immediately for service in the multiplying Norwegian-American settlements throughout the Midwest dominated his thinking, and a lengthy period of ministerial training worked against this goal. Weenaas conceded that a comprehensive educational program might be appropriate for younger men, but mature students, he thought, should be permitted to qualify for the ministry as soon as possible.[10] Significantly, he did not argue that a modern college education might subvert the faith of the theological candidate; after the founding of Augsburg he showed a willingness to experiment with a variety of designs for pre-theological education.

The stipulation in the 1869 Marshall Academy purchase agreement obligating Augsburg Seminary to operate the academy as an American institution created the setting for the first preparatory school experiment. In the autumn of 1869 the Augsburg board of directors, with Weenaas as chairman, framed a constitution for Marshall Academy which the October, 1869 Racine meeting of the Scandinavian Augustana Synod's Norse division approved with a number of significant changes. The original draft of this document reflects the kind of relationship that Weenaas and his associates sought to establish between academy and seminary.[11]

The Racine convention adopted the first paragraph of the constitution in its proposed form: "The Norwegian division of the Augustana Synod establishes in combination with the theological seminary an academy based on the American model which, as soon as circumstances permit, will be expanded into a full-fledged college." However, convention action profoundly altered paragraph two, the original draft of which defined the task of the academy as being "partly to serve as a preparatory school for the theological seminary, partly and chiefly to educate proficient teachers for the public schools, and partly to provide young men and women with a good general education." The convention deleted the phrase "partly to serve as a preparatory school for the theological seminary," a change that made the projected relationship between academy and seminary much less intimate.

The board of directors' proposal to require acceptance of the Augustana Synod creedal statement as a pre-condition for permanent tenure of academy teachers also was revised in favor of a specification that "at least one of the academy teachers must be a member of the Lutheran church in order to satisfy the need of students for religious instruction." The resolution proposing this change stated the reason for it as being that many delegates "regarded the academy as a free school for the Norwegian people in America which should maintain an external (*ydre*) rather than an organic (*indre*) relationship with the synod."[12]

The influences responsible for these changes in the original board of directors' design are elusive. Helland suggests that the stipulation in the Marshall Academy purchase agreement requiring the Augsburg administration to operate the academy as an American institution may have been an obstacle. In other words, the Racine delegates possibly were persuaded that the proposals, particularly the all Lutheran faculty requirement, violated the terms of the purchase agreement.[13]

Weenaas' memoir tends to support the Helland interpretation. The Augsburg president recalls that "grave difficulties" were inherent in the "unique combination of a Norwegian Lutheran divinity school and a non-sectarian English institution to which the purchase of Marshall Academy had committed us." He further notes that his initial interest in the academy, which he confesses was slight, rested on the assumption that under certain conditions it could serve as the seminary's preparatory institution. This assumption, he writes, soon proved to be mistaken.[14] Unfortunately, Weenaas does not specify what led him to this conclusion. That the relationship between the academy and seminary established at Racine was a factor seems reasonable. Other circumstances, including the developing rift within the Norse division of the Scandinavian Augustana Synod, and the president's failure to establish friendly rapport with the non-Scandinavian academy students, no doubt reinforced his disillusionment with the academy.

TO FILL THE GAP created by the failure to establish Marshall Academy as the preparatory school of the seminary, Weenaas instituted a two-year preparatory department, generally called the pro-seminary (*proseminariet*). Its curriculum consisted of courses in Norwegian, German, Latin, Greek, English, religion, world history, geography, and mathematics.[15] Obtaining faculty to handle this program proved to be difficult. In the 1869–70 school year, Nils C. Brun a seminary student who also served as a Marshall Academy instructor, taught English to students who had only slight experience in that language. Those who had a basic knowledge of English took further work in the language within the academy, an arrangement that maintained the only tenuous tie between academy and seminary.[16] The exclusion of the seminary from the academy building in October, 1870 terminated all relationship between the two institutions.

From 1869 to 1872, when Augsburg moved to Minneapolis, a young Norwegian scholar named Caesar Boeck taught the pro-seminary

17

courses in German, Latin, and Greek. According to Weenaas, Boeck, who happened to be available for a teaching post at the start of the 1869–70 school year, was especially skilled in Greek and Latin. He was not, writes Weenaas, particularly interested either in Lutheranism or the work of the church, but nonetheless respected the seminary's goal, and established a cordial relationship with the president. Shortly after Augsburg left Marshall, Boeck returned to Norway where he accepted an appointment in government service.[17] The remaining pro-seminary teaching load — including the courses in Norwegian, history, geography, and mathematics — was taught by the "best qualified among the students." [18]

Neither Weenaas nor his associates thought of the pro-seminary as anything but a temporary arrangement. But they did not at first contemplate the founding of a full-fledged academy and/or college. Instead, they sought to relocate near a state university, hoping that it could serve as a preparatory school.

In his report to the 1871 convention, Conference President Claus L. Clausen, a prominent churchman who had separated from the Norwegian Synod primarily because he disagreed with its position on slavery, and who later would become an adversary of Georg Sverdrup within the Conference, noted that the choice of a new Augsburg location had narrowed to Madison or Minneapolis. The governing factor in determining location, said Clausen, was proximity to a state university so that the Conference could avoid the burden of a preparatory school "similar to the one maintained by the Norwegian Synod at Decorah." [19]

Clausen then went on to describe what he regarded as the shortcomings of Luther College. It was costly to operate. Moreover, it failed to meet the needs of the time. Nearly all the instruction utilized either Norse or German, and English was neglected despite its growing popularity within the church, particularly among the younger generation. Clausen argued that enrollment in university courses would enable the potential clergyman to become thoroughly proficient in English, while his subsequent study at the seminary would provide sufficient preparation in "our own mother tongue."

The 1871 convention shared Clausen's enthusiasm for the university solution to the preparatory school problem. One of its resolutions noted with gratitude that the University of Minnesota had offered to provide instruction in English to Augsburg students without cost. Another stipulated that students taking classes at the University should live on the Augsburg campus and remain under the jurisdiction of the seminary faculty.[20] While these decisions looked toward 1872–73, when Augsburg would be relocated at Minneapolis, Weenaas took immediate steps to put the university arrangement into effect. He reported to the 1872 convention that the urgent need to train English-speaking clergymen had been met in part by the enrollment during 1871–72 of three Augsburg students at the University of Minnesota and three at Wisconsin. Formally, these six young men had remained under the control of the seminary, even though Madison and Minneapolis were too far distant from Marshall to permit effective supervision by Weenaas and his assistant. The president affirmed that this arrangement sufficiently safeguarded the students' "religious and doctrinal point of view." [21]

The relationship with the University of Minnesota was maintained through the 1873–74 school year; thereafter Augsburg launched its own complete preparatory program. However, Weenaas still spoke glowingly of the agreement in his report to the 1873 Conference convention. During the preceding year, he pointed out, six of Augsburg's "most advanced" students had taken university classes in English and advanced Greek and Latin, permitting Augsburg to limit its classical language responsibilities to beginning courses. He praised William W. Folwell, President of the University of Minnesota, for his accommodating friendliness. In addition, Weenaas reiterated his own confidence in the soundness of the relationship. Seminary supervision of the students' extra-curricular and devotional life, he assured the delegates, preserved them for Lutheranism; and university training of the quality available at Minnesota gave them the proper intellectual foundation for theological study.[22]

Despite Weenaas' enthusiasm, the arrangement nearly lapsed in 1873–74, when only two Augsburg students took classes at the university. The reason for this development is to be found on the university campus rather than at Augsburg. In 1870 President Folwell formulated an educational blueprint known as the "Minnesota Plan," which the board of regents unanimously adopted. Among other things, the Folwell design called for university concentration on post-collegiate and professional education, together with a gradual shift of responsibility for secondary and junior college education to other institutions, primarily the public high schools. Experience demonstrated that the Folwell plan could not be carried out completely; the university continued to offer junior college work. But it did phase out secondary education, a process completed in 1879 with the elimination of the subfreshman class.[23]

Although Weenaas failed to mention the Minnesota Plan in his reports to the Conference conventions of the early 1870s, implications of the Folwell design are clear. In effect, it drastically limited the extent to which the university could serve as Augsburg Seminary's preparatory school. The plan also raised the question of whether Augsburg should

19

assume the responsibility of preparing Norwegian-American youth for university entrance as well as for the seminary.

Weenaas alluded to this responsibility in his 1873 report. After noting the possibilities of Minneapolis as an urban center, he called attention to the heavy influx of Norwegian settlers into the region. "Minnesota," he said, "is no doubt already the most Norwegian state in the Union, and the strong tide of immigration is strengthening the Norwegian element. . . ." He commented that "no city is better suited than Minneapolis as the locale for an institution of higher learning serving our countrymen." The University of Minnesota, observed Weenaas, offered rich educational opportunities, but English proficiency was the most pressing Norwegian-American need. He went on to say that if Augsburg and the Conference failed to help the immigrant with the language transition, Norwegian-Americans would leave Lutheranism and embrace the Reformed churches. "It should be our desire," he continued, "to do all in our power to meet our countrymen's need in this respect. . . ." He suggested that consideration be given a program of institutional expansion for both faculty and plant.[24]

THESE REMARKS anticipated formulation of the previously mentioned 1874 plan, which included a building program and the appointment of Gunnersen and Sverdrup to the faculty, along with an expansion and restructuring of the curriculum. Development of the plan's curricular section passed through three stages: 1) during 1873–74 the board of directors drafted a set of proposals adopted by the 1874 Conference convention; 2) on the last day of August that year the directors approved a curriculum fitting the specifications of the proposals; and 3) a month later the faculty drafted and endorsed a document entitled: *A Program for Augsburg Seminary and Its College Departments, Adopted by the Board of Directors on August 31, 1874, Together with an Interpretative Statement by the Faculty.* As the title suggests, the document includes two sections: a catalog of the courses offered under the new program; and an analysis of its educational philosophy.[25]

According to Oftedal the program was "not the work of a single individual." [26] This would seem to be correct. Weenaas, who was chairman and dominant member of the board of directors, affirms that he took the lead in the first stage.[27] As a member of the faculty in 1873–74, Oftedal may have been consulted, but he was not a member of the board of directors. Sverdrup and Gunnersen came to Minneapolis in mid-August, too late for involvement with the first stage.

Despite the brief period between their arrival and stage 2 — board of directors approval of the curriculum — the new professors, along with Oftedal, participated in its formulation. Sverdrup later recalled that "the course of study was arranged by the Theological Faculty and thereupon laid before the directors, who adopted it in joint meeting with the faculty held at Augsburg Seminary, August 31st, 1874." [28] Thus, the second stage involved all four members of the faculty.

The third stage — drafting the *Interpretative Statement* — was managed, writes Weenaas, by Sverdrup, Oftedal, and Gunnersen.[29] Evidence indicates that Sverdrup played the dominant role. Years later he claimed authorship of the section on the Greek (pre-theological college) department, and the content and style of the statement, especially on theological education, bears the mark of his pen.[30] However, Gunnersen and Oftedal were active participants. Weenaas recalls weekly faculty meetings at which the document was the central point of discussion.

Despite the division of responsibility among men who shortly would be at odds with one another, development of the new program proceeded from stage to stage without any perceptible interrruption. Most important, the *Statement,* particularly the section written by Sverdrup, suggests no retreat from the broad educational responsibility assumed by the program, although this would develop after Sverdrup became president in 1876. As defined in the Weenaas proposals, the new preparatory program had a double objective: pre-theological education; and providing students not headed for the ministry with the knowledge and skills required for effective participation in the affairs of an "enlightened secular community." [31]

In addition to accepting full responsibility for general education of both clergy and non-clergy, the *Statement* indicated a hope that Augsburg would become a major Norwegian-American cultural center (*et aandelig foreningspunkt for de Norske i Amerika*).[32] It also suggested that the "unique status of the seminary as a Norwegian-American institution" had implications for Augsburg's mission:

We believe that our people, who have left their native land to establish homes within a nation that will play a predominant role in world history, must be given an opportunity to develop their potentialities. We believe that not a single one of the many nationalities in this country should lose its identity before having an opportunity to make a distinctive contribution to our evolving American culture. Hence, it is the obligation of our school to help Norwegian-Americans find their place in the emerging American nation. . . .

This obligation defined two goals: preservation of the Norwegian heritage; and preparation of Augsburg students for full participation in

American life. Norwegian history, literature, and culture definitely belonged in the curriculum, as did the study of American history and institutions. The educated Norwegian-American had to be bilingual, both in speech and culture. As the *Statement* put it, "Our college must . . . place equal emphasis on Norwegian and English." [33]

The expanded program created a preparatory school with three departments. A beginning preparatory department (*faellesavdelingen*), to which a student with "common school," or elementary preparation could gain admission offered courses in Norse, English, world history, geography, religion, and arithmetic. Until the late 1880s, students enrolling in this department normally completed their work in one year. The course of study was expanded to two years in 1888, to three years in 1900, and to four years in 1910, a change that elevated the department to the status of a private high school, or academy.[34]

Also established were two parallel advanced preparatory, or college level departments. The Greek department (acually the forerunner of Augsburg College), served pre-ministerial students who had completed the beginning preparatory course. It offered a four-year program, the completion of which led to the Bachelor of Arts degree and eligibility for admission to the three-year theological course.[35] A department of practical studies (*realavdelingen*), also offered a four-year course and the B.A. degree; it was planned to accommodate students headed for careers other than the ministry.[36] Subsequent failure to get this department started was the major departure from the 1874 school plan.

The Greek department of study approved by the board of directors on August 31 emphasized languages and history, and offered no electives. In his freshman year the student took five hours in each of three languages: Norwegian, English, and Greek; four hours of history, three hours of geography; and three hours of religion. With the exception of Greek, which was added, and arithmetic, which was dropped, the freshman program was a continuation of the beginning preparatory course of study. Sophomore offerings eliminated geography, added Latin, reduced the work in Norwegian and English, shifted emphasis from world to American history, and added church history to the course in religion. In the junior year, literature partially displaced grammar and composition as the central concern of the English and Norwegian courses. Latin and Greek were continued, and German grammar made its first appearance.

No new disciplines were introduced during the senior year. The history of literature became the chief preoccupation of Norwegian and English. Latin concentrated on a "Latin Church Father," Greek emphasized

New Testament study, and German turned from grammar to literature and composition. Neither in the senior year nor earlier did the Greek department student have an opportunity to study natural science, and his work in mathematics was confined to the beginning preparatory course.

To some extent, courses designed for the department of practical studies paralleled that of the Greek department. On the beginning preparatory level, the curriculum was identical. Thereafter each included courses in Norwegian, English, history, and religion. However, in place of Latin, Greek, and German, the practical studies department proposed to offer three years of Old Norse; four years of mathematics, the third being "pure and applied mathematics"; three years of geography beyond that required by both programs during the freshman year; a year each of accounting and American government; and two years of natural science.

Although the department of practical studies would soon be abandoned, Sverdrup, Oftedal, and Gunnersen initially regarded it as an important program. The *Interpretative Statement* conveys the impression that failure to include such a department in the design would seriously impair the work of the school. Only a few young men, the *Statement* pointed out, would enter the ministry. To place the entire burden of communicating Augsburg's principles on them would court the danger of clericalism (*religiøs tvangsaag*), "precisely what we are battling against." The Augsburg constituency, the *Statement* argued, embraced all Norse-Americans who were not ashamed of their origin and were proud of investing their "national talents" in the building of an American civilization. "We must," affirmed the *Statement*, "reach the farmer, the worker, and the businessman. . . . We must seek to encourage everyone, irrespective of occupational or professional status, to adopt a liberal cultural outlook (*et frit aandelig blik*) . . . and we must educate school teachers, officials and legislators. . . ." [37]

THE YOUNG PROFESSORS who constructed Augsburg's 1874 program believed it was highly experimental. The opening paragraph of the *Statement* predicted that the many departures from established educational norms would invite discussion and attack. It was written, in fact, to inform potential critics, forestall misinterpretation, and assure that conflict, if and when it came, would be joined on issues of principle, rather than on questions of detail.[38]

Sverdrup and his colleagues exaggerated the disparity between their educational ideas and traditional practice. A comparison of the new Augsburg program with that of Luther College discloses that courses offered by the two institutions were strikingly similar. Greek, Latin, English, Norwegian, German, religion, and history dominated the curricula both of Luther and the Augsburg Greek department, although, significantly, not of the proposed department of practical studies. In his history of Luther College written in the late 19th century, Professor Gisle Bothne, for many years a member of the Luther College faculty, and later Professor of Norwegian at the University of Minnesota, remarks that the Luther academic program laid primary emphasis on language and history.[39] The same was true of Augsburg.

There were, however, subtle differences between the programs of the two institutions. The Luther College people strongly affirmed the inherent worth of language study apart from its instrumental value for theological and other disciplines. The role of Greek and Latin was particularly exalted, with no noticeable difference in the status of the two. Bothne concedes that "in our day [1897], knowledge of Greek and Latin cannot be equated with a sound education." Nevertheless, he affirms that a truly superior education necessarily included knowledge of the two classical tongues. Bothne adds:

We are not here speaking of the practical benefit which knowledge of Greek and Latin confers, for example, on the theologian by enabling him to read the New Testament in the original. We are speaking of the liberalizing potentialities of these languages . . . they . . . unite us organically — as only languages can do . . . with the past, thereby shaping our intellectual and moral outlook by incorporating the past into contemporary life.

Modern language study, according to Bothne, could not yield the advantages inherent in Greek and Latin. Preoccupation with contemporary language and recent history would, he writes, encourage the student to overemphasize the "phenomena" of the present and inhibit his discovery of "the correct" historically based world view. Bothne also discounts the importance of "other ancient languages, Indian and Chinese, for example," which do "not reflect our past." [40]

Although the 1874 program required pre-theological students to devote considerable study time to Greek and Latin, the Augsburg professors attributed less significance to classical languages than their Luther College brethren. The *Statement* held that the educated man was one whose grasp of ultimate truth had reached the point where it dominated his personal life, and served as a frame of reference for understanding the world. Academic disciplines concerned with "truth in itself," and mankind's struggle to possess truth and use it as a force shaping humanity were of greatest value.* It followed that religion — primarily Biblical studies — and history, rather than classical languages, commanded top priority "in the Greek department as well as the department of practical studies." [41]

At the same time, an extensive language program was essential. According to the *Statement*: "It is obvious that our students in the Greek department will derive substantial educational benefit from study of the five languages in our curriculum. . . ." In this connection Greek held a position of such "overwhelming" importance that Augsburg had to "discard the old customary Latin school name and substitute Greek school in its place." Greek, the *Statement* continued, was truly the foundation language of European civilization and the free mind, while Latin was identified with intellectual authoritarianism and divisive rationalism (*en tyrannisk aandsretning og en sønderskjaerende systematik*). Grammatically and structurally, too, Greek was far superior to Latin, the *Statement* argued.

After paying its respects to Latin, the *Statement* explained why this language, along with German, merited inclusion in the curriculum: "we perceive that a comprehensive study of Protestant theology would be impossible, or at any rate extremely difficult, without knowledge of these languages. . . ." The faculty also wanted students to become familiar with the spirit of the Latin and Germanic people; and the five prescribed languages would establish contact "with all the cultural elements presently shaping world development." [42]

The curriculum formulated for the department of practical studies did not include Greek, Latin, and German, a gap filled by courses in natural science, mathematics, American government, and Old Norse. Although this department's failure prevented the offering of Old Norse, the rationale for its inclusion is interesting. Ancient language study, the *Statement* observed, could be intellectually rewarding. The question was: which

Den virkelige aandsdannelse, der bestaar i den personlige indtrængen i sandheten, saaledes at denne blir livsmagt i hjertet til bestemmelse av tanke og vilje, og handling, idet verdens-utviklingen og menneskelivet sees i dens lys, med andre ord i den personlige frihet, den kan ingen skole vaere sikker paa at meddele sine elever; ti mange naar den aldrig, mange tilkjæmper sig den først gjennem livets alvorlige erfaringsskole. Men skolens midler til at føre eleverne henimot den, er fremstillingen av sandheten i sig selv — og av menneskeslegtens kamp for at tilegne sig den og gjennemføre den i livet, — og til samme tid av de avveie og feiltrin, som er begaat i denne utvikling.

language would most effectively promote Norwegian immigrant assimilation into American life?

Without hesitation, the *Statement* favored Old Norse. This "sister tongue" of Anglo-Saxon possessed the attributes of a great language. It combined the finest qualities of Greek and Latin, and culturally its worth equaled that of the two Mediterranean languages. In addition, serious study of Old Norse would yield insights about the Norwegian national character, and at the same time illumine the development of English speech. Old Norse was an admirable foundation for instruction in both modern Norwegian and English.[43]

Departures from traditional methods of language instruction also were proposed. The goal, said the *Statement*, "should be to give the students actual reading proficiency in the languages offered." Work in Greek and Latin would be limited to prose study so that emphasis could be centered on the "period in the development of these languages that corresponds to the rise of Christianity. . . ." The *Statement* predicted that traditionalists would contend that concentration on classical literature could utilize the time reserved for language study. The Augsburg faculty rejected this contention on two grounds: the futility of reading "a little here and . . . there in Greek and Latin literature"; and the pagan world view presented by classical authors. "In principle [we] are not humanists," affirmed the *Statement*.

The Augsburg Program of 1874 articulated several tenets of the reform movement that had shaped the thinking of Sverdrup, Oftedal, and Gunnersen before they left their native land. For one thing, it implicitly rejected the "humanist" educational standard that held up the cultivated gentleman trained in Greco-Roman studies as an ideal type. Years earlier Johan Sverdrup had assailed Norwegian university training for producing lawyers separated from the masses instead of educating committed servants of the people; the *Statement's* critique of established theological education sounded an identical note. For another, the statement exalted truth gained from experience over preoccupation with "glossaries, citations . . . and crammed memories. . . ." [44] To be worthy of the name, education had to be practical. In this connection it is interesting that Georg Sverdrup's paternal grandfather led a movement to establish agricultural schools for Norway's peasant class.

Norwegian folk nationalism also permeated the program. The claim that Old Norse, the language theoretically undergirding the speech of plain Norwegians, merited equal status with Greek and Latin was a bold assertion of Norse cultural worth *vis a vis* the European aristocratic classical tradition. Contrary to what might be inferred, the *Statement's* endorsement of assimilation was compatible with this nationalistic spirit — hopefully, Norse contributions would become part of the mix produced by the American melting pot, but to assure such an outcome, Norwegian-Americans were obliged to preserve and cherish their heritage.

Although the broad frame of reference running through the 1874 program would guide Augsburg's educational policy for many decades, only part of the blueprint became operative. Development of the beginning preparatory and Greek departments followed the program's specifications, but the department of practical studies never got underway, nor was Old Norse introduced. Augsburg also failed to become a major Norwegian-American cultural center guiding a moderately paced immigrant assimilation into American life. Instead, for more than four decades the institution remained essentially what it set out to be in 1869: a divinity school serving a minority wing of Norwegian-American Lutheranism.

"EXCLUSIVELY...A DIVINITY SCHOOL"

 ALTHOUGH ITS provisions were only partially realized, the 1874 plan marks a turning point in the history of Augsburg Seminary. The building program was approximately on schedule when the Conference convention met in 1875. Two additional wings of the main building, due for dedication immediately following adjournment of the convention, would be ready for service by September. Completion of the three-apartment residence housing the Oftedal, Gunnersen, and Sverdrup families filled a vital need. The permanent faculty had doubled with the appointment of the latter two men, enabling the theological department to offer a reasonably complete program.

With an enrollment of 30 in September, 1874, the beginning preparatory department went into full operation. As scheduled, both advanced preparatory departments offered work on the freshman level. Six students enrolled in the Greek department, a sufficient number to assure its future. The department of practical studies was less secure — only two students chose its program.[1] Records fail to indicate the size of practical studies enrollment in 1875–76, but the department offered no work on the sophomore level that year, and was discontinued entirely in September, 1876.[2]

In 1875–76 the student body nearly doubled, from 53 to 102. Although information on the number of men living off campus is lacking, the plant could provide adequate lodging and classroom space for only about 80 students. Consequently, either a number of them found housing elsewhere, or the dormitories were badly overcrowded, a factor that may have contributed to the high incidence of illness reported by Weenaas that year.[3]

Six men constituted the 1875–76 faculty. An enrollment of 102 meant a student-faculty ratio of 17 to 1 — fairly satisfactory by 20th century standards. However, in 1875 teaching responsibilities ranged from elementary arithmetic and beginning English on the one hand, to advanced theological courses on the other, and the level of student age, maturity, and educational preparation varied widely. Professors also were involved in such non-academic ventures as fund-raising, writing for the religious press, serving congregations temporarily without pastors, and assuming a share of the Conference's administrative burden.

John Blegen includes a profile of each member of the faculty in his memoir. Weenaas commanded overwhelming respect, an attitude encouraged by his dignified bearing, teaching effectiveness, and a quick temper that inspired a body of early alumni lore. An enlarged faculty relieved Weenaas of part of his previous duties, but remaining responsibilities demanded his continuous effort.

Concerning Sverdrup, Blegen reports that students "held only one opinion . . . he was an exceedingly skillful and inspiring teacher." Oftedal enjoyed a less exalted reputation: "One sometimes got the impression that he came to class unprepared." Nevertheless, most students admired Oftedal's versatility and colorful personality. "Gunnersen was in many respects an interesting teacher . . . but not as coherent in expressing his thoughts [as Sverdrup and Oftedal] and also very absent-minded."

In addition to the four theological professors, all of whom taught in both preparatory and seminary departments, the faculty included two instructors on one-year appointments who worked exclusively on the preparatory level. Jørgen Jensen, a recent graduate of Christiania University, taught mathematics, geography, and Norse. Blegen remembers Jensen as a competent teacher, but his failure to observe Augsburg's total abstinence code shortened his term of service. He left in February, 1877. I. H. Stenersen, the second instructor, was a graduate of Osage College in Iowa. He taught English and possibly a number of other courses. Like Jensen, Stenersen terminated his connection with the school in 1877.[4]

ALTHOUGH Sverdrup replaced Weenaas as president of Augsburg Seminary in 1876, several patterns established during Weenaas' last year persisted through the following decade. Total enrollment from 1875 to 1885 averaged 103, with a low of 92 in 1876–77, and a high of 111 in 1884–85. Within the departments seminary enrollment rose, and the beginning preparatory tally declined, in part due to limitation of new admissions until an additional dormitory could be constructed. After the full college program was initiated in September, 1878, Greek department enrollment averaged 49. The first college commencement in May, 1879, awarded five young men the B.A. degree. In the next six years, the number of graduates varied from two in 1882 to six in 1884. Due to small enrollment and insufficient faculty, the Greek department offered no junior level work in 1883–84; consequently, there was no class of 1885.[5]

In the curricular area, too, the 1875–76 school year set the direction for the next ten years. The beginning preparatory and Greek department courses of study proceeded according to the 1874 program. However, because of a wide variation in the educational backgrounds of entering students, the faculty in 1875 extended the beginning preparatory course to two years, an extension maintained until 1878, when it reverted to the original one-year program. Additional faculty required by this modification necessitated a one-year delay in organizing the first Greek department junior class. By 1878, however, one beginning preparatory and four Greek department classes were meeting, and both conformed to 1874 specifications.[6]

The transition from Weenaas to Sverdrup also brought change. Assumption of leadership by Sverdrup and Oftedal widened internal Norwegian-Lutheran warfare which, in turn, profoundly influenced Augsburg's long-range development. However, the young professors did not initiate the conflict. Since its founding in 1870, the Conference had battled the Norwegian Synod on a variety of issues, and Weenaas was recognized as a leading Synod critic. The arrival of Oftedal, Sverdrup, and Gunnersen provided him with a team of resourceful allies.

Unfortunately, relations between Weenaas and the younger men cooled soon after they joined the faculty. An unpleasant misunderstanding developed in 1874 between Weenaas and Oftedal concerning their roles as interim pastors of Trinity Congregation.[7] A year later the faculty, under the signature of Sverdrup as secretary, presented its own report to the Conference convention. While it carried no suggestion of hostility to Weenaas — who, as usual, delivered his own message to the delegates — a faculty report was a departure from custom.[8]

In 1875 Weenaas submitted his resignation, effective the following spring. He insists this action was not related to tension between himself and the faculty, nor was the decision hasty. For several years Weenaas had considered re-establishing his career in Norway. Although he admired American technical efficiency, differences between Old and New World ways of life baffled and sometimes appalled him, and he found expatriation impossible: "One can indeed never forget [his homeland], and however well he may prosper in a foreign country, he is still an alien among strangers and longs for a return to his people and native soil." [9]

Despite Weenaas' impending departure, faculty dissension became so acrimonious in 1875–76 that Pastor Johan Olson, president of the Conference, intervened.[10] His effort to secure a reconciliation failed. At the 1876 Conference convention, disagreement between Weenaas and Sverdrup became public. As in the previous year, Sverdrup delivered a separate report, this time as Conference treasurer. One of his recommendations clashed directly with a proposal advanced by Weenaas, who reported both for the board of directors, and on his own behalf. The issue was whether the teaching post left vacant by Weenaas' resignation should be filled. Citing the school's precarious financial situation, Sverdrup argued against appointment of a successor.

Speaking for the board of directors, Weenaas recommended that the professorship be filled, and that Sverdrup be elected president "for one year." To these proposals Weenaas added his own suggestion that Pastor Bottolf B. Gjeldaker, vice-president of the Conference, be appointed theological professor. If Gjeldaker accepted, said Weenaas, the convention should consider electing him president of Augsburg; heavy responsibility already burdened Sverdrup.[11]

The substance of Weenaas' recommendations, in opposition to Sverdrup, reflects the deep animosity that had developed within the faculty. Their presentation also altered the relationship of Weenaas to a growing rift within the church. Since 1874 a number of Conference pastors, with Gjeldaker as their spokesman, had sharply criticized the Public Declaration with which the Augsburg faculty, including Weenaas, was closely identified. By recommending Gjeldaker for both the professorship and presidency Weenaas, in effect, shifted sides in the controversy. Before departing for Norway, he underscored this change of position by retracting his signature from the Public Declaration.[12]

Neither Sverdrup nor Weenaas won total victory on the convention floor. After approving continuance of a fourth professorship, the delegates selected Gjeldaker for the post. In the contest for president, however, Sverdrup received 47 votes to 16 for Gjeldaker, with five abstentions.[13] Sverdrup continued to serve as president until his death in 1907.

Taken as a whole, these decisions comforted Sverdrup more than Weenaas. The size of Sverdrup's margin in the presidential race attested to the reputation established by the 27-year-old professor in less than two years. Nevertheless, the new president faced a difficult challenge. Following his election dissension within the Conference grew, rather than abated. Weenaas hoped that his own disavowal of the Public Declaration would quiet the controversy; actually, the opposite happened. Critics of the document, who soon would be called the Old School (*gamle retning*), as distinguished from its defenders, the New School (*nye ret-*

ning), now had Weenaas' prestige, if not his presence, on their side. In Gjeldaker they had representation on the Augsburg faculty. Gunnersen, too, seemed to be moving in their direction. After Gjeldaker joined the faculty, a Gjeldaker-Gunnersen combination opposed the Sverdrup-Oftedal team on at least one significant issue.[14]

In responding to the situation, Sverdrup might have sought accommodation with the Old School. Characteristically, he chose, with the help of Oftedal, to make a fight for what he regarded as basic ecclesiastical principles. Before the battle reached its decisive stage in the early 1880s, however, Augsburg passed through a critical financial crisis.

Considered in relation to the resources of Augsburg's constituency, financial reports submitted to the 1877 Conference convention make sober reading. A special fund out of which salaries were paid registered a deficit of more than $4,000 — an increase of $790 over the previous year. In addition, a debt of $10,720, most of it a legacy from the 1874–75 building program, encumbered the physical plant. Worst of all, calamities of nature combined with economic depression to limit the financial capacity of the predominantly rural Conference churches.[15]

An account published in 1893, and obviously composed by Oftedal, describes how Augsburg supporters responded to the 1877 crisis. It interprets, from a New School viewpoint, the significance of this episode in the history of the school:

The financial condition of the institution became every year more entangled, the indebtedness had in 1877, reached $16,000. The churches that never had evinced any great substantial zeal for the school grew more and more indifferent; the school as well as the society [Conference], threatened to split up in parties and go under.

Something had to be done this year; 1877 is, therefore, the great turning point in the history of Augsburg Seminary. A large and enthusiastic convention in Wilmar [*sic*], consisting of one-third ministers and two-thirds lay delegates . . . took the matter in their hands. It was a remarkable assembly; determined Norsemen and earnest Christian farmers, the large majority of them. Apparently irreconcilable discussions and an insurmountable debt stared them in the eyes. All around, the fields were in June dark with the ravages of grasshoppers, that . . . infested the entire Northwest, the main support of the school. But nothing deterred them from taking the steps that seemed necessary to save both Seminary and society. After long and earnest debates . . . the convention discharged the last appointed Professor [Gjeldaker], and resolved to raise $16,000 cash, on condition that if it was not all paid in before January 1, 1878, the whole amount collected should be returned to the contributors. It was live or die. Professor Oftedal was appointed Chairman of a Committee to collect this money, with authority to select the Committee.

He went about the work in dead earnest. He first started a paper [*Folkebladet*], and printed . . . 10,000 copies. Through this instrumentality, chiefly, and with very little traveling, he organized Committees in every Church, gave them detailed instructions, and wrought up in two or three months an enthusiasm hitherto almost unknown amongst a cool-headed, conservative people like the Norwegians. The results followed. From the beginning of October, most of the Committees were ready to work, and in three months the whole amount, $16,000, and some to spare, was subscribed.

In three weeks, from the 1st to the 21st of January, 1878, after having given orders to send in the amounts subscribed, Professor Oftedal received cash $18,000, contributed by over 30,000 individuals.

The school was saved and more; from now on Augsburg Seminary was not the concern of some ministers or of a clique, but — as of right it ought to be — the school of the Churches, of the people. The farmers got the habit of calling it "Our School." [16]

Completion of Oftedal's successful financial drive brought only temporary relief. Outgo exceeded income again the next year, not because expenditures were reckless, but because church contributions lagged.[17] To avert another crisis, and to relieve Augsburg professors of money-raising responsibility during summer vacations, Oftedal, as board of trustees president, launched an endowment fund campaign, with a goal of $50,000. Prudent investment of this sum, it was hoped, would yield sufficient income to pay salaries, thus obviating the need for a special salary fund entirely dependent on yearly contributions.

Oftedal presented his proposal to the 1878 Conference convention which selected an endowment fund committee, but failed to give the plan final approval. Rising factionalism within the church also prevented positive action the following year, when a mounting deficit again threatened Augsburg's solvency. Before the 1880 convention met, members of the board of trustees began solicitation on their own. Following an interminable debate consisting of 66 speeches, the 1880 assembly adopted a resolution authorizing creation of an endowment fund to be used specifically for payment of the salaries of theological professors "and one teacher in English." Two years later, when the endowment committee had collected or subscribed more than $50,000, the campaign terminated.[18]

Meanwhile, controversy between the Old and New Schools was becoming increasingly bitter. Both secular and religious Norwegian-American newspapers carried blasts from one side or the other, and every

Conference convention from 1879 through 1883 included at least one confrontation between representatives of the two groups. As might be expected, the endowment campaign became entangled in the hostilities. Old School spokesmen charged that soliciting funds in advance of Conference approval violated the constitution. Oftedal and his associates countered by accusing congregations partial to the Old School of delaying final Conference approval, and of failing to contribute as fully as they should have when the drive got underway.[19]

Other issues were aired. New School spokesmen contended that a developing hierarchy threatened the God-given right of individual congregations to carry on their ordained tasks, manage their own affairs, and select their own pastors, who "must be servants, not rulers, of the congregation." In response, Old School representatives accused their adversaries of failing "to differentiate between the pastoral office and the spiritual priesthood" — of denying the clergy its rightful prerogatives. Another disagreement related to the role of theological discussion in the life of the church. Sverdrup opposed preoccupation with minute doctrinal issues which, he said, was contrary to a Christianity based on simple scriptural truth and personal commitment. His opponents rejected the charge that they stood for a sterile, intellectualized Christianity, and counterattacked by arguing that New School indifference to doctrinal discussion courted the danger of "throwing the baby out with the bath water." [20]

In 1882–83 a crisis, carrying overtones of Old and New School controversy, developed within the Augsburg faculty. Since Gjeldaker's departure in 1878, Gunnersen had managed a reasonable coexistence with Sverdrup and Oftedal. On December 11, 1882, however, he submitted his resignation, effective at the close of the school year. He attributed this action to a conviction "that the professors at Augsburg Seminary do not work well together." This insight, Gunnersen implied, was a recent development; it had come to him since "a double editorship" assumed control of *Folkebladet*.[21]

The reference to *Folkebladet* linked Gunnersen's resignation to an important Old School complaint. Oftedal had founded the Norwegian language weekly newspaper in 1877 as a publicity organ for the financial campaign of that year. He suspended publication briefly at the conclusion of the fund drive, then revived it with Sverdrup as his partner. At this point, *Folkebladet* became a vigorous exponent of the New School point of view. It aroused resentment, not only because its editorial view displeased the Old School proponents, but also because they believed the theological faculty should not associate with a journal taking one side of a highly charged controversy.[22]

After hearing of Gunnersen's resignation, Conference President Theodor H. Dahl advised Oftedal that his resignation would quiet suspicions of a Sverdrup-Oftedal combination against Gunnersen which, if allowed to grow, might inflict severe damage on Augsburg and the Conference. Oftedal complied with a letter of resignation dated December 24, whereupon a prominent churchman with Old School leanings suggested that the crisis was now amenable to settlement. If Gunnersen could be persuaded to withdraw his resignation, Oftedal's should be permitted to stand, and every effort should be made to retain Sverdrup.[23]

Sverdrup, however, refused to countenance such an arrangement; on April 11 he, too, resigned. His communications to Conference leaders and the 1883 convention stressed the president's responsibility for faculty discontents like those voiced by Gunnersen, and strongly hinted that unless Oftedal were retained, he could not continue at Augsburg. Sverdrup's action forced the 1883 Conference convention to choose between Sverdrup and Oftedal on the one hand, or Gunnersen on the other.[24]

The convention selected the two-man team. A motion requesting all three professors to withdraw their resignations passed by a substantial margin, but both Sverdrup and Oftedal steadfastly refused the request. Parliamentary confusion followed. Ultimately the convention adopted the premise that three vacancies did, indeed, exist, clearing the way for a new election with all three professors in the running. Since Sverdrup and Oftedal polled more than the required two-thirds vote, their faculty status was restored and they accepted the convention mandate. Gunnersen, on the other hand, received less than two-thirds, an outcome that terminated his connection with Augsburg. New School dominance both at Augsburg and within the Conference was now an established fact.[25]

FOLLOWING THE 1883 convention, the Conference enjoyed seven years of comparative peace. Tension still fermented beneath the surface, but Old School spokesmen, aware of their minority position, avoided direct clashes with the other party. At the same time, Conference relations with other Lutheran bodies improved, with the exception of the Norwegian Synod. Discussions looking toward synodical union got underway which, in 1890, were successful.[26]

Augsburg, too, achieved a measure of prosperity and stability. An improved financial situation permitted expansion of the physical plant. In 1884 a three-story dormitory (the future North Hall) accommodating forty men was constructed. Three years later, a two-apartment residence, later known as Morton Hall, was added to the campus. This structure, which stood on the corner of Eighth Street and 22nd Avenue, served for many years as the home of the Sverdrup and Oftedal families.[27]

Enrollment also increased. By 1889–90 the total count was 160: 41 seminarians, 58 college men, and 61 beginning preparatory students. From 1885 through 1890 enrollment averaged 142, compared to 103 in the preceding decade. This trend is due to a number of factors, including expanded campus facilities, an increasing Norwegian-American population, a growing Conference constituency, the lure of Minneapolis, and a somewhat improved Upper Midwest economic situation.

With its more secure base Augsburg, after 1883, might have worked for achievement of an unrealized goal that ranked high in the 1874 program: providing broad educational opportunity for young Norwegian-Americans not headed for the ministry.[28] Actually, the administration moved in an opposite direction. Sverdrup's report to the 1884 Conference convention affirmed that Augsburg in the future, more than it had in the past, should seek to become "exclusively" a divinity school. (*Skolen maa mere en hidtil laegge udelukkende an paa at blive en presteskole.*) A resolution fully endorsing this policy statement won convention acceptance, apparently without debate.[29]

The next annual convention clarified the meaning of Sverdrup's 1884 statement. In his message to the delegates Conference President Dahl urgently recommended a new personnel policy for the preparatory departments:

There is a handicap [*ulempe*] that has burdened our school since its founding. This is with respect to our instructors. It has always been difficult to recruit men for these posts who possess, not only the necessary academic qualifications, but also the earnest Christian spirit which is so important for a divinity school teacher to have. . . . If our school is to avoid irreparable harm . . . it is necessary to work our procedures for filling these teaching posts more satisfactorily . . . they should be placed on the same basis as our theological professorships. . . . The college teachers are the first to have an impact on incoming students, and if these teachers are not themselves committed to the Kingdom of God, their influence on the young men will not serve the goal of a divinity school.[30]

Whatever may be said about Dahl's basic premise, his remarks called attention to a serious weakness in the Augsburg operation. The preparatory teaching load until then had been shared by the overburdened theological professors, a corps of part-time teachers (mostly seminarians), and low-paid instructors on temporary appointments. Since 1874 twelve men had served as instructors, most of them for periods of one or two years. These individuals were more heterogeneous in background than their successors — a circumstance that may have exerted a healthier influence on the student body than Dahl or Sverdrup believed. Only two of them held Augsburg's B.A. degree: John J. Skørdalsvold, and John T. Bugge. Several had attended Christiania University. The group also included two University of Minnesota men; J. W. Perkins, and Thomas R. Newton.[31]

Newton's status is especially interesting. An active Baptist layman of early American ancestry, and the father of future Congressman Walter H. Newton, he taught Latin, English, history, and geography during his four years at Augsburg. Colleagues and students remembered Newton as "an able and conscientious teacher" after his resignation in 1882.[32]

Although the Augsburg preparatory faculty of the late 1870s and early 1880s included a number of capable instructors, its level of academic preparation was no more impressive than that of most 19th century teaching staffs. The sketchy data available indicates that only Jørgen Jensen had taken graduate work in disciplines other than theology. Unfortunately, the problem of poorly trained faculty was, to a considerable extent, insoluble. The typical American college professor of the 1870s has been characterized as "a nondescript, a jack of all trades, equally ready to teach surveying and Latin eloquence." [33]

Nevertheless, the situation at Augsburg was open to a limited improvement. The administration realized that more secure tenure and better pay would reduce an excessively high turnover and stimulate better morale among preparatory teachers. In 1882, for example, Newton drew a salary of $500 a year compared to the $1,250 received by the theological professors.[34] Inadequate resources precluded munificent raises, but a reduction in the disparity between theological and preparatory salaries was possible.

Sverdrup also recognized that his hopes for Augsburg's future depended largely on the commitment of his faculty. He reminded the 1885 Conference convention of the previous year's decision to operate Augsburg "exclusively" as a divinity school. The time had now come, he said, to institute faculty and student recruitment policies consistent with this objective. On behalf of the board of directors, he then moved the election of John Blegen and Theodor S. Reimestad as college professors at an annual salary of $600. A second motion proposed that the fund maintained for payment of the theological professors, and subsidized by endowment income and by contributions from Conference churches, be assessed an additional $1,200 for preparatory salaries. This motion aimed to give the Blegen-Reimestad professorships the same prestige and financial security — such as it was — as the theological posts enjoyed.[35]

A minority report, presented as a substitute for the board of directors' proposal, called for election of an additional theological professor from Norway instead of Blegen and Reimestad. Sponsors of this proposition assigned highest priority to the needs of the theological department; they believed that three theological professors and a staff of instructors could satisfactorily handle the preparatory work. Sverdrup, on the other hand, wanted to strengthen the preparatory branches and, in the process, integrate them more closely with the theological department.[36]

The two young pastors sponsored by Sverdrup seemed admirably suited for this purpose. Reimestad, like Blegen, was an Augsburg alumnus; they had been classmates from the time they entered the beginning preparatory department in 1875 until they completed the theological course in 1883, when they were graduated with distinction. Neither had taken graduate work beyond seminary training, but both had served as part-time instructors during their college and seminary years. Two years in the parish ministry had exposed them to the realities of congregational life, a valuable experience for divinity school teachers.[37]

Although presentation of opposing faculty expansion plans touched off a lengthy debate, the 1885 Conference convention adopted the Sverdrup proposal, and Blegen and Reimestad joined the faculty in the fall. Reimestad remained at Augsburg until 1900, Blegen until 1916, both of them teaching a variety of courses. However, Blegen's principal fields came to be Greek, German, and Norse; Reimestad concentrated on Latin and Norse.

In his memoir Blegen recalls the sense of challenge he felt on assuming his new responsibilities. His first teaching assignment included a Norwegian course in the preparatory department; the freshman and sophomore Greek offerings; ancient and medieval world history taught on the sophomore level; and the junior-senior German courses. For one without special teaching preparation, he remarks, "it was no light matter to assume responsibility for all these courses, with five hours instruction each day. There was no time to relax." [38]

The appointment of Reimestad and Blegen set a precedent for stabilizing the preparatory faculty. In 1886 the Conference convention elected John Bugge to a permanent professorship, and three years later Wilhelm M. Pettersen who, like Bugge, had served for several years as an instructor, was similarly promoted. Both were Augsburg alumni. Bugge, whose fields included Norwegian, Greek, and history, graduated from the college in 1879 and the theological department in 1882. Pettersen, a member of the college class of 1884, also taught Norwegian and history, along with mathematics.[39]

Meanwhile, Anders M. Hove, a Luther College graduate with public school experience, had joined the faculty. Under a one-year appointment, Hove in 1887–88 taught a number of Bugge's and Blegen's courses so these men could substitute in the theological department while Oftedal was on leave. The administration discovered a need for Hove's continued service in 1888–89, particularly as a teacher of English. In addition, a planned extension of the beginning preparatory program from one to two years dictated faculty expansion. Accordingly, in response to a recommendation by the board of directors, the 1888 Conference convention elected Hove to a full professorship.[40]

Staffed by a permanent faculty of five men who approved of Sverdrup's policies, Augsburg's preparatory departments moved into a closer relationship with the theological program. Statistics of the period indicate the trend. Of the Greek department graduates from 1879 through 1884, 59 per cent went on to complete the theological course; in 1885–90 the proportion rose to 82 per cent.[41]

But the institution stopped short of becoming exclusively a divinity school. Students who had completed the beginning preparatory course were eligible for certification as elementary teachers, and the administration could hardly ignore this need, nor neglect the opportunity to augment tuition income. Moreover, many boys otherwise qualified to enter the beginning preparatory program were uncertain about vocational choice. Therefore, in setting admission requirements, Augsburg found it more expedient to favor applicants with "some thought of entering the service of the Church" than to insist on a firm ministerial commitment. The hope that campus influences would lead to such commitment was frequently realized, but a substantial number of students chose other callings. These considerations influenced both educational policy and self-image. A recruiting advertisement of the period represented the institution as being "essentially" rather than "exclusively" a divinity school.[42]

AUGSBURG'S DECISION to concentrate — whether "exclusively" or "essentially" — on ministerial education confirmed a retreat from the broad goals of 1874 that placed equal emphasis on training clergy and educating young men bound for other careers. The program's *Interpretative Statement* called attention to the danger of clericalism inherent in a segregation of ministerial and non-ministerial students. The *Statement* also pointed to the general educational value of the Greek department course of study: "Since we reject the view that theology is separate from life, we feel that every Greek department offering is potentially useful both to the students who will take no further academic work and those who plan additional study in fields other than theology."[43]

The goals of 1874 seem more consistent with Sverdrup's and Oftedal's thought than the guidelines that shaped their educational policy in the 1880s. In scores of public addresses and published articles, Sverdrup proclaimed the inseparability of theology from life. He frequently counseled Norwegian-Americans not to forget who they were, but at the same time urged them to participate fully and courageously in American life. In an 1883 speech to the Augsburg Student Society, he analyzed the psychological plight of Norwegian immigrants, and also subjected contemporary American society to a remarkably informed critique. On the negative side, both he and Oftedal accused Norwegian Synod leaders of attempting to confine Norse immigrants within a ghetto of ignorance and provincialism, the walls of which had to be destroyed if Norwegian-Americans were ever to become full-fledged citizens of their adopted land.[44]

It is difficult to square these concerns with the policy Augsburg followed after 1884. Limiting the institution basically to ministerial education courted the danger of erecting a barrier between clergy and laity, even though Augsburg aimed to produce a democratic ministry. A wide gap also separated Sverdrup's and Oftedal's anxiety concerning Norse-American preparation for American life, and the school's virtual abandonment of lay education at a time when the Conference had no other institution of higher learning. A faculty hiring policy that gave overwhelming preference to Augsburg alumni with New School leanings scarcely encouraged establishment of communication with other groups in American society, a value often extolled by Augsburg's leaders.

The key to the paradox is found in Sverdrup's primary commitment: church reform. With a passion rivaling that of a 17th century Puritan divine recently settled in New England, he came to the heartland of Norwegian-American Lutheranism determined to work for the same polity and theological orientation as the church reform party in Norway was unsuccessfully seeking to establish there. The Public Declaration, which appeared before he left Norway, vaguely defined Sverdrup's position, and soon after his arrival the emerging New School movement began more concretely to articulate his hopes.[45]

Like most church reformers, Sverdrup realized the strategic importance of theological education, and the passage of time expanded his conception of its significance. However, in the first year of his presidency he believed that the school could offer both general education and pastoral training. In an 1876 article profiling Augsburg, he noted that the institution "in its new form is organized not only for the education of pastors, but also congregational members." The article indicated at least mild enthusiasm for the innovation. It suggested that the Conference "as a congregational synod" would derive "blessing" from educated lay people, "since God's kingdom is not built by clergy alone. . . ." [46]

A year later Sverdrup was more pessimistic about Augsburg's capacity to fulfill its double commitment, for 1877 marked the climax of a major financial crisis. Other problems, too, plagued the new administration. Heavy non-academic responsibility burdened the faculty. Experience had disclosed that the educational level of incoming students was lower than anticipated, a discovery that dictated more courses on the beginning preparatory level. Circumstances demanded retrenchment and, given the priority Sverdrup assigned to ministerial education along with the urgent need for more Conference pastors, curtailment of the theological department was out of the question.

In his report to the 1877 Conference convention, Sverdrup proposed that the Conference circuits promote regional two-year academies on the Norwegian Folk High School model. "There is no cause," he added, "which at the moment deserves more consideration than this one. Our people must take a position over as against Catholicism* and the moneyed aristocracy, and they must work valiantly against the parasitic influences that are gnawing at the roots of freedom, and the best countervailing force is popular enlightenment in the Protestant spirit." Folk high schools could also help Augsburg. Their establishment would relieve pressure on the institution's beginning preparatory department, thereby permitting a commitment of costly instructional resources to "higher education." [47]

Although the Conference endorsed Sverdrup's regional academy recommendation, nothing developed on the circuit level.[48] Nor did the president renew the proposal. But a wide disparity between means and ends persisted. Limited resources dictated a selective response to the demands being made on the institution, and of these the training of clergy ranked first. A *Folkebladet* article of January 20, 1881, announcing that a lack of facilities precluded acceptance of any more students during that school year, is illuminating. According to the article, Augsburg could not assume responsibility for Norwegian-American education at a time when thousands of immigrants were flocking into the region. Other institutions, particularly the public schools, had to shoulder a larger part of the burden, and in the process develop more efficient techniques for teaching English to mature foreign-born students already possessing the rudiments of learning. At the same time *Folkebladet* counseled young men

* In using this term, Sverdrup was referring more specifically to an ecclesiastical tendency than to the Roman Catholic church.

aspiring to become "servants of the congregation" to file application for admission to Augsburg well in advance of their first school year.

Developments in the 1880s sharpened the administration's preoccupation with ministerial education. For a time Sverdrup and Oftedal opposed the holding of intersynodical conferences designed to promote the merger of existing Lutheran church bodies. This stance presently gave way to acceptance of the church union concept, providing merger could be accomplished on terms consistent with the New School position. In a series of articles published in 1882, Sverdrup discussed the three foundations which, in his view, could support a united Norwegian Lutheran church in America. The first was the autonomous congregation, free of hierarchical domination and in full possession of its God-given rights. The second was *Børnelaerdommen*, the simple tenets of the Christian faith as set fourth in the Lutheran Catechism without abstruse doctrinal interpretation. The third was *Presteskolen,* the divinity school.[49] A moment's reflection suggests the dependence of the first two foundations on the third. Congregational autonomy could scarcely be achieved without a parish clergy firmly committed to it, and the divinity school was the agency most likely to produce such a commitment. *Børnelaerdommen* was a matter of theological emphasis which a potential clergyman's seminary training would either reinforce or undermine.

Sverdrup's treatment of Augsburg in relation to the divinity school foundation is revealing indeed. "Perhaps the greatest source of mischief within our church," he wrote, "is the varied education of our clergy." Lutheran congregations, he pointed out, drew their pastors from at least seven seminaries in the United States, Christiania University, the Mission School at Stavanger, Norway, and from "Lay-preaching circles." "Anyone," commented Sverdrup, "can understand the impossibility of harmonious cooperation among these divergent elements." In his opinion, a united Lutheran church should concentrate its resources on "one or at the most two divinity schools." He added that the Conference's efforts on behalf of Augsburg and its endowment fund had contributed as much to the cause of church union "as anything else." Sverdrup envisaged Augsburg as *the* ministerial training school for a united Norwegian Lutheran church, an ambitious goal that left little room for involvement with other educational programs.[50]

As their awareness of the importance of pastoral education for their program of church reform grew, Sverdrup and Oftedal became increasingly protective of Augsburg's divinity school role, and more sensitive to trends that threatened its effectiveness. By 1880 the Norwegian cultural milieu, with which they maintained close contact, was beginning to challenge a number of their basic premises. Most important, the alliance between political liberalism and low-church Christianity was becoming severely strained. Their brothers, Jacob Sverdrup and Lars Oftedal, both of them clergymen and leaders of the Liberal party's church reform wing in Norway, were battling with conservative churchmen on the one hand, and agnostic reformers on the other.[51]

In the late 1870s a number of Norwegian intellectuals, notably the famous poet and dramatist, Bjørnstjerne Bjørnson, who for many years had championed Norwegian liberalism, repudiated orthodox Christianity. Within a few years Darwinism, naturalism, and related streams of thought, all of which were regarded as antithetical to confessional Christianity, seemed on the point of capturing the mind of Norway. One Norse church historian compares the descent of these movements on his country to a "deluge" that inundated the land, sweeping away much that was traditional." [52]

Bjørnson toured the American Middle West during the winter of 1880–81, speaking in most major Scandinavian-American centers, and outraging Lutherans of all schools by subjecting cherished dogmas to satiric attack.[53] Before the furor aroused by the great poet's visit subsided, another threat appeared. Kristofer N. Janson, a popular literary man and social reformer who, like Bjørnson, had rejected traditional Christian doctrine, settled at Minneapolis in the autumn of 1881. Janson presently became a Unitarian clergyman and a crusader for several reform causes, including the drive against liquor.[54]

Augsburg's leaders reacted strongly to these developments. On January 6, 1881, *Folkebladet* deplored the advance of "agnosticism" (*fritaenkeri*) and its appeal to young people. Sverdrup and Oftedal took pains to refute the message preached by Bjørnson during his American tour; nearly every issue of their journal during the winter and spring of 1881 carried reports of his lectures along with arguments against his major contentions. The arrival of Janson in Minneapolis elicited an equally unenthusiastic response. "It is disconcerting," said *Folkebladet*, "to see a Norse champion of freedom become a clergyman in the United States for the purpose of advocating a doctrine [rationalism] that was preached by those who imprisoned [Hans Nielsen] Hauge. . . . It is sad to see an able and talented man from the Norwegian church openly declare that he will base his position on premises that the Christian church has never recognized as its own." [55]

Janson responded with a letter to the editors which, after attempting to minimize the theological differences between Unitarianism and Lutheranism, requested that he be accepted as a "neighbor." The letter suggested that his group and the Conference could work "side by side" without accusing one another of heresy. *Folkebladet* brusquely rejected this offer of friendship. "For us," replied the editors, "the Christian faith is not a minor issue," adding that they found it impossible "to talk about working 'side by side' with any man or movement rejecting the divinity of Christ." [56] The Janson mission, which continued for about a decade, established a number of Unitarian societies in the area, but most Norwegian-Lutherans remained loyal to their traditional religious allegiance. Nevertheless, dedicated Lutherans kept a wary eye on Janson's operation. Pastor Elias Aas, who attended Augsburg in the 1880s, recalled that he and his peers "liked to hear Janson because of his style, but his teaching we despised." [57]

Whether the Sverdrup-Oftedal reaction to Norway's new intellectual climate — and to Bjørnson and Janson — had an impact on Augsburg's educational policy cannot be ascertained. However, it is probable that the two professors became less sanguine about cooperation with the world beyond church and campus, and more inclined to construct defenses of their own developing tradition.

Church reform in Norway during this period also took a disappointing turn from the Sverdrup-Oftedal point of view. In the parliamentary elections of 1882 the Norwegian Liberal party won a decisive victory that catapulted Johan Sverdrup into the prime ministership. From the beginning of its tenure, which continued until 1889, the Sverdrup ministry was plagued by a profound division between the Liberal party's pietist and "European" — or agnostic — wings. The appointment to the cabinet of Jacob Sverdrup, a nephew of the prime minister, disturbed the "Europeans," who felt that Jacob's church reform program threatened to establish a pietist brand of clericalism as oppressive as the high church variety.[58]

The Liberal party schism soon became entangled with emotional issues. Parliamentary deputies belonging to the pietist faction voted against a stipend for Norway's distinguished writer, Alexander Kielland, on the ground that Kielland, whom they regarded as an agnostic, did not represent the country's true spirit. This stance sharpened "European" antagonism to Jacob Sverdrup's proposals for ecclesiastical reform which called for greater congregational autonomy and aimed to augment the influence of "believing" laymen within the church.[59] Although the prime minister backed his nephew, a coalition of Conservatives and "Europeans" defeated Jacob Sverdrup's program. Far-reaching repercussions followed. The Sverdrup ministry disintegrated; indeed, Johan Sverdrup's own political career went into eclipse, and the pietist Liberals, led by

Jacob Sverdrup and Lars Oftedal, seceded from their party to found a "moderate" Liberal grouping. Some observers concluded that the influence of traditional Christianity on Norwegian life was rapidly waning.

Georg Sverdrup's personal involvement with the travail of Norwegian church reform may have influenced his course as a churchman and educator. The Norwegian clergy, he argued, was mainly responsible for the destruction of his brother's program. Many theologians and clergymen had backed religious revival in the 1850s and 1860s, but anxiety to preserve a basic core of clerical privilege had inhibited their full acceptance of the congregation's rightful role in the life of the church. Consequently, even sincere and conscientious pastors had allied themselves with the opponents of genuine church reform, thus depriving it of the support it needed to prevail.[60]

Whatever the validity of this analysis, Sverdrup's interpretation reinforced his conviction that the future of Norwegian-Lutheranism in America depended on the production of a new breed of clergy, and he believed Augsburg's program responded to this challenge. By 1890 church union was imminent on terms that promised an expansion of the divinity school role. Unfortunately for Sverdrup, his educational design failed to win general acceptance within the new church created by the merger of 1890.

WHAT IS A DIVINITY
SCHOOL?

 THE POSSIBILITY of achieving Norwegian-American Lutheran unity seemed dim in 1880. Eleven years earlier the Norwegian, Scandinavian Augustana, and Eielsen synods had competed for the allegiance of a rapidly growing flock. During the next decade further proliferation had taken place. Division of the Scandinavian Augustana body into its Swedish and Norwegian components in 1870 led to the founding of two Norse synods: the Conference, and the Norwegian Augustana Synod. A few years later the Eielsen group split in two, the larger calling itself Hauge's Synod, the smaller retaining the Eielsen name. At the same time, growing controversy between the Old and New Schools began to threaten the Conference with disruption.

By the early 1880s, internal dissension also was plaguing the Norwegian Synod. A group, led principally by Frederick A. Schmidt, a theological professor, contended that the Missouri Synod, with which the Norwegian Synod maintained close relations, was veering toward Calvinistic determinism and away from traditional Lutheranism. For a few years Schmidt's Anti-Missourians fought a battle within the Norwegian Synod, but their establishment of a separate seminary on the St. Olaf campus in 1886 led to a parting of the ways. The Norwegian Synod convention of 1887 declared the Anti-Missourians to be schismatic, leaving them no alternative but a formal severance of affiliation with the main body. For the time being they constituted themselves as a "Brotherhood," which gained the allegiance of approximately one-third of the congregations adhering to the Norwegian Synod.

Paradoxically, this schism reinforced the drive for unity within Norwegian-Lutheranism, a drive that had gained considerable momentum by 1887. Reluctant to create another synod, the Anti-Missourians launched a merger campaign. At a meeting in Minneapolis late in February, 1888, they not only endorsed the unity idea, but also appointed a number of committees to promote it. The most important of these was a contact committee which requested and secured the privilege of presenting the case for merger before the 1888 conventions of the Conference, the Norwegian Augustana Synod, and Hauge's Synod. All three responded favorably to the Anti-Missourian initiative by selecting members to serve on a joint union committee charged with the responsibility of developing a blueprint for a united Norwegian Lutheran church.

At a meeting in Eau Claire, Wisconsin, from August 15 to 23, 1888, the joint union committee successfully fulfilled its mandate. Its deliberations produced three basic documents: a doctrinal settlement (*Opgjør*) reconciling differences in theological viewpoint among the participants; a constitution for the merged church, and articles of union dealing with such practical issues as synodical schools and finances. In accordance with arrangements made at Eau Claire, a convention made up of delegates from the four participating groups met at Scandinavia, Wisconsin, in November to consider the union committee's blueprint. After amending the documents in several particulars, the Scandinavia meeting referred them — and the entire merger question — to the 1889 conventions of the negotiating bodies. When these met Hauge's Synod withdrew from the projected union, but the other three groups endorsed the work done at Eau Claire and Scandinavia. By prearrangement they met at Minneapolis for their 1890 conventions, which formally brought the merged church into being by adopting the constitution drafted at Eau Claire. Following this action, they convened as a single delegate assembly, the first annual convention of the United Norwegian Lutheran Church in America.[1]

THE ARTICLES of Union designated Augsburg Seminary as the divinity school (*Presteskole*) of the new church. They further specified that salaries of theological professors be funded from interest earned by an endowment fund to which the Conference agreed to contribute $50,000, the Anti-Missourian Brotherhood an equal amount, and the Augustana Synod, $15,000. In addition, they stipulated an expansion of the theological faculty, with the Conference providing two professors (Sverdrup and Oftedal), the Anti-Missourians two, and the Augustana Synod one, thereby consolidating the Anti-Missourian and Augustana seminaries with Augsburg. Legal incorporation of the new church was to be accomplished as soon as possible, after which the merging synods would transfer their school property to United Church ownership. Augsburg's preparatory departments and the academy at Canton, South Dakota (Augustana College), were to continue their established programs "for at least one year" after achievement of the merger.[2]

47

The founding of the United Church seemed to open broad vistas for Augsburg Seminary. With a constituency more than twice as large as the old Conference, a broadened financial base, and an enlarged faculty, the institution appeared destined to become Norwegian-American Lutheranism's major divinity school. Unfortunately, disruptive forces were present in the new church from the beginning of its existence. Most important, the term "divinity school" meant one thing to Augsburg's leaders and something else to Schmidt and the Anti-Missourians. The latter equated it with a three-year theological seminary admitting applicants with a college background. Sverdrup, on the other hand, assumed that the divinity school specified in the articles of union included Augsburg's beginning preparatory and college departments, along with the three-year program of specialized theological study.[3]

This difference in concept became evident less than a week after formal declaration of the 1890 union. On June 17 the first annual convention of the United Church considered the report of its committee on educational institutions. Two resolutions raised the divinity school issue. The first delegated to Augsburg's board of directors and theological faculty the responsibility of formulating "the necessary regulations with respect to the division of labor among the theological professors at the school." [4]

Sverdrup objected vigorously to this proposal, arguing that it infringed on the role of the faculty. The directors, he asserted, were not qualified to decide such questions. He noted further that the resolution implied limitation of the theological faculty's teaching responsibilities to the seminary department, a limitation that ran counter to Augsburg's policy of integrating preparatory and theological study. Despite Sverdrup's strong stand, the delegates passed the resolution with an understanding that it did not infringe on the faculty's right to establish the teaching schedule.[5]

The other controversial resolution in the education committee's report was to prove even more explosive. It proposed that "St. Olaf's College at Northfield, Minnesota, shall be the college of the United Norwegian Lutheran Church." [6] Again Augsburg partisans saw a threat to their divinity school concept. Adopting St. Olaf as *the* college of the church did not necessarily mean liquidation of Augsburg's preparatory departments, but discussion on the convention floor suggested that it might mean this. Professor Schmidt expressed the view that Augsburg would be "too small to be both a seminary and a college," and that it might be "more to the point if the preparatory division could be separated from Augsburg and be an independent school." He added a thought which directly challenged Augsburg's central educational principle: "Men have always come back to the conclusion that it is best not to have the two institutions [college and seminary] together." [7]

Sverdrup, apparently absent from the session, did not reply to Schmidt's remarks. Nor did any other Augsburg spokesman explicitly oppose the St. Olaf resolution. Oftedal expressed regret that such an important matter had to be decided on short notice, particularly since it involved unknown financial commitments, but his comments seemed to acknowledge the church's need for a college as well as a seminary. Following Oftedal's presentation, Bernard Tollefsen, a former Conference pastor with New School leanings, moved that the resolution be referred to the Augsburg board of directors for consideration until the next convention.

This motion failed to win any significant support. Speaker after speaker asserted that a gift like St. Olaf could not be spurned at a time when the new church faced a critical educational problem. Johan A. Bergh, a prominent Old School clergyman, suggested that since the convention had welcomed Augsburg Seminary with a vote of unanimous approval, it should extend the same courtesy to St. Olaf. Before Bergh could complete his remarks, enthusiastic voices in the assembly called for the question. The motion to refer the St. Olaf issue to Augsburg's board of directors lost overwhelmingly, and the original resolution was adopted by acclamation. By convention action, St. Olaf had been made the college of the United Church. [8]

Augsburg partisans were soon convinced that this was the first step in the execution of an underhanded scheme to liquidate Augsburg's preparatory departments in order to provide wider opportunities for St. Olaf, both with respect to students and financial resources. The more extreme version of this conspiracy theory held that even during the merger negotiations, Anti-Missourian leaders had cherished the hope of substituting St. Olaf for Augsburg's preparatory departments. According to the theory, Augustana and Old School Conference representatives combined with the Anti-Missourians to achieve this end. Circumstances dictated secrecy until merger was an accomplished fact. Had the articles of union included St. Olaf among the schools to be adopted by the United Church, the merger proposal could not have mustered sufficient support to prevail — or so the Augsburg men reasoned. Completion of the union created a new situation. At the 1890 convention, enthusiasm generated by merger festivities put the delegates off guard, making it easy for the "conspirators" to push through the St. Olaf resolution before its implications could be weighed. [9]

Like most conspiracies, this one existed more in the minds of its proponents than in the real world. The suspicion of an Anti-Missourian, Augustana, and Old School intrigue against Augsburg is not supported by available evidence. Nor did the exclusion of St. Olaf from the articles of union, coupled with Anti-Missourian advocacy of its adoption by the United Church after merger, add up to a sinister combination of circumstances. Although the Anti-Missourians regarded St. Olaf as their institution, a private corporation legally controlled the school. Consequently, the articles of union could make no stipulation regarding St. Olaf "because it was only indirectly connected with one of the contracting parties." [10]

The premise that a monolithic majority within the new church intransigently opposed Augsburg and its divinity school concept is equally untenable. Until 1893, when the "Friends of Augsburg" separated from the United Church, the school controversy involved three, not two, parties. These included the followers of Oftedal and Sverdrup, who fought for maintenance of Augsburg's *status quo*; an enthusiastic coterie of St. Olaf supporters who worked openly for consolidation of Augsburg's preparatory departments with their institution; and a middle group whose leaders earnestly searched for a compromise that would preserve synodical unity. In the final showdown at the convention of 1893, the St. Olaf party reluctantly accepted a settlement that, among other things, revoked adoption of St. Olaf by the United Church. Rightly or wrongly, the Augsburg people spurned the attempted compromise of 1893 because they believed it failed to offer adequate guarantees that their cherished program of ministerial education would be continued.

IMMEDIATELY AFTER the 1890 convention the school question seemed unlikely to disrupt the United Church. For a few weeks Sverdrup refused to accept the unanimous election to Augsburg Seminary's presidency which the convention had tendered him, but at a mid-July meeting of the school's board of directors, he announced his willingness to serve. At about the same time the board of trustees resolved a number of financial questions, including temporary administration of the Anti-Missourian school endowment fund.[11] It also appeared that Schmidt and Marcus O. Bøckman, the professors selected by the Anti-Missourians to represent them on the Augsburg faculty, were establishing a satisfactory relationship with the administration. In addition to their seminary instruction, Bøckman and Schmidt accepted teaching responsibility in the beginning preparatory and college departments, where they taught religion courses. The new professors accommodated themselves to Sverdrup's divinity school concept without necessarily accepting its validity for all time.[12]

The school year got off to a promising start. In accordance with traditional Augsburg routine, theological instruction began on September 15, and preparatory classes on October 1. Enrollment rose moderately over the preceding year, from 160 to 188. The seminary tally accounted for most of the increase: it expanded from 41 to 72. College enrollment declined slightly — from 58 to 51 — and the beginning preparatory count totaled 65 compared to 61 in 1889–90. Perhaps the one-sided increase in seminary enrollment boded ill for the nine-year divinity school program. Nevertheless, the divergent elements in the student body seemed to be developing a sense of community.[13]

Unfortunately, divisive issues boiled to the surface early in 1891. On January 7 *Skandinaven* published an incendiary letter signed by "A. Erickson," a pseudonym employed by Albert Erickson Egge, a St. Olaf professor, whose identity was soon exposed. From beginning to end, the Egge letter was an attack on Augsburg's academic program. The writer professed little knowledge of the school, but he claimed to have received an unsolicited letter about it from an Augsburg student who, on request, had authorized "A. Erickson" to publish the letter. According to the student's alleged testimony, Augsburg's environment encouraged a spirit of lax anti-intellectualism. Augsburg students, he wrote, had "entirely too much freedom." They were at liberty to take as many or few courses as they pleased, an option that extended to Latin and Greek. When a young man left the institution, he took with him a positive "distaste for rigorous intellectual labor." Nor was there, the letter contended, much hope of improvement. Ambition and vanity — evidently on the part of Augsburg's leaders — precluded moving the college, and dictated that the United Church's educational program be located on the Augsburg campus.[14]

These accusations precipitated a lively Norwegian-American press war of several years' duration. Influential newspapers, including *Norden* and *Amerika*, elaborated the Egge attack, and *Folkebladet* replied in kind. Before long, a uniformly dreary pattern of assault and defense emerged. Augsburg spokesmen claimed that their institution fostered true Christian piety, while St. Olaf nurtured a dangerously "humanistic" view of the world. Proponents of the Northfield school characterized Augsburg as a "humbug" institution, and pointed with pride at St. Olaf's strides toward achieving academic stature.[15]

The Augsburg campus became a storm center of the growing controversy. Students of Conference background — particularly the New School variety — often found themselves in disagreement with those whose antecedents were Anti-Missourian or Augustana. The administration, too, reacted strongly, and its efforts to uncover the identity of Egge's informant injected additional issues into the argument. Shortly after the *Skandinaven* piece appeared, the theological faculty requested the students to sign a statement affirming that they had not written to "A. Erickson." A number of them regarded this procedure as inquisitorial, and anti-Augsburg spokesmen, including Egge, took up their cause.[16]

Meanwhile, discussion of issues related to Egge's allegations had driven a divisive wedge into the faculty. On February 18, 1891, *Folkebladet* published a letter from Professor Schmidt reiterating the position he had taken at the 1890 convention during debate on the St. Olaf resolution. According to Schmidt, the articles of union did not oblige the United Church to maintain the preparatory departments on the Augsburg campus forever. He acknowledged that a case could be made for the Augsburg divinity school concept, but also insisted that there were powerful arguments for the maintenance of colleges and seminaries as separate institutions. The church, Schmidt contended, needed independent minds (*selvstaendige Karakterer*) within the ranks of its clergy. Whether a system of ministerial education that placed the candidate under the influence of the same teachers from the time he began his preparatory work until his ordination contributed to this end was extremely debatable. An integrated program like Augsburg's, he suggested, could produce clergymen conforming to a single pattern and possessing such undesirable characteristics as "one-sidedness," and a narrowly partisan spirit.

Schmidt's letter invited rebuttals, to which the professor responded with comments that provoked further reaction. Unfortunately, extraneous issues, including personalities, soon became part of the exchange. For example, an unsigned *Folkebladet* article replying to Schmidt's first communication included unflattering references to the professor's role in earlier controversies.[17] Such treatment may have been responsible for the angry Schmidt letter published by *Skandinaven* on April 1, that accused Sverdrup's administration of being oppressive and unfair to faculty and students outside of the Conference tradition. Schmidt shortly retracted this letter, explaining that it had been written under the pressure of emotional stress and physical illness, but the impression of disharmony within the faculty persisted, and off campus the conflict continued to accelerate.[18]

THE DELIBERATIONS of the United Church's second convention, held at Kenyon, Minnesota, from June 17 to 25, 1891, intensified rather than ameliorated the mounting crisis. In his message to the opening session, President Gjermund Hoyme dealt at length with the issues in controversy. He refrained from making a recommendation with respect to Augsburg's preparatory departments, but unmistakably asserted the right of the United Church to separate these departments from the institution if this seemed prudent and wise. Hoyme rejected the contention of some Augsburg spokesmen that the divinity school — which the articles of union obligated the United Church to maintain — necessarily included Augsburg's preparatory departments, a contention that affirmed a contractual obligation on the part of the church to continue these departments.[19]

Sverdrup's report to the Kenyon convention did not take issue with Hoyme's assertion of full United Church authority over Augsburg's preparatory departments. On the contrary, it implicitly accepted this authority. At the same time, Sverdrup presented an elaborate argument for his divinity school concept. He thought it would be unwise for the convention "to initiate any significant changes in the school's program this year." To this observation he added a lengthy comment, again as a statement of "the president's" opinion:

Under present conditions it is necessary to continue the preparatory departments in as close a relationship with the theological department as possible. Instruction in these departments is arranged in such a way that it provides the best preparation for fruitful theological study; and so far as can be ascertained, it presently is the only way to assure the theological department a sufficient number of adequately trained students. The theological professors and seminarians exert an extremely beneficial influence on the younger boys in the preparatory departments. But apart from these important considerations, the synod cannot effect any significant change in educational policy without launching an extensive building program, and this cannot be done just now. Prudence undoubtedly suggests preservation of what we have until the United Church has calmly weighed all aspects of the school question and until the synod is confident of its capacity to carry the building program that necessarily has to accompany any forward step in the educational area.[20]

With Sverdrup conceding the United Church's authority to order Augsburg's educational program, and Hoyme calling for responsible debate on the issues relating to the institution's preparatory departments, it would seem that the way lay open for a satisfactory settlement of the school question. Unfortunately, several developments at the 1891 convention and in its aftermath intensified mutual suspicion and hostility to the point where negotiation was impossible. Most important, Augsburg partisans more than ever became persuaded that they were victims of a conspiracy, the aim of which was to undermine their institution's program of ministerial education.

Convention proceedings disclosed that St. Olaf College enjoyed considerable favor within the church. Hoyme referred glowingly to the Northfield school and its work. Its administration and faculty had instituted an educational program that placed St. Olaf graduates "side by side" with students holding degrees from the nation's leading colleges. Hoyme regretted that St. Olaf hitherto had not received more support from the church, remarking that limited resources made the school's achievements all the more impressive. He strongly urged the delegates to appropriate a generous sum for its support.[21]

The convention heeded Hoyme's request. It bestowed $7,000 on St. Olaf, compared to the $4,500 earmarked for Augsburg. Since endowment fund income financed a substantial portion of Augsburg faculty salaries, the disparity was not as substantial as it might seem.[22] Nevertheless, Augsburg spokesmen complained bitterly about the additional monetary burden that St. Olaf imposed on the church at a time when their institution needed more support.[23] Assumption by the United Church of responsibility for a deficit in St. Olaf's current budget heightened chagrin within Augsburg circles, as did transfer of provisional control of the Anti-Missourian endowment fund from the Augsburg to the United Church board of trustees.[24]

Had the Augsburg men regarded St. Olaf as a "safe" institution, they might have accepted its competitive status with more grace. As it was, Sverdrup and Oftedal genuinely distrusted the Northfield school, and events at Kenyon reinforced their suspicion. The report presented to the convention by Thorbjørn N. Mohn, president of St. Olaf, articulated a view of Christian higher education with which they disagreed. Specifically, Mohn failed to mention religious commitment as a goal of St. Olaf's program; apparently he assumed that this was implicit. In addition, he defended the traditional Latin school course of study, remarking that since Greek and Latin culture had produced modern civilization, a study of the two ancient languages and their literature belonged at the core of a well-ordered college curriculum.[25] Augsburg's leaders had explicitly rejected this idea in 1874, and during the intervening years their dislike of what they called "humanist" education had increased.

Convention deliberation on the school question — meaning the future of Augsburg's preparatory departments — brought hostilities between St. Olaf and Augsburg into clear focus. Three options were presented to the delegates. The first, formulated and recommended by a majority of Committee No. 1 (responsible for drafting resolutions on the basis of the principal convention reports), was essentially a compromise proposal. It read: "Because of existing circumstances, the preparatory departments of Augsburg Seminary shall continue to operate for the time being in conjunction with the divinity school of the church body."[26] A Committee No. 1 minority report proposed a merger of Augsburg's preparatory departments with St. Olaf. The Augsburg board of trustees formulated a third alternative. It laid down a number of conditions for the transfer of Augsburg property to the United Church. These included maintenance of the preparatory departments "essentially" in their present form, an annual appropriation of at least $4,500 for their support, and a guarantee that the church would not mortgage Augsburg property except for the school's direct benefit. The trustees' proposal further specified that none of these arrangements could be altered by simple majority action at a United Church convention. Before any projected change could go into effect, it had to be adopted by one convention and ratified by a two-thirds majority at the next.[27]

When these rival resolutions reached the floor for deliberation, a lengthy and spirited debate developed. An exchange between Egge and Sverdrup at one session illumines the basic issue in controversy. Egge contended that St. Olaf was well equipped to provide pre-theological training, since he believed theological study did not require special preparation. Up to now, he argued, ministerial candidates had been denied sufficient exposure to the liberal arts (*humane Fag*), a deficiency that St. Olaf could correct. He noted that while the school did not train ministers nor, for that matter, doctors or lawyers, it did provide "an education for all." In Egge's view, a general liberal arts education was the best possible preparation for theological study.

Sverdrup, who spoke immediately after Egge, totally rejected the latter's basic premise. For 17 years, he said, the primary goal of Augsburg's preparatory departments had been to train young men for theological study. Upon arriving on campus, most Augsburg students began working in congregations "as teachers of religion and in other capacities." According to Sverdrup, Augsburg's preparatory branches and St. Olaf College were "entirely different" types of institutions. Educating ministers was one thing, and training lawyers and doctors was another, he insisted. "Schools with different goals," he added, "need not impede each other . . . either financially or otherwise."[28]

By an overwhelming vote the delegates chose the Committee No. 1 majority report. While this decision assured continuance of Augsburg's *status quo*, it left the school's partisans apprehensive about the future. Sverdrup complained that while the majority report did not explicitly characterize Augsburg's program as deficient, it created that impression. Moreover, the phrase, "for the time being," clearly implied a liquidation of the preparatory departments "sooner or later." Postponement until the next annual convention of action on a proposed constitution for Augsburg Seminary, a document that called for maintenance of the existing academic arrangements, further reinforced pessimism concerning the long-range prospects of Sverdrup's divinity school concept.

FOLLOWING ADJOURNMENT of the Kenyon convention, the journalistic exchange between St. Olaf and Augsburg spokesmen grew more intense. In the summer of 1891 Egge publicly acknowledged the A. Erickson pseudonym, asserting at the same time that he had written strictly on his own and not as a representative of St. Olaf or the Anti-Missourian Brotherhood. Accompanying circumstances led Augsburg spokesmen to reject Egge's claim that he spoke only for himself. More important, individuals with tangible St. Olaf connections joined the newspaper war. Peer O. Strømme, a well-known Norwegian-American journalist and former St. Olaf teacher, invented a correspondent named Peter Olson Vraadal, a fictional Augsburg student with marked intellectual deficiencies, whose ungrammatical composition, weak argument, and damaging admissions left the impression that an Augsburg education was worthless. A typical Vraadal statement conceded that "the nastiest accusations made against our dear Augsburg are what in Latin is called *veritas* (truth), and nothing less." [29]

Anonymous *Folkebladet* articles replied in kind to these blasts. A correspondent identifying himself as "the father of a family," wondered why Egge had not been dismissed from his post. "If this man is retained," affirmed the writer, "we will be obliged to believe not only that the school is rationalistic, but something worse." From this the father drew a painful conclusion: "Obviously we . . . are obliged to withhold our contribution from St. Olaf . . . because we can have no assurance that we are supporting a Christian school." [30] Other considerations reinforced this reasoning. "What direct or indirect benefit," asked the writer, "does the church body derive from St. Olaf with its luxurious facilities, its doctors of philosophy, its masters of arts, and the deficits that it imposes on the synod year after year? What do we gain by appointing teachers with glittering titles and perhaps impressive theoretical knowledge when it is fairly clear that they are no more effective in the classroom than ordinary instructors with less academic preparation?" [31]

These polemics created grossly distorted stereotypes of both Augsburg and St. Olaf. Although Augsburg spokesmen exalted religious commitment over formal learning — a tendency that would become more pro-

56

nounced after the schism of 1893 — an Augsburg education was not as deficient as Egge and "Vraadal" contended. *Folkebladet* treatment of St. Olaf was equally unfair. Whatever would be true in the future, the Northfield school in 1890 was not equipped with luxurious facilities. The Mohn administration cherished lofty ambitions, but at the time St. Olaf was a struggling institution coping with the problem of survival.[32]

The charge that "rationalism" dominated St. Olaf was even more ludicrous. While there were some differences between the two institutions, these scarcely warranted the accusations made by Augsburg partisans. St. Olaf was coeducational, its curricular program included both lay and pre-theological education (as Augsburg's had initially), and its leaders were less hostile than Sverdrup to traditional European higher education. In addition, the St. Olaf administration was working to establish the school as a recognized modern American college, while Augsburg's leaders interpreted their own mission as being the creation of a unique divinity school. The hiring policies of the two institutions reflect this difference in aspiration. Augsburg recruited its faculty from alumni firmly committed to the New School Conference tradition. St. Olaf, on the other hand, attached relatively greater importance to the formal academic preparation of its teachers, but not at the expense of theological acceptability. Negotiations between Mohn and Thorstein Veblen, the controversial economist who applied for a position at St. Olaf in 1890, terminated promptly after Mohn received from Veblen a frank exposition of the latter's unorthodox religious views.[33]

Beyond its effect on settlement of the transfer question, the St. Olaf-Augsburg newspaper war of 1891–92 undoubtedly influenced the images and self-images of the two institutions for years to come. The "humanist" bugaboo dampened the enthusiasm of many United Church people for St. Olaf, thereby intensifying the school's financial difficulties, which were unusually grave in the 1890s. In the long run, however, Augsburg suffered a more painful loss of reputation. Both the friends and detractors of St. Olaf cultivated the impression that the school was seeking to achieve academic excellence. Augsburg's developing image was less flattering. The position taken by St. Olaf supporters — which, due to wide circulation of papers like *Skandinaven*, gained the attention of many Norwegian-Americans — nourished suspicions that Augsburg tended to substitute piety for scholarship. Statements by spokesmen for the Minneapolis school sometimes reinforced this view. The catalog for 1900–01 flatly stated that at Augsburg, "Spiritual life and Christian character are considered of infinitely higher importance than mere knowledge." [34]

SVERDRUP ENLISTED as a regular participant in the newspaper feud in the autumn of 1891. Beginning on November 18, *Folkebladet* carried his series of articles dealing with the principal issues in controversy. The first two contributions leveled a bitter attack on St. Olaf. Adoption of the school by the 1890 convention, Sverdrup charged, was an unwise decision foisted upon the assembly by unprincipled manipulation. St. Olaf's financial needs, he added, were threatening the United Church with catastrophic debt. Worse yet, the bitter controversy unleashed by the school's partisans was sapping the inner vitality of the new church even before merger of the three synods could be transformed into a genuine union. According to Sverdrup, two parties stood in angry confrontation within the United Church: a group of St. Olaf "humanists," animated by "enthusiasm for the Latin school on the one side, and the divinity school and congregation on the other."

Subsequent articles developed an argument against "Latin School humanism," the educational perspective that allegedly held sway at St. Olaf. As in other controversies, the Augsburg president based much of his analysis on Norwegian experience. Two parallel conflicts, he wrote, had dogged his native land since early in the century. The first separated caste-conscious clergymen from the main body of Christian believers; the other aligned an "aristocratic officialdom" against the plain people. A common educational experience helped forge an alliance between pastors and officials. From the Latin school both had acquired a distinctively humanist orientation.[35]

As every writer who employs a word like "humanism" should do, Sverdrup undertook to explain the sense in which he used the term. Academically, he asserted, humanism was a system of education which "utilizes the old Greek and Latin classics as its essential instructional material." Language study — "whether . . . Greek or Latin or Norse or English" — for the sake of "practical" need should not, he insisted, be equated with humanism. The term denoted rather a training of the intellect based on the thought and values set forth in Greek and Latin literature. Humanism also assumed that "man is good by nature." A sound education required only that unspoiled nature be adorned with "Greek and Roman forms." Thus attired, the "natural" became the "humane," and the "good and beautiful" were united.[36]

Sverdrup's indictment of humanism and its institutional sponsor, the Latin school, included two principal counts. First, their educational canon set up knowledge of Latin as the boundary separating the "uncouth" masses from society's "upper" or cultivated classes, an emphasis that tended to perpetuate the aristocratic ideal in a democratic age.

Shielded by the protective "screen" of a "mysterious" language, Latin school alumni often amused themselves "with Latin witticisms at the people's expense." For those who required the language as a tool — students of theology, for example — Latin study was entirely appropriate, according to Sverdrup. But humanist enthusiasts saw its value in other terms. They regarded Latin "as the narrow way from crude ignorance to cultured refinement, from the undifferentiated mob to a select elite."

While fulminating against Latin's alleged supremacy as a learned discipline, Sverdrup strongly recommended the pursuit of "useful" knowledge. It was, he wrote, socially responsible (*folkeligt*) for a prospective physician to study medicine, an aspiring carpenter to master house construction, or a future lawyer to learn jurisprudence. "But it is socially irresponsible (*ufolkeligt*)," he continued, "for a student to acquire knowledge simply because possession of this knowledge elevates him above his fellowmen, irrespective of whether or not he derives any practical benefit from it." [37]

The second major count in Sverdrup's indictment of humanism charged that it endangered the religious commitment of Christian students. In a pious home, he pointed out, beneficent influences protected and nourished the child's spiritual life. "But in the learned school the situation is entirely different," he added. Here the dominating aim of instruction was to "awaken the intellect," which meant "raising questions and instilling doubt." Humanists, wrote Sverdrup, gloried in the greatness and beauty of the human spirit, a value reinforced by the works of pagan classicists who held up ambition as humanity's proper driving force. Humanist education exalted "free inquiry" over "simple faith," and insisted that "a question mark be attached to everything possible." Initial exposure to such learning might "trouble the conscience a little," but gradual adaptation was predictable. Before long the Christian student would become a skeptic (*Tviler*), and ultimately — providing he persisted on the humanist road — a confirmed agnostic (*Fritaenker*).[38]

Although Sverdrup directed most of his fire at Norwegian higher learning, American education did not escape his censure. Humanists might assert, he wrote, that the American college and Norwegian Latin school were fundamentally different institutions. Sverdrup conceded a difference, but denied its relevance: "American humanists, who are drawn chiefly from the ranks of polished . . . Congregational clergymen, bear the mark of classical rationalism to an even greater extent than do European humanists. We admire the rhetoric of American humanists . . . but nevertheless must conclude that their message is not the best. Among many of them, eloquent expositions of human wisdom overshadow the Cross of Christ. And this is a consequence of their faulty educational system." [39]

Natural science, which was winning a significant place in American colleges and universities, was as suspect as classical literature, according to Sverdrup. Many Norwegian-American students were yielding to agnosticism. This deplorable reality, he wrote, was "most often" attributable to the ribald (*smudsige*) works of pagan antiquity which undermined morality, and to the insistence of science on the inexorable sovereignty of natural laws (*Naturvidenskabens Lovmaessighed*), a mode of thinking that rendered the concept of Christian freedom unbelievable. He also quoted a church historian to the effect that the course of study open to most American college students left them Biblically illiterate. In short, the American college was an inadequate model to follow in constructing a suitable pre-theological program.[40]

After expressing dissatisfaction with prevailing patterns of higher education — whether European or American, classical or scientific — Sverdrup shifted his discourse to Augsburg's mission. Much of what he wrote reiterated previous pronouncements. The school's supreme aim was to train clergymen attuned to the needs of the congregation and completely identified with it (*Menighedsmaessig Presteuddannelse*). Therefore, potential ministerial candidates had to meet the test of personal religious experience and commitment. Equally important, Augsburg's academic program from the beginning preparatory through the college and theological departments was designed to strengthen personal commitment and rapport with the congregation.

Sverdrup's specifications for achieving this goal were similar to those set forth in the 1874 program. The basic disciplines included Biblical studies and history, "God's revelation and mankind's self-revelation," together with the "absolutely essential languages." However, even this unadorned course of study, though presumably free of humanist virus, could alienate the ministerial student from his future flock. "One can become so preoccupied with the congregation's history that he loses vital contact with the congregation that he is to serve," wrote Sverdrup. To avert this peril, Augsburg encouraged its students to engage in such vacation-time activities as teaching in congregational religion schools and assisting pastors even to the point of filling pulpits on Sunday morning. Relatively long vacation periods assured maximum benefit from this "exchange between divinity school and congregation." [41]

Sverdrup frankly recognized that involvement of Augsburg's college department with the kind of ministerial education he advocated precluded claiming college status for the department. "The congregations," he wrote, "need a divinity school oriented to their needs (*en menigheds-maessig Presteskole*)." All instruction had to be placed within the framework of Christian commitment and directed toward training servants of the congregation. Anyone familiar with higher education would know that a college was not designed to meet such a challenge, added Sverdrup. Similarly, "every schoolman knows that an educational institution organized along these lines is not a college, but another type of school, the most appropriate name for which is the one we use, divinity school." [42] In the judicial proceedings of a few years later between the United Church and Augsburg's board of trustees, Sverdrup reiterated the same point. The goal of his administration, he asserted, had been "to build a school for educating ministers through an eight years' course, not to try to build a college and theological seminary at the side of each other." [43]

Whatever else might be said about the line of argument in Sverdrup's *Folkebladet* series, it is clear that his articles, along with other pronouncements on his side of the controversy, helped create a troublesome legacy for Augsburg College. His defined goals excluded seeking full American college status for the Greek department in favor of maintaining that department as an integral part of a divinity school model which failed to win the admiration of theological educators. The unfair attack on St. Olaf, which can be understood though scarcely justified as an angry reaction to considerable provocation from the Northfield camp, guaranteed prolonged disharmony between two sister schools, and alienated many Norwegian-Americans who otherwise might have been staunch Augsburg supporters. Finally, Sverdrup's assault on prevailing systems of higher education — particularly the proscription of classical literature and modern science because these disciplines allegedly threatened the Christian faith — left the impression that a narrow anti-intellectualism dominated Augsburg's academic policy.

It is impossible fully to dismiss this impression. However, any evaluation of Georg Sverdrup must take into account his commitments in relation to the milieu of his own time. He was hostile to aristocratic privilege, whether ecclesiastical or secular; sympathetic to the democratic aspirations of his age; suspicious of those brands of theology that in his view unduly intellectualized religious faith; and perhaps overly inclined to project his Norwegian experience into an American setting. It is also probable that the defection from Christianity of prominent Norwegians who shared the Sverdrup family's zeal for democratic reform heightened his fear of the de-Christianizing tendencies inherent in the new thought currents of the period.

There is an unmistakable congruence between these concerns and the major theses argued in Sverdrup's articles. His protest against "Latin school humanism" was that of a theologian-educator who wanted to break with tradition but was worried about the emerging present, and felt himself under siege within the United Church fraternity. One additional comment is appropriate: Sverdrup was not compensating for any personal academic deficiencies. As both friend and adversary unreservedly recognized, he had an admirable command of the tools of scholarship. He was an acknowledged member of the Norwegian-American community's intellectual elite who chose to champion an anti-elitist position.[44]

SCHISM

 BETWEEN THE United Church conventions of 1891 and 1892, the intrusion of a thorny legal problem added another dimension to the Augsburg controversy. Formally the Conference, an unincorporated body, had never owned Augsburg Seminary. By action of its board of trustees, the school had been incorporated under Minnesota law in 1872. In reality this step imposed no limitation on Conference control over the institution. Annual conventions continued to elect trustees, directors, and permanent faculty, and also retained authority over broad school policy. To quiet fears that this control might not be strictly legal, the Minnesota legislature of 1877 enacted a special law ratifying past Conference decisions with respect to Augsburg, and adding to the articles of incorporation a proviso that empowered the Conference to select future trustees.[1]

When negotiators of the 1890 merger formulated the articles of union, they hoped to vest in the United Church basically the same control over Augsburg that the Conference was exercising. However, there was a technical difference between the two situations. Unlike the Conference, the new church was to be incorporated, a step that union negotiators hoped would establish a tidier legal relationship between church and seminary than had existed before 1890. Since Minnesota law frowned on the direct transfer of one non-profit corporation's property to another, this hope could not easily be realized.

Hoyme and his intimates became aware of the transfer question's complexities shortly before the Kenyon convention. In a communication dated June 4, 1891, Judge Andreas Ueland, who had been engaged as attorney by the United Church, informed Hoyme of a delicate legal problem. "I cannot but come to the conclusion," wrote Ueland, "that the proposed transfers [of Augsburg and St. Olaf] would be beyond their [boards'] corporate power to make, and that the transfers could be hindered or set aside at the instance of a donor of the property or of the state if an attempt was made to do this. . . . But while the transfers would thus be voidable, they would not be void. Until attacked and set aside by the court they would be operative and vest title in the new corporation." [2]

For reasons that were not entirely clear, Hoyme chose not to inform the 1891 convention of Ueland's pessimistic assessment. From the United Church's point of view, this was a serious blunder.[3] The crux of the Ueland opinion would inevitably become known; Oftedal said he learned of it in November, 1891.[4] As should have been anticipated, the Augsburg men interpreted Hoyme's concealment of legal information that potentially strengthened their bargaining position *vis a vis* the United Church as additional evidence of a conspiracy against their school.[5]

FOLLOWING THE Kenyon convention United Church leaders gingerly approached the legal problem connected with the school transfer question, a development that focused attention on Sven Oftedal, president and dominant member of the Augsburg board of trustees, and also a member of the United Church board of trustees. At a series of separate but interlocking meetings of the two boards held at Minneapolis on July 8 and 9, 1891, the church trustees delivered a double request to Augsburg's board: that it shift to the United Church board provisional control of the Anti-Missourian endowment fund as the Kenyon convention had ordered; and that it transfer Augsburg's property to the United Church as soon as this could be done. After considerable haggling, the Augsburg trustees acceded to the first request. They declined to act on the second, arguing that the church convention had failed to authorize negotiation of the requested transfer.[6]

In response to pressure from two members who favored early transfer of Augsburg's property, Oftedal called his board together on January 5, 1892, the meeting being held on the Augsburg campus. By this time he had obtained the text of Judge Ueland's opinion which provided him with plausible legal grounds for opposing immediate transfer. With the support of two other members of the five-man group, Oftedal secured passage of a resolution postponing consideration of transfer until "necessary negotiations" with the United Church could be conducted at its next convention, and until the same assembly could weigh the legal issue raised by Ueland.[7]

Two months later President Hoyme activated a nine-man college committee that the 1891 convention had authorized him to appoint. A broad responsibility rested on this committee. The resolution providing for its creation instructed it to conduct a thorough investigation of the "college question," including the legal complexities connected with establishment of United Church control over both St. Olaf and Augsburg. Hoyme's appointments to the committee included Sverdrup, Mohn, and Anders G. Tuve, president of Augustana College; three prominent clergymen, Theodor H. Dahl, Ole J. Hattlestad, and John N. Kildahl, St. Olaf's future president; and three laymen, Ole O. Aanstad, A. A. Klove, and Iver Larsen. In terms of definable groups within the United Church, these appointments created a balanced body; they accorded representation to the church's three major educational institutions as well as the three former synods that had merged. Nevertheless, Sverdrup declined to serve on the grounds that the committee was not legally competent to discharge the responsibilities laid on it by Hoyme.[8]

The committee held its first meeting at Minneapolis from March 22 to 25, 1892. After consulting two prominent attorneys — Dean William S. Pattee of the University of Minnesota College of Law, and Selden Bacon of Minneapolis — it endorsed an approach to the transfer question which came to be known as the Pattee-Bacon plan. This plan accepted the premise that a direct transfer of Augsburg and St. Olaf property to the United Church would be of "doubtful validity," a confirmation of Ueland's view. However, the two lawyers suggested a practical way out of the difficulty: making "the members of (delegates to) the Annual Meeting of the United Church the members of the several corporations . . . and the sole members thereof. . . ." Technically the three corporations — Augsburg, St. Olaf, and the United Church — would retain their separate legal identities; actually "the delegates to the United Church" would "also be the members of the other two Institutions ex officio." Business meetings of the three corporations, although conducted by the same assembly, would have "to be called to order separately and their transactions . . . kept separate. . . ." But the "practical result," according to Pattee and Bacon would be to give the United Church "full control of the Institutions." [9]

On May 24, 1892, Pattee and Bacon submitted to the college committee a second communication which elaborated their plan. Among other things, this document dealt with the problem of how annual conventions of the United Church could legally become the Augsburg and St. Olaf corporations. The essential step, stated by the attorneys, was an amendment to the articles of incorporation of the two institutions sanctioning the proposed arrangement. At this point the lawyers detected what they regarded as a minor difficulty: "The articles of Augsburg Seminary were originally so drawn as to render it highly doubtful where the power of amendment of the articles lies." In their opinion, authority to amend resided "in the five gentlemen who originally sought to incorporate them-

65

selves as Augsburg Seminary." To resolve doubt, Pattee and Bacon suggested adoption of the amendment "by these five gentlemen and by the five gentlemen now occupying the position of Trustees, by each body at a meeting regularly called for that purpose." [10]

A halfhearted effort by United Church leaders to act on this counsel failed. Shortly before the 1892 convention Hoyme and Dahl, chairman of the nine-man college committee, requested Ole Paulson, who had served as chairman of the board of trustees that had incorporated Augsburg Seminary in 1872, to call a meeting of his fellow incorporators for the purpose of initiating the desired amendment. Paulson complied but, since only one other incorporator appeared, the meeting could take no action.[11] A few weeks later Oftedal more successfully utilized the legal authority which Pattee and Bacon believed to be vested in the original incorporators and current board of trustees.

AS INFORMED Norse-Americans expected the school controversy dominated the 1892 United Church convention assembled at Dawson, Minnesota, on June 15. A heavy influx of delegates from congregations previously unrepresented at annual conventions, Norwegian-American journalists in quest of exciting copy, and interested spectators raised attendance far beyond Dawson's housing capacity. To accommodate the overflow, convention officials pressed facilities in neighboring Madison into service, and a special train provided transportation between the two villages several times daily.[12]

Convention proceedings did not disappoint those expecting pyrotechnics. Theoretically the Pattee-Bacon plan, which the college committee presented as the heart of its report, served as the basis of discussion and decision. In reality debate frequently moved into peripheral areas, and a number of spirited personal exchanges enlivened the deliberations. One journalist recalled Sverdrup's devastating reply to an effort at self-justification by Professor Egge as "the worst or best of its kind" that he had ever witnessed.[13] Oftedal, too, spoke at length on nearly every issue before the convention. His colorful rhetoric and ready wit held audience interest and often evoked appreciative laughter. However, it is doubtful that his participation strengthened Augsburg's cause. His mock humility, frequent outbursts of self-righteousness, and occasional resort to specious reasoning — as when he sought to discredit incorporation of the United Church by appealing to agrarian dislike of big business corporations — infuriated his adversaries and failed to win the uncommitted.[14]

Following a lengthy debate extending through several sessions when a number of substitute resolutions and motions to amend were introduced and rejected, the convention endorsed the college committee's basic proposal. The key paragraph of the resolution embodying this decision recommended "that the board of trustees of Augsburg Seminary transfer Augsburg Seminary's property to the United Church in accordance with the plan presented by W. S. Pattee and Selden Bacon." To forestall undue delay in accomplishing transfer, the resolution requested an official or unofficial response from Augsburg's board before convention adjournment if possible, and by September 1, 1892, at the latest.[15]

The Augsburg party regarded this decision as wholly unacceptable. According to Oftedal, the Pattee-Bacon plan was so riddled with imperfections that compliance could not be squared with the obligations under which the Augsburg board operated. Augsburg spokesmen also objected to what they called the assumption that the United Church corporation could "dictate" a course of action to the Augsburg corporation instead of "negotiating" a new agreement. An arrogant majority, they charged, was ruthlessly trampling a helpless minority whose leaders were righteously faithful to a moral and legal trust.[16]

These allegations exaggerated the cohesiveness of the so-called convention majority. On a number of questions, moderate supporters of the Pattee-Bacon plan voted with the Augsburg bloc in opposition to an ultra St. Olaf party. This coalition defeated an effort to expunge from the official convention report a critical reference to Professor Egge in Sverdrup's presidential message.[17] It also rejected a minority recommendation from the nominating committee proposing Bøckman instead of Sverdrup as president.[18] Similarly, the delegates turned down an amendment "demanding" rather than "recommending" compliance by the Augsburg board with the Pattee-Bacon plan.[19]

Convention approval of a resolution submitting the school question to a congregational referendum provides the clearest evidence of a strong impulse within the church to seek a compromise of the St. Olaf-Augsburg controversy. In presenting the referendum proposal from the floor on June 23, closing day of the convention, John Kildahl articulated a longing for harmony shared by most of the delegates. "I believe," said Kildahl, "that there will never be peace within the synod until the congregations decide the issue." His resolution called for determination of two questions: 1) Shall the United Church operate and support both St. Olaf and the college department of Augsburg Seminary? 2) If the synod is not to operate and support both these schools, which of them should the United Church operate and support?" Kildahl's proposal further specified that the congregations should report their results to President

Hoyme by December 31, 1892, and that either or both of the schools —
depending on the referendum's outcome — should be supported by the
United Church.[20]

Although Sverdrup had suggested submission of St. Olaf's status to a
congregational vote, neither he nor Oftedal backed the Kildahl motion
which, incidentally, gained the reluctant assent of St. Olaf spokesmen.
During debate on the proposal Oftedal and Sverdrup questioned whether
the United Church constitution authorized referring such an issue to
congregational determination. This doubt may have been genuine —
though it had a strange ring coming from uncompromising advocates of
congregational autonomy — but from their point of view, there was another objection. Even if the referendum went in Augsburg's favor (as it
would), Kildahl's resolution included an unacceptable stipulation: "The
church body shall have the right to organize, order and operate (*ind-
rette, ordne og drive*) the school which the congregations adopt in accordance with decisions taken by the synod's annual conventions." The
referendum proposal, which the closing session approved by an overwhelming majority, failed to provide suitable guarantees against modification or even ultimate liquidation of Augsburg's divinity school program by a United Church convention majority.[21]

ON AUGUST 3, 1892, approximately six weeks after adjournment of the
Dawson convention, Oftedal assembled a joint meeting of Augsburg's
original incorporators and the institution's board of trustees at Minneapolis for the purpose of amending the Augsburg articles of incorporation.
Four of the five original incorporators and all five of the trustees were
present. Although Oftedal agreed with Pattee and Bacon that the power
to amend the incorporation articles resided in this combined group, the
meeting, following his leadership by a margin of seven to two, recast the
articles along very different lines than suggested by the two attorneys.
The most important change reconstituted the Augsburg corporation. Article II of the amended document stipulated:

> Any . . . member in good standing, of a Norwegian Lutheran Church,
> connected with the United Lutheran Church . . . may become a member
> of this Corporation by being elected as such a member by the then mem-
> bers of the Corporation . . . and whenever the members of this Corpora-
> tion equal or exceed thirty . . . a two thirds . . . vote of such members
> shall be necessary in order to elect new members.

Articles I and IV defined the responsibilities and powers of the corporation. "Its general purpose" was to be "the training and education of
young men in the ministry of the Lutheran Church . . . by . . . estab-

lishing and maintaining . . . a Theological Seminary at Minneapolis," which was to "include a preparatory school substantially as heretofore maintained." The officers were to include a five-man board of trustees elected for a term of five years by the corporation at its annual meetings; a president who was to be a member of the board of trustees; and a secretary and treasurer who "in the discretion of the Trustees" could "be members of this Corporation or not."

On the assumption that the board of trustees and original incorporators jointly constituted Augsburg's corporation, the August 3 meeting elected 21 new corporation members, bringing the total to 30. In recruiting this group, the Oftedal majority made no effort to distribute representation among various United Church factions. The expanded corporation was, on the contrary, heavily packed with former Conference men of New School leanings. One of the two minority board members recalled that when he objected to his imbalance, Ole Paulson, a firm Oftedal partisan, replied that the meeting had been called to build a wall around Augsburg which would protect the institution from Anti-Missourians, Augustanans, and Old School Conference adherents.[22]

Public explanations of the August 3 meeting developed a different rationale. According to *Folkebladet*, no settlement of the transfer question could be anticipated until the 1893 United Church convention assembled. Meanwhile, legal uncertainties menaced the school. "The terms of a majority of its board of trustees have expired, and should they or the original incorporators pass from the scene," Augsburg's title to its own property could be seriously compromised. *Folkebladet* also advanced a claim frequently made by Oftedal: that the August 3 action, far from being a planned hindrance to transfer, was meant to facilitate establishment of United Church control of Augsburg on "mutually acceptable terms." [23]

These comments and claims were not as cynical as Paulson's remark might indicate, or as United Church officials chose to believe. Jackson and Atwater, a law firm retained by Augsburg's board of trustees, advised their client that the death of incorporators and trustees would create "a most serious deadlock, and one which would be difficult, if not impossible, to remedy." The attorneys also raised a number of practical objections to the Pattee-Bacon plan, the most important being that a body as large and fluctuating as a United Church convention would find competent discharge of corporation responsibilities difficult. "For these and other reasons," concluded the attorneys, "it has, we think, been the general experience of Protestant churches . . . that the interests of . . . institutions under their control are best subserved by placing the management of their affairs in the hands of a body of men like those that will be secured for Augsburg Seminary under these amendments, who will preserve an active and continuing interest in that corporation, and, being members of and in sympathy with the purposes of the United Church, will conduct the business intrusted to them with due regard to the mutual and harmonious interests of both bodies." [24]

Fortified with this legal opinion, Oftedal and his associates were less inclined than ever to comply with the Pattee-Bacon resolution. The September 1 deadline passed with no visible sign of action by the Augsburg board. On September 26, Iver Larsen, president of the United Church board of trustees, sent a communication to Oftedal asking for a response to the convention mandate "as soon as possible." In a reply dated October 3, Oftedal informed Larsen that Augsburg's board had taken no action on Pattee-Bacon, explaining convention submission of the school question to congregational referendum had in his opinion "annulled" the earlier resolution. According to Oftedal, no further steps could be taken until the 1893 convention, when the outcome of the referendum would be known. [25]

United Church spokesmen took sharp issue with Oftedal's logic. As they saw it, the referendum resolution left the Pattee-Bacon decision intact. The issue submitted to congregational referendum was whether the church should operate and support both Augsburg's preparatory department and St. Olaf College, and if not both, then which one. Transfer was a separate question. Even if the congregations chose to maintain only St. Olaf, Augsburg's theological department would remain the United Church's divinity school and as such was subject to transfer in conformity with Pattee-Bacon specifications.

On March 7, 1893, Iver Larsen sent Oftedal a second communication requesting the Augsburg board to indicate "as soon as possible" whether it was prepared to negotiate with the United Church board as recommended by the 1892 resolution. In responding Oftedal called attention to his reply of October 3. The resolution in question, he added, made no provision for negotiation, but merely recommended that "the relationship between the United Church and our board with respect to Augsburg Seminary" be arranged according to definite specifications set by the convention. "There is no doubt," concluded Oftedal, "that the Augsburg board is prepared to negotiate with the United Church board concerning the future relationship of the United Church and the Augsburg board whenever a mutually satisfactory meeting can be scheduled." [26]

The problem was not that simple. Finding an agreeable time and place was the least serious issue facing the two boards. The question

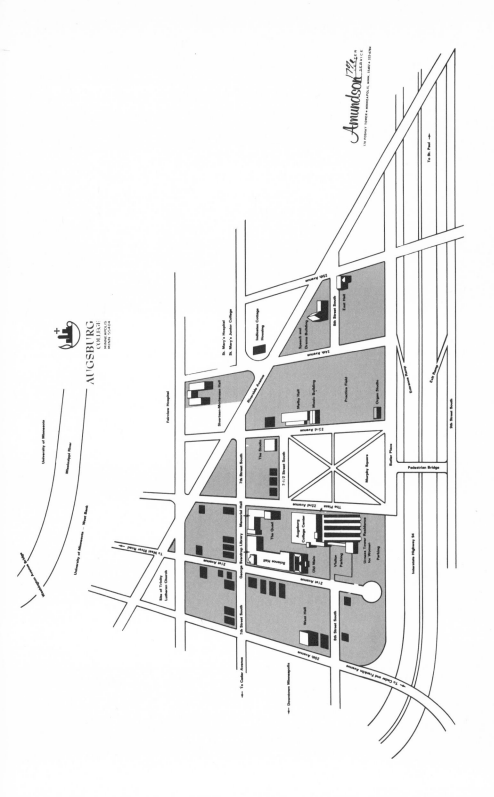

August Weenaas (1869–1876)

Augsburg

Georg Sverdrup (1876–1907)

Sven Oftedal (1907–1911)

George Sverdrup (1911–1937)

Presidents

Oscar A. Anderson (1963–)

Leif S. Harbo (1962–1963)

Henrik N. Hendrickson (1937–1938)

Bernhard M. Christensen (1938–1962)

This Academy Building at Marshall, Wisconsin, was Augsburg's first home for one year in 1869.

Augsburg College is located above the embankment to the left in this early painting by Edwin Whitefield. St. Anthony Falls and the Suspension Bridge crossing the river at what became East Hennepin Avenue are in the distance. From the Minnesota Historical Society Picture Collection.

Carl H. Chrislock, a professor of history at Augsburg College, is the author of its centennial history.

Andreas Helland, theological professor at Augsburg from 1905 to 1940, wrote the school's fifty-year history.

This photograph shows the first building constructed on the present site of Augsburg College. A center and east wing were added in 1875.

An early scene of the Augsburg Block taken from Murphy Square. In the center is Morton Hall. Main is shown at left; North Hall is to the right.

This student's room in Old Main during the 1880s displayed an ornately framed painting of President Georg Sverdrup.

John O. Evjen, a gifted and versatile professor, taught theology at Augsburg from 1909 until 1919.

Hans A. Urseth began teaching English theology and literature at Augsburg in 1898. He was Dean of the College from 1907 until his death in 1909.

Page 9 from the 1924 Augsburgian.

was: What would the two parties negotiate if and when they met? United Church officials contended that the articles of union — particularly point 23 requiring the merging synods to transfer their educational properties to the new church — imposed on the Augsburg board a contractual obligation to accept the Pattee-Bacon formula. It followed that any negotiation would have to accept Pattee-Bacon as an established precondition, with only routine details remaining to be determined.

Shortly after the second Larsen-Oftedal exchange, Hoyme announced the results of the congregational referendum. Although some respondents clouded the outcome by attaching extraneous qualifications, a reasonably clear mandate emerged. A preponderance of congregations, 557 out of the 582 participating, voted for only one preparatory school, and of these, 404 elected Augsburg, 138 St. Olaf, and 15 refrained from designating a choice. Of the 404 pro-Augsburg congregations, a substantial majority (239), indicated that their choice was contingent on transfer of Augsburg's property to the United Church. The remaining 165 voted unconditionally for Augsburg.[27]

While these returns comforted Augsburg more than St. Olaf, they failed to endorse the Oftedal board's position. St. Olaf partisans could, in fact, argue that the referendum favored their school should the Augsburg board persist in its refusal to transfer. In addition to the 138 congregations voting for St. Olaf as a first choice, a total of 116 specified a preference for the Northfield institution if Augsburg was not transferred. This meant that unless the Augsburg board changed its position, St. Olaf was favored by a vote of 254 to 165.

PRESIDENT HOYME'S report to the 1893 convention meeting at Minneapolis from June 7 to 15, outlined a five-point solution of the school question based on his interpretation of the referendum outcome. The first point affirmed that the United Church would neither recognize nor support any school not under its control. Point two asserted that the United Church should "maintain and operate only one college." The third called for revocation of the 1890 resolution adopting St. Olaf as the United Church college. Number four committed the United Church to support and maintain Augsburg, providing the Augsburg board complied with the Pattee-Bacon plan by June 30, 1893 — a date extended to July 15, by convention action.

Point five undertook to calm Augsburg apprehensions by offering a triple guarantee to the institution. First, "under no circumstances" would the United Church mortgage Augsburg property to fund synodical debt.

Second, "Augsburg Seminary's college" was designated as "the preparatory institution of the seminary," and would "be operated essentially as heretofore." (If this appeared to concede a key Oftedal-Sverdrup demand, point five also imposed what Augsburg supporters regarded as an unacceptable condition: "The synod reserves the right through Augsburg Seminary's corporation* to institute such improvements [in the preparatory program] as annual conventions and the corporation may from time to time designate.") The third guarantee pledged that the United Church endowmend fund, together with its income, would be utilized exclusively for the payment of Augsburg theological salaries.[28]

Committee No. 1, the group responsible for preparing recommendations on the basis of major convention reports, incorporated Hoyme's five points into its report, and added two more. Point six authorized the United Church board to yield minor concessions to the Augsburg board within the Pattee-Bacon context. Number seven stipulated that if the Augsburg board failed to transfer the institution's property "in accordance with the present convention's resolutions" before expiration of the July 15 deadline, the United Church board of trustees and school directors should "as soon as possible institute the necessary arrangements for moving the divinity school and providing for its support until the next annual convention." [29]

Although this last point carried an ominous threat, several so-called majority spokesmen on the convention floor argued that rejection of the proposal as a whole by Sverdrup and Oftedal would be inconceivable, since so much was conceded to the Augsburg party. The resolution cut St. Olaf adrift, a step protested by several supporters of that school, though reluctantly accepted by President Mohn and his board of trustees.[30] Only one college was to enjoy the support of the United Church: Augsburg. Moreover, the proposal pledged maintenance of Augsburg's preparatory program "essentially" as it was, subject only to improvements by the church. To one participant in the debate it seemed evident that all the demands advanced by Oftedal two years before at Kenyon were being met.[31]

Nevertheless, Augsburg spokesmen emphatically rejected the Committee No. 1 report. They regarded the threat to end financial support of Augsburg if its board refused to accept the Pattee-Bacon plan as intolerable. For three years, they argued, Augsburg Seminary had faithfully served the United Church, and it would continue to do so irrespective of

* The corporation referred to was not the one established by Oftedal in July, 1892, but the annual conventions of the United Church, as envisioned by the Pattee-Bacon plan.

whether the transfer question was settled in 1893 or 1894. Nor did the concessions in the convention resolution impress them. A few months after the convention Oftedal remarked that "humanistic St. Olaf" had been sacrificed so that "Augsburg Seminary's preparatory departments could be transformed into a college of the same character." Promises to maintain Augsburg's *status quo* notwithstanding, the vital core of the 1893 Pattee-Bacon formula placed the school's future in the hands of transient United Church convention majorities not bound by understandings reached in a particular year.[32]

Worse yet, Augsburg spokesmen professed to lack confidence in the pledged word of their adversaries. An exchange between Oftedal and Professor Bøckman on the afternoon of June 14 suggests how wide the gap between the parties had become after three years of charge and countercharge:

Prof. Bøckman: . . . when he [Oftedal] says that we want to take possession of the property and change the entire set-up at Augsburg and tear the school apart, then that is —

Prof. Oftedal: I believe that.

Prof. Bøckman: You believe that —

Prof. Oftedal: [In English] Yes sir!

Prof. Bøckman: But when we pledge that we will keep our promises.

Prof. Oftedal: I do not believe that.[33]

The militant bitterness displayed by Oftedal and Sverdrup failed to shake the decisive convention majority favoring Hoyme's program. Test votes taken during the opening sessions on such matters as election of synodical officials disclosed that less than one-third of the delegates adhered to the Augsburg party, a proportion which did not change significantly as the convention proceeded.[34] With the outcome assured, the important question was how Sverdrup and Oftedal would respond to their inevitable defeat. To minimize the disastrous probability of a synodical split, United Church leaders proposed a number of last-minute concessions. These included an arrangement permitting the Augsburg party to name the school's initial board of trustees, and a delegation to the United Church trustees of discretionary authority to depart from the Pattee-Bacon formula on details which would not basically compromise the plan.[35]

Although these concessions seemed excessive to ultra St. Olaf supporters who resented the orphaning of their school, they left Sverdrup and Oftedal unmoved. Immediately following convention adoption of the Committee No. 1 report on the afternoon of June 14, the two Augsburg leaders submitted their resignations as theological professors of the

United Church, but not as Augsburg Seminary professors. On the following morning a resolution accepting the resignations was adopted without debate.[36]

Oftedal's letter of resignation asserted that the unjust treatment to which a big majority within the church had subjected him indicated that he did not command the confidence required for productive work at a theological institution. Sverdrup took a slightly different and less personal tack. His letter accused the United Church of refusing "by an overwhelming majority" to consider all proposals for amicable settlement of the controversy. This refusal, continued Sverdrup, was attributable to a fundamental disagreement "with the principles of ministerial education and ecclesiastical activity represented by Augsburg Seminary." [37]

That same evening delegates sympathetic to Augsburg held an unofficial meeting on campus. After hearing several speeches, the assembly approved a set of resolutions that specifically: endorsed the course being followed by the Augsburg board; counseled against transfer of Augsburg property to the United Church without "full and binding guarantees" protecting the school's academic program; asserted that even if the United Church withdrew all support Augsburg Seminary should continue; instructed the Augsburg board to mobilize financial assistance for the institution; asked Sverdrup and Oftedal to retain their posts at Augsburg Seminary; pleaded for "free negotiations" between the Augsburg board and the United Church; and called upon congregations supporting Augsburg to remain within the United Church and work for its welfare.[38]

This meeting in reality presaged formation of the Lutheran Free Church. Presently the "Minority," in whose name the resolutions were passed, would become "The Friends of Augsburg," a loose federation of congregations that functioned as a de facto church body while maintaining for a time the fiction of United Church affiliation. However, failure of negotiation to accomplish anything, pressure by the United Church against congregations adhering to the Friends of Augsburg, and eventual legal action by United Church officials to gain possession of Augsburg property soon destroyed even the fiction. In 1897 the Friends of Augsburg converted their organization into the Lutheran Free Church, an unincorporated association of congregations that continued until 1963, when it merged with the American Lutheran Church.[39]

Following adjournment of the 1893 convention, controversy shifted for a time to Augsburg Publishing House, a United Church enterprise housed in Augsburg Seminary's dormitory (North Hall). The argument involved several issues. One of these was whether ownership of the publishing firm — the assets of which consisted of a stock of books, two church papers, and printing equipment — was vested in the United Church or the Augsburg board of trustees. Another concerned the position of Lars Swenson, manager of the publishing enterprise, and treasurer both of Augsburg Seminary and the United Church. From his office in the Augsburg dormitory, Swenson conducted business relating to all phases of his triple role. Since he responded more willingly to the authority of United Church officials than to that of the Augsburg trustees, under whose supervision the publishing house technically operated, Augsburg spokesmen believed he could not be trusted with their interests.

On June 15 the Augsburg board decided on a course of direct action. It dismissed Swenson as treasurer of Augsburg Seminary, elected Halvor Engemoen in his place, and determined to take possession of publishing house assets. Swenson refused to recognize the validity of these resolutions. Apparently the Augsburg men were not surprised — at any rate, they were prepared for the contingency. On Saturday, June 17, while Swenson was temporarily absent from his domain, Oftedal and Engemoen entered, ordered publishing house employees to leave, changed the combination of the office safe and, with the assistance of an expert, placed a new lock on the outer door. Upon returning to campus in midafternoon, Swenson attempted and failed to secure police intervention, whereupon he addressed an emergency message to Iver Larsen, president of the United Church board of trustees. This body met in special session on June 19, a day marked by a series of legal moves and countermoves, and a tense confrontation between adherents of the two parties near the dormitory.

A temporary agreement designed to remain in effect until the courts determined rightful ownership resolved the immediate crisis. This agreement placed the contested property under control of a three-man committee, one representing the United Church, another the Augsburg board, and the third a neutral outsider. The publishing house and Swenson were to move to another location, and Engemoen surrendered to Swenson control of all notes, cash, and financial records belonging to the United Church. Swenson retained his post as manager under a bond of $25,000, and both sides agreed to refrain from any acts damaging to the business. Litigation to determine legal ownership terminated on June 5, 1894, with a decision in favor of the United Church.[40]

By this time the schism had split Augsburg Seminary asunder. In a communication addressed to the United Church and dated July 11, 1893, the Augsburg board of trustees formally refused compliance with the synod's transfer plan. The effect was anticlimactic. Although the

Augsburg reply was lengthy, it advanced no new arguments. Basically, it confirmed the message Sverdrup and Oftedal had delivered a month earlier when they resigned their positions as theological professors of the United Church.[41]

Shortly after expiration of the July 15 deadline, the board of trustees and school directors of the United Church met jointly for the purpose of responding to the Augsburg board's refusal to accept the transfer plan. Since the 1893 convention had instructed trustees and directors to find a new location for "the United Church's divinity school" if the Augsburg faction remained adamant, the question was not whether a new seminary would be established, but where. Before the end of the summer a six-man committee composed of three directors and three trustees rented a building on the corner of 26th Avenue and East Franklin where classes opened in September, 1893. Three of Augsburg's theological professors, Schmidt, Bøckman, and Emil G. Lund, joined the new seminary's faculty; the five preparatory teachers remained at their old posts.[42]

Significantly, the new seminary patterned its organization on that of Augsburg. It established a six-year preparatory course as an integral part of its total program, engaged four preparatory teachers, and assigned to the theological professors responsibility for sharing preparatory instruction. As might be expected, St. Olaf supporters sought a reconsideration of the decision that had set their school adrift. Eventually they succeeded, but only after lengthy and sometimes spirited argument. Not until 1899 did the United Church liquidate its seminary's preparatory program and formally readopt St. Olaf as its college.[43]

The dispute accompanying this action has a bearing on what might have happened had Sverdrup and Oftedal accepted the mandates of the 1893 convention. It is often assumed that Augsburg compliance with the Pattee-Bacon plan would have been followed by a synodical decision to liquidate the school's preparatory departments in favor of St. Olaf. However, this is far from certain. If the congregations which in 1897 organized the Lutheran Free Church had remained within the United Church, it is conceivable that St. Olaf's restoration to grace might have been blocked. In that event, Augsburg College and Seminary, possibly operating as two institutions on the same campus, would have been provided with a substantial supporting base which, together with the advantages of location in Minneapolis, could have made a significant difference in the subsequent history of the school. Obviously, no one can prove what would have happened had 1893 brought reconciliation instead of schism, but it is clear that the decisions taken during that year had a decisive influence on Augsburg's future.

RALLY AND SLUMP– 1893-1911

 THE SCHISM of 1893 left Augsburg Seminary in a precarious position. Only a small part of the enlarged constituency created by the 1890 merger remained. Along with the services of three theological professors, the institution lost about $4,000 income from that part of the United Church endowment fund which had been contributed by the Anti-Missourian and Augustana synods. Provisionally, the Augsburg board retained control of the $50,000 that had been furnished by the Conference, but permanent possession was in grave doubt. So, indeed, was the legal title of Oftedal's corporation to any Augsburg property. Within three years the United Church would institute court proceedings to determine whether it, as legatee of the Conference, possessed a valid claim to all assets belonging to the institution.

For the time being, however, both sides continued to hope that an amicable settlement could be negotiated. The Augsburg board presented to the 1894 United Church convention an offer to vest in this and subsequent annual United Church conventions the authority to elect the Augsburg board of trustees, providing the church would assume "the obligation to carry the expenses required for [Augsburg Seminary's] conduct and maintenance, without running it into debt, and that the United Church recognize the principle for education of ministers heretofore followed at Augsburg, and for this reason acknowledge the preparatory departments thereof as an essential part of the divinity school." [1]

Although this formula failed to meet Pattee-Bacon specifications, it conceded something. As Oftedal noted, the incumbent Augsburg trustees could not have anticipated re-election had it gone into effect.[2] Nevertheless, the convention declined acceptance. On the premise that vesting annual conventions with the right to elect Augsburg's board restored the authority exercised by the old Conference, the assembly endorsed this part of Oftedal's plan. In addition, it selected a special committee to expedite negotiations between the United Church and Augsburg boards.

However, it also reaffirmed the right of annual conventions to "make such improvements" in the school's academic program as they might "from time to time" deem appropriate, and ignored the provision recognizing "the principle for education of ministers hitherto followed at Augsburg." The basic issue that had precipitated schism in 1893 remained as intransigent as ever.[3]

Subsequent developments confirmed this dreary reality. In reporting to the 1895 convention, Hoyme noted no progress whatsoever, confessing a virtual abandonment of hope that a "voluntary" transfer of Augsburg's property to the United Church could be achieved. Sentiment for a legal test of the church's right to possess Augsburg was growing, he said. He rejected this alternative, suggesting instead that the controversy be left unresolved "for the time being." The congregations were weary of the conflict, and a new initiative from the synod's side promised only more bitterness and strife.[4]

If Hoyme expected this stance would reduce tension, he was mistaken. By 1895 the dispute between the United Church factions extended beyond the Augsburg transfer question. Officially the United Church had branded formation of the Friends of Augsburg as an infraction of the synodical constitution. It also called upon congregations that had passed resolutions accusing the church of having violated the articles of union to withdraw such accusations or face expulsion from the synod. Missionaries found themselves under pressure to conform to the majority position on pain of losing financial support, and heated arguments developed concerning whether Augsburg Seminary graduates were eligible for ordination within the United Church. The convention of 1895 refused to seat Oftedal and Sverdrup as delegates representing Trinity Congregation, an action regarded by Augsburg partisans as an unforgiveable affront.[5]

Whether the situation warranted such a determined policy can be debated endlessly. Before long charges that the United Church was encroaching on the right of congregations to manage their own affairs became the central issue in the ongoing controversy. The "Guiding Principles and Rules" of the Lutheran Free Church, formulated and adopted in 1897 when the church body was organized, underscored the rights of individual congregations and severely circumscribed synodical authority. Point 5 of the "Guiding Principles" affirmed that "The congregation governs its own affairs, subject to the authority of the Word of God and of the Spirit, and recognizes no other ecclesiastical authority or government above itself." Point 10 proclaimed: "Free and independent congregations have no right to demand that other congregations shall submit to their opinion, will, judgment, or decision; therefore all domination of a majority of congregations over a minority shall not be tolerated." [6]

At its 1896 convention the United Church embarked on a course terminating in a final solution of the transfer question. On the premise that the United Church had inherited the authority over Augsburg exercised by the Conference, the assembly elected an Augsburg board of trustees which it authorized to gain possession of the school, by legal process if necessary, by other means if possible.[7] As was anticipated, the Oftedal board refused to surrender its prerogatives, whereupon the new trustees requested an advisory opinion from the attorney-general of Minnesota. He ruled for the Augsburg board. In his view, the Conference had not constituted the Augsburg corporation; therefore the United Church did not have authority to elect a board of trustees.[8]

Undeterred by this rebuff, the new board instituted a legal suit which the Hennepin County District Court agreed to adjudicate. On October 18, 1897, Judge Robert D. Russell decided in favor of the United Church. "The members of the Conference," Russell pointed out, "alone exercised rights of ownership and authority over [Augsburg Seminary], and up to 1892 their right and authority was never challenged or disputed by anyone." Consequently, the amended articles of incorporation adopted on August 3, 1892, by joint action of trustees and incorporators were invalid, since this group did not constitute the Augsburg corporation.

After making these points, the court discussed the relationship between the Conference and United Church. "The members of the Conference did not lose their membership and their rights in the corporation by going into the union," affirmed Russell. "The Conference simply changed its name and associated its members with other Norwegian Lutheran ministers and congregations." It followed that the United Church possessed full legal control over Augsburg, and the board elected by the 1896 convention, rather than the one headed by Oftedal, had jurisdiction over the school.[9]

The old board appealed this ruling to the Minnesota Supreme Court and on June 9, 1898, while the second annual conference of the Lutheran Free Church was in session, the court announced its decision. To the intense satisfaction of Augsburg supporters, it reversed the lower court's contention that authority to elect Augsburg trustees resided in United Church conventions. After hearing this news from Oftedal, the LFC conference, meeting in Trinity church at Minneapolis, held a spontaneous service of thanksgiving, concluding with the hymn, "Now Thank We All Our God." [10]

Jubilation was premature. While denying the right of United Church conventions to select Augsburg's trustees, the higher court avoided the complex issue of what claims the synod had on Augsburg, and left the status of Oftedal's corporation undefined and doubtful. The possibility of continued litigation loomed. Augsburg supporters realized that a renewal of legal hostilities could be expected when the 1898 United Church convention adopted a resolution setting up an Augsburg committee authorized to institute further court action.[11]

Fortunately, however, battle fatigue and the high cost of adjudication predisposed both sides to negotiate. Following an approach by the United Church committee to the old Augsburg board, a series of joint sessions between these two bodies terminated in a compromise agreement. Incorporation of the terms in a judgment issued on August 27, 1898, by the District Court of Hennepin County invested the agreement with legal force.[12]

The 1898 settlement balanced one major concession to the Augsburg party with two less important ones to the United Church. The latter yielded title to all Augsburg Seminary real estate, both land and buildings, thereby placing the campus under the uncontested ownership of Oftedal's corporation. In return, the Augsburg board surrendered claim to the endowment fund contributed by the Conference at the time of the union, an asset estimated to be worth approximately $49,000, that Augsburg had controlled and utilized since 1890. Augsburg also agreed to a division of the library. The so-called Augustana Synod library — volumes acquired from Augustana College and Theological Seminary at the time Augsburg was founded — together with books procured prior to January, 1876, were transferred to the United Church; Augsburg retained all other library holdings.[13]

WHETHER SVERDRUP and Oftedal or Hoyme and his group were ultimately responsible for placing the church in court, the prolonged litigation of the 1890s imposed an additional burden on resources already seriously depleted by loss (or forfeiture) of the greater part of Augsburg's constituency. Other circumstances intensified the hardship. Following the Panic of 1893, a severe depression of four years' duration that struck the Midwest wheat belt with particular force reduced the capacity of loyal Augsburg adherents to contribute financial support. As a result, the institution faced an acute test of its will to survive.

For a time the school responded admirably to this challenge. Sverdrup keynoted the festivities commemorating Augsburg's 25th anniversary by proclaiming a "new springtime" in the history of the institution.[14] Like most claims of its kind, this was exaggerated, but at the moment Augsburg Seminary was faring well within the context of an unpromising situation. It would continue to do so for another six years.

Enrollment statistics indicate development trends. Immediately preceding the schism, the student body consisted of 167 young men. The following year marked a decline of 54, distributed fairly evenly among the three departments. By 1895-96 enrollment had reached 165, two less than before the break. The following year it rose to 187, and to 194 in 1897-98. Following a slight decline during the next year, it increased to 201 in 1899-1900, a total that would not be exceeded until 1923.[15]

Financially, too, Augsburg weathered the immediate post-schism era more successfully than might have been expected. To be sure, retrenchment was required. A reduced current operations budget had to absorb substantial legal costs while maintaining the same level of instructional activity as before 1893. Endowment income also declined. Part of the fund consisted of notes held by congregations remaining loyal to the United Church, and understandably officials of these congregations argued that the United Church Seminary rather than Augsburg was entitled to receive payments on the notes. In addition, depressed economic conditions reduced the return from that portion of the endowment remaining under Augsburg control until 1898. In 1895-96 for example, the fund yielded $2,261.59; the following year, only $1,876.35.[16]

Nevertheless, unmanageable deficits were averted. The sense of being under siege strengthened the willingness of both leaders and followers to make substantial personal sacrifices. In 1895 Sverdrup and Oftedal volunteered to accept salary reductions — Sverdrup from $1,650 to $1,200, and Oftedal from $1,500 to $1,200. Members of the preparatory faculty also remained doggedly loyal; in the same year they contributed more than ten per cent of their meager salaries to the school treasury.[17]

This example encouraged openhandedness within what remained of Augsburg's constituency. So did the mission of Pastor Peder Nilsen who, in 1894, accepted appointment as an emissary of Augsburg to its supporting congregations. Nilsen, an effective evangelist, interpreted his responsibility as including more than fund raising. Sensing symptoms of religious revival within Norwegian-American Lutheranism, he launched an evangelistic crusade that gained considerable momentum. In the minds of many people Augsburg Seminary became synonymous with spiritual revitalization, an identification that spurred both student recruitment and monetary contribution.[18]

The financial reports soon reflected the impact of Nilsen and his revival. From June 1, 1895, to June 1, 1896, congregations adhering to the Friends of Augsburg contributed nearly $4,000 to the school, a sum comparing favorably to the $4,500 appropriated for Augsburg by the United Church convention of 1892. Response to the financial gap created by transfer of the endowment fund to the United Church in 1898 was even more impressive. A special fund drive launched by the Lutheran Free Church conference of 1898 yielded more than $6,800.[19]

Encouraged by enrollment trends and an apparently improved financial situation, the LFC conference of 1899 authorized the most ambitious building project in Augsburg's 30-year history, a structure that later generations would know as Old Main. Two conditions were attached to this authorization: cost of the building was not to exceed $30,000; and construction was to proceed as funds became available.[20]

THE ROSY OPTIMISM of 1899 began to erode after the turn of the year. In reporting to the LFC conference of 1900, Augsburg officials pointed with pride to the unprecedented high enrollment, but expressed anxiety about the financial situation. Fund-raising since June, 1899 had yielded approximately $20,000 in cash and pledges. Although this was a courageous performance, it fell short of requirements. The current operating budget needed about $10,000 to remain in balance, and revised building estimates raised the cost of the new facility to $40,000.[21]

Since construction could not proceed ahead of fund-raising, work begun on the new building in the autumn of 1899 remained in abeyance through 1900. Students returning to the campus in September came upon the same dismal scene they had left in May, an untidy excavation on the corner of Eighth Street and 21st Avenue. Many did not return at all. Due in part to cramped facilities and in part to poor harvests in North Dakota and western Minnesota, enrollment declined 15 per cent — from 201 to 170.[22]

Before long an even more serious blow fell. In December, 1900, the saga of Melchior Falk Gjertsen began to unfold. Technically, Gjertsen, who had served as pastor of Trinity Congregation at Minneapolis since 1881, was not directly affiliated with Augsburg, but he had retained an active identification with the school since its founding. In 1873 he accompanied Weenaas on the mission to Norway that recruited Oftedal. During the 1890s he remained a steadfast and effective ally of Sverdrup and Oftedal. No one could question that Trinity and Gjertsen contributed substantially to Augsburg's survival through this critical decade.[23]

Gjertsen's prominence as a community leader further enhanced the value of his identification with the school. His many roles included participation in Republican politics, membership on the Minneapolis School Board, championship of Scandinavian-American ethnic interests, and involvement in the crusade against liquor. On Sunday mornings the Trinity church usually was filled with worshippers, including many non-members drawn there by the pastor's reputation for eloquence.[24]

In the summer of 1900 Gjertsen toured Norway on a preaching mission. A few weeks after his return to Minneapolis, a Norwegian churchman wrote to Sverdrup and to Gjertsen himself, preferring serious charges against the Trinity pastor. Specifically, Gjertsen was accused of having authored and posted a salacious, anonymous letter to a married woman with whom he allegedly had established a romantic relationship during his stay in Norway.[25]

Gjertsen responded with a bitter attack that widely publicized the charges. Shortly afterward he booked passage for Norway, announcing to his congregation and to the Minneapolis community that he intended "to meet these accusations, and, if possible, bring the instigators to justice." [26] This he conspicuously failed to do. A Norwegian police investigation, initiated soon after his arrival in mid-January, vindicated the accusers rather than the accused. Competent handwriting experts concluded that Gjertsen indeed had composed the anonymous letter, and several witnesses contradicted his version of the relationship. Even worse from the Gjertsen point of view, Norwegian authorities instituted proceedings against him for having maligned the woman and the two churchmen who had made the charges. To avoid arrest, he hastily left Norway by a different route than prescribed by his return ticket.[27] He later admitted having deliberately eluded the police, explaining that intense emotional pressure had impelled him to act rashly.[28]

When Gjertsen returned to Minneapolis early in April he found a state of turmoil that would continue for several months. The most controversial issue was whether Trinity should retain him as its pastor. Following refusal of the membership to accept his resignation, he stoutly opposed congregational investigation of the affair, claiming that nothing could be uncovered that he had not already clarified. Initially, Gjertsen had his way. A meeting held on April 24 formally dissolved a committee created earlier to probe the accusations.[29]

However, a group of Trinity parishioners led by Sverdrup and his Augsburg colleagues succeeded in reversing this decision. On July 31 a congregational meeting directed a joint committee of trustees and deacons to examine available documentary evidence in the case, most of which had been collected by Sverdrup. After holding more than a dozen sessions, the joint committee reported to the congregation on August 28.

With respect to the accusation that Gjertsen had authored the improper anonymous letter, it affirmed: "We find that the charges are not in accord with the truth, and we cannot say that he is guilty." At the same time, it called upon Gjertsen to render "a more lucid explanation" than already given of another communication which he admitted having sent to the lady. Gjertsen, interpreting these findings as a vindication, thereupon submitted his resignation, a step that appeared to terminate the sordid controversy.[30]

Unfortunately, further difficulty lay ahead. When Trinity turned to the problem of finding a replacement for Gjertsen, his supporters insisted that he be restored. For a time the Gjertsen faction commanded a majority both within the board of deacons — which had authority to employ a minister temporarily — and the congregation, but it was unable to muster the two-thirds majority required to extend a permanent pastoral call. Consequently, Gjertsen continued to serve temporarily while his adversaries, led by Augsburg faculty members, campaigned against him. By January 15, 1902, when Trinity held its annual meeting, the anti-Gjertsen party had gained enough strength to prevail, whereupon the pastor's supporters seceded to found Bethany Lutheran Congregation in south Minneapolis. A declaration of withdrawal issued by Gjertsen spokesmen included an angry attack on the Augsburg professors whom they accused of having promoted private and public circulation of "slanderous falsehoods about . . . Rev. M. Falk Gjertsen." [31]

This accusation grossly misrepresented the role of Sverdrup and his colleagues. When the charges were first leveled against Gjertsen a year earlier, Sverdrup and Oftedal, though refusing to prejudge the case, supported the pastor's effort to clear himself. Oftedal served as a kind of personal business agent for Gjertsen while the latter sought vindication in Norway.[32] The break between the clergyman and his faculty parishioners was precipitated by Gjertsen's adamant opposition to any congregational investigation. As controversy mounted during the spring of 1901, other issues widened the breach. Critics of Gjertsen contended that his assault on the reputation of the woman, coupled with his attack on Norwegian justice, passed the bounds of propriety, and they branded his explanations for leaving Norway in such haste as unacceptable.[33] Irrespective of whether the original charges against Gjertsen were true or false, these issues were of legitimate concern. To insist that they be weighed was a responsible act, not a descent into scandalmongering.

Nevertheless, the Gjertsen affair created serious problems for Augsburg. The alienation of Gjertsen from Sverdrup and Oftedal, the most tragic aspect of which was the destruction of two long-standing personal friendships, deprived the institution of an effective supporter. Inevitably, too, some critics of the school linked the alleged scandal with Augsburg. In announcing the "fall" of "The mighty Pastor Falk Gjertsen," *Fargo Posten* of April 19, 1901, described him as "the Augsburgers' chief cornerstone." *Skandinaven* commented in more restrained fashion, but the implication of Augsburg involvement was equally strong.[34] Augsburg's narrow supporting base was threatened; rumblings grew louder within the LFC to the effect that Sverdrup and Oftedal were exercising "dictatorial" authority. Financial contributions to the school declined. Delegates to the LFC conference of 1901 learned of a $5,000 deficit in the operating budget of the preceding year.[35]

Augsburg's relationship with the Minneapolis community also suffered. In explaining the failure of local businessmen to participate in a drive to raise funds for construction of the new building, Amasa C. Paul, president of the Minneapolis Commercial Club, pointed to "the trouble . . . in connection with . . . Gjertsen, which if we had foreseen, would have prevented us from taking up the [fund-raising] matter at all." According to Paul, "A number of businessmen [had] refused contributions on that account." [36]

AN ATMOSPHERE of gloom dominated the opening sessions of the LFC conference of 1901 which, contrary to initial plans, met at Willmar instead of Minneapolis, a change dictated by the turmoil within Trinity congregation.[37] Official reports on details of Augsburg's operation disclosed a seriously unbalanced current budget, a lagging building fund campaign, and a significant drop in enrollment. Exchanges among delegates reflected dissatisfaction with the unstructured relationship between Augsburg and the LFC — did the congregations indeed own and control the school as official ideology affirmed? Neither Sverdrup nor Endre E. Gynild, president of the LFC, officially alluded to the Gjertsen case in their conference reports, but its disruptive impact came into the open when delegates approved a resolution urging Trinity Congregation to investigate the affair.[38]

To its credit, the 1901 conference responded realistically to the most pressing problems facing Augsburg. It selected a committee to draft a proposal that would share authority over Augsburg between the corporation and annual LFC conferences, with the former retaining ultimate legal responsibility for the school. A year later the annual conference adopted a series of recommendations proposed by the committee with only minor modifications.[39]

Essentially, this arrangement restored the relationship between Augsburg and the church that had prevailed up to 1890, and that would continue until 1963. It revived the board of school directors, a body consisting of the Augsburg president and four members elected by annual conferences for staggered terms of two years, and vested with a supervisory role in academic affairs. Together with the faculty, directors were responsible for nominating three candidates whenever a professorial post fell vacant. Authority to select one of the three was delegated to the next annual LFC conference, a two-thirds majority being required for election. The annual conference also was empowered to nominate from within the corporation's membership two candidates for each vacancy on the board of trustees between whom the corporation would make a final choice.

The willingness of Augsburg's leadership to accord the LFC a larger role in managing the school encouraged the 1901 conference to act decisively on the stalled building program. One resolution adopted by the Willmar assembly authorized immediate completion of New Main and called upon the LFC fraternity to contribute $19,000, the estimated deficit in the building fund. Another requested members of Augsburg's preparatory faculty to devote the remainder of the summer to fundraising.[40] This they consented to do, and results were gratifying. By the turn of the year New Main was ready for occupancy.

Completion of the building strengthened morale within the Augsburg community. The dedication ceremonies, held on January 1–3, 1902, reflected considerable pride in the new facility, a spacious structure compared to other buildings on campus. An article by Professor Hans A. Urseth published in a volume commemorating the dedication stressed New Main's commodious dimensions. "It is," wrote Urseth, "built practically on a level with the other buildings . . . and presents a rather imposing elevation when seen from the street below." Urseth also admired the interior. "There are no low ceilings, not even in the basement, and no dark halls," he remarked. "Broad halls, the entrances to which are so arranged as to admit a rich flow of light through glass-paneled doors and well lighted vestibules, run through the whole length of all floors, and from these halls every part of the building is conveniently reached." [41]

Other improvements in physical arrangements reinforced the impression of progress. Since New Main accommodated all classes along with the library, gymnasium, and chapel, Old Main became available for other uses. Its classrooms were converted into dormitory space, and the dining facilities were moved from the basement to the third floor of the east wing, a space where the main auditorium had been located. The ground floor of the dormitory building (North Hall), an area that earlier had housed Augsburg Publishing Company, was partially converted to student lodging. Modern plumbing was installed in all campus buildings, making possible the removal of what Oftedal called "the old unsightly . . . out-houses" that had usurped valuable space on the seminary block for a generation.[42] Although central heating was not yet a reality, the campus by 1903 had assumed the general appearance that it would retain until 1938, when Sverdrup-Oftedal Memorial Hall was constructed.

ENCOURAGING AS these physical innovations were, an Augsburg renaissance failed to develop in the aftermath of the crisis of 1900–02. Enrollment continued to dwindle. In this respect, the contrast between Augsburg and St. Olaf is dramatic indeed. Excluding students in the theological department, Augsburg's enrollment in 1898–99 was 146 compared to 184 at St. Olaf. By 1914 the Augsburg count had fallen to 103, while St. Olaf's had risen to 545.[43]

Disparities in the curricular advance of the two institutions were equally striking. St. Olaf significantly broadened its course offerings, introducing natural science as a "serious study" in 1900, and adding economics in 1903, sociology in 1909, and political science in 1910. By 1914 the Northfield school had adopted a modern college program based on the free elective system, the great educational reform of the age initiated at Harvard in the 1870s. Academic recognition rewarded this and other forward steps; in 1915 St. Olaf was admitted to the North Central Association of Colleges and Secondary Schools.[44]

Despite a commitment to traditional classicism, Luther College, too, was moving toward modernization, although not at a sufficiently rapid pace to suit its more progressive supporters. The Decorah institution introduced chemistry in 1891, its first course in natural science on the college level, and three years later the catalog listed offerings in French and economics, Luther's first electives. After 1900 a controversy developed between a conservative faction and a reform party that endorsed the affirmation that Luther should not remain "a theological preparatory school," but become "a college proper." The reformers won only a limited victory but, like St. Olaf, innovation proceeded far enough to qualify Luther for North Central accreditation in 1915.[45]

Compared to its sister institutions, Augsburg remained relatively unresponsive to curricular change. To equalize the qualification of Augsburg's beginning preparatory students entering the college department with that of public high school graduates who were enrolling in larger numbers, the beginning preparatory department was by stages transformed into an American secondary school, or academy. In 1888 the beginning preparatory course was expanded from one to two years. In 1900 it was increased to three, and in 1910 to four years. Concurrent with this extension, academic offerings corresponded with the standard high school program of the period.[46]

The college department curriculum, however, remained unaltered for more than a decade after 1900. Essentially, the course of study formulated in 1874 — which emphasized Greek, Latin, Norwegian, English, German, history, and religion — continued in force until the World War I period. The few concessions made to modernization were relatively insignificant. Physics was introduced in 1898, but dropped in 1903; a year of French offered during that same time evidently was meant to equip candidates for the mission station in Madagascar, rather than for general cultural enrichment. Other innovations had to await the administration of George Sverdrup, Jr., which formally began in 1911.

Notwithstanding a substantial shift in membership, the faculty, too, retained much of its traditional tone and spirit. Of the five professors manning the preparatory departments in 1890, only John Blegen and Wilhelm Pettersen held their positions in 1905. John Bugge, who died in 1891, was succeeded by Johannes L. Nydahl. Henrik N. Hendrickson joined the faculty after Theodor Reimestad resigned in 1900. The appointment of Samuel O. Severson in 1904 filled a gap created by the departure three years before of Anders M. Hove, whose chief responsibility had been English. Since the theological professors continued to teach college and academy courses, two changes on the theological faculty also affected preparatory instruction. Hans Urseth was elected to a newly created theological professorship in 1899. Before long Oftedal's determination to retire, publicly expressed during the New Main dedication ceremonies in January, 1902, created another vacancy which Andreas Helland filled in 1905.[47]

Unquestionably the addition of these men, who ranged in age from 27 to 36, strengthened the faculty. Urseth soon developed a warm rapport with his students, becoming in their eyes an apostle of "Americanization," and desirable change. Hendrickson, Urseth's intimate friend, held no advanced degrees (he would obtain his M.A. years later), but he had attended institutions other than Augsburg, including the University of Minnesota. Helland broadened his theological preparation with a year of study in Norway, and Severson held an M.A. degree from the University of Minnesota.

However, the recruitment and retention of the new professors was based more on their identification with the Augsburg tradition than on

88

their competence as academic specialists. Without exception, all were products of Augsburg's college program, and all but Severson were ordained graduates of the theological department. Sverdrup's policy of employing faculty members firmly committed to his educational philosophy remained vigorously in force. At least one alumnus questioned this policy. In writing to his close friend, George Sverdrup, Jr., on July 9, 1902, Charles E. Stangeland remarked: "Piety and frock coats are well enough, but they are not sufficient. To put in men with only the training rec'd at Augsburg . . . is apt to breed narrowness, and we don't want that."

There are other evidences that Sverdrup continued to assign considerably higher priority to Augsburg's divinity school mission than to any suggestion that the Greek department be transformed into an American college. His published articles and presidential messages to annual LFC conferences during the last decade of his life consistently affirmed the soundness of the principles guiding education at Augsburg. From Sverdrup's point of view, the major challenge facing his administration was not re-examination of these principles, but greater achievement of their promise.[48]

At the same time, bitter inter-synodical controversy that had never abated since the early 1890s diverted attention from other problems. Shortly before his unexpected death on May 3, 1907, Sverdrup became involved in a spirited exchange with United Church spokesmen on issues raised by the decision of several recent Augsburg Seminary graduates to accept pastorates within the United Church. Preoccupations of this kind tended to lock him into positions he had taken earlier.[49]

Nevertheless, in the closing year of his life Sverdrup demonstrated a mild recognition of the need for change. His last message to the LFC delivered in June, 1906 noted that Augsburg had achieved a closer relationship with other educational institutions than ever before in its history. Increasingly, Sverdrup added, Augsburg students were continuing their work at other schools, a circumstance dictating that academic standards meet those prevailing at other schools of the same class. To evade this responsibility, he said, would reflect discredit on both the students and their professors. However, he failed to recommend any specific departures in curricular policy.[50]

Since Sverdrup died before the end of the next academic year, it cannot be determined whether these remarks presaged a shift in his thinking. Nor is it certain that even his leadership could have promoted a modernization program. A precarious financial situation left little room for maneuver. Oftedal, whose flair for money-raising had served Augsburg well for a generation, still chaired the board of trustees, but since retiring as theological professor in 1904 he had committed his energies to the study of modern Greek, a pursuit that drew him to Greece for long periods at a time.

Moreover, no solid consensus favoring innovation was apparent within the LFC. On the contrary, vocal opposition to broadening and reforming the college program continued until as late as 1923. By questioning the suitability of American college training as a preparation for theological study, and by arguing that Augsburg should remain "essentially" if not "exclusively" a divinity school, Sverdrup had helped to instill within his following a suspicion of contemporary higher education favoring maintenance of the *status quo*. To some degree, this defense of the existing order reflected competitive institutional interests. Supporters of Oak Grove Lutheran Ladies Seminary, founded in 1906 at Fargo, North Dakota, and Bethania College at Everett, Washington, a coeducational academy aspiring to become a full-fledged college and established in 1904, were not hostile to Augsburg's claims, but the hopes associated with them understandably diminished their enthusiasm for expanding the role of the Minneapolis school.

IN THE EARLY hours of Friday, May 3, 1907, a shattering communication spread quickly through the Augsburg circle: "Professor Sverdrup is dead." On Monday and Tuesday the president had met with his classes and tended to administrative routine. Illness kept him from campus on Wednesday, and his absence from the graduation ceremonies of the preparatory departments held on May 2, dampened the festivity of that occasion. However, his appearance on the veranda of his home on that day, and the fact that the diplomas handed out by Oftedal were signed in Sverdrup's "usual firm handwriting" precluded serious alarm. During the night of May 2, his illness took a critical turn and at 3:15 a.m. he died, the apparent victim of a heart attack.

An elaborate funeral memorialized the beloved leader. To some extent this reflected the standards of 1907, but the grief was genuine. Not only was Sverdrup's death unexpected, but at fifty-eight he had scarcely filled a normal life span. Nevertheless, for more than a generation his leadership, loyally seconded by Oftedal, had directed every facet of Augsburg's development.[51]

Finding a successor turned out to be a formidable problem. Soon after Sverdrup's death a drive to select Urseth gained considerable student support but evoked a negative response from conservatives, who distrusted Urseth's alleged theological liberalism and his insistence on rapid

"Americanization." Instead, they preferred Andreas Helland because they believed he "would more wholly follow in the footsteps of the late president." The divisive possibilities inherent in this situation alarmed Oftedal. As he saw it, a contest between a "younger element" backing Urseth and the "older folks" who favored Helland potentially threatened LFC unity, despite the warm personal relationship between the two men. To avoid such a disaster, Oftedal advocated a temporary arrangement that would permit a delay in the election of a permanent president. The possible availability and acceptability of George Sverdrup, Jr., as his father's successor — which at the moment was not established — strengthened the case for an interim solution, according to Oftedal.[52]

The LFC conference of 1907 adopted a course of action conforming to Oftedal's recommendation. For one thing, it delegated to the school directors and faculty authority to elect a "temporary president" and to procure the instructional assistance needed to fill the gap left by Sverdrup's death. For another, it requested the same group to "take the necessary steps" with respect to electing Professor Sverdrup's successor. "In this connection" it "directed . . . attention . . . to Georg [sic] Sverdrup Jr." [53]

Three weeks after adjournment of the conference, faculty and school directors met to discharge the responsibilities given them by the LFC, and in the course of a single day completed their assignment. With a few modifications, the plan formulated by the joint group went into effect during the 1907–08 school year. In accordance with the plan, Oftedal consented to serve as acting president, but declined a request to teach in the theological department. That post was filled by the interim appointment of Pastor Elias P. Harbo, who would be elected permanent theological professor two years later. To lighten Oftedal's administrative burden, two deanships were created: Helland was given jurisdiction over the seminary, and Urseth was named head of the academy and college departments. George Sverdrup accepted appointment as "temporary" college professor, an indication of his willingness to become identified with Augsburg.[54]

The administrative arrangement created by this plan was awkward. In most respects the students enrolled in the three departments constituted an integrated community — as Helland comments, they "not only utilized the same classroom building, but also occupied the same dormitory rooms." A separation of supervisory authority in the academic realm might have been feasible, but the division of responsibility between Urseth and Helland extended to all areas of student life. No tension developed between the two deans, although Helland notes that the situation required exercise of considerable "caution and tact" by both men.[55] The deans also found their relationship with Oftedal delicate. Impatient with administrative routine, determined to devote as much time as possible to his Greek studies, and somewhat disoriented by the loss of Georg Sverdrup, the old leader delegated broad responsibilities to his subordinates without surrendering a vague right of intervention which he sometimes invoked unpredictably.[56]

In the summer of 1908 Oftedal returned to Greece to resume his interrupted studies. During his absence, Urseth was to assume the acting presidency in addition to the preparatory deanship and a normal teaching load. Helland continued as seminary department dean. Unfortunately, Urseth, whose health had been precarious for several years, was disabled by illness shortly after the school year began, and by faculty decision Helland took command. Urseth's death on April 3, 1909, at the age of forty-two accentuated the leadership crisis which many Augsburg supporters had hoped he could help resolve.[57]

THE VACANCY left by Urseth's death, coupled with pressure for extending the college program, generated a difficult problem for the LFC conference of 1909. Everyone agreed that a new theological professor had to be elected to fill the Urseth vacancy. At the same time, advocates of college expansion argued that the establishment of an additional permanent college post was essential. Since finances justified selecting two new faculty members, the election of one theological and one college professor seemed a reasonable solution.

However, two strong candidacies for the theological professorship developed: Pastor Harbo, who had taught on an interim appointment for two years, and Dr. John O. Evjen. In proposing nominations for the vacancy, school board directors presented the names of both men, a tactic that imposed on the conference responsibility for choosing between them. The directors also advanced two other proposals, both relating to college and academy needs. One requested the conference to consider adding a course in practical studies (*Realkursus*) — a college program geared to non-ministerial students — "as soon as financial resources and faculty are available." The other recommended that William Mills, who had served for one year on a temporary appointment, be elected to the rank of college professor with permanent tenure.[58]

Conference deliberations modified this array of recommendations beyond recognition. The assembly approved the establishment of a new theological professorship, thereby opening the way for electing both Harbo and Evjen, but also precluded on financial grounds permanent status for Mills. However, to avoid a possibly critical academy-college faculty shortage, the conference authorized the board of trustees to appoint Mills for one year "if it finds this necessary." Discussion of the practical studies proposal was deferred until the next conference.[59]

These conference actions were designed partly to avert a painful contest between Harbo and Evjen. In addition, floor discussion of issues relating to Augsburg disclosed a deep reluctance to sanction any innovation in school policy. The committee appointed to formulate recommendations on the basis of the reports on Augsburg's activities presented a resolution reaffirming the "integral" relationship of the school's three departments, and the commitment of all three to ministerial education. During discussion of this resolution, Helland directed a query to its sponsors: Was there a threat to the continued solidarity of the three departments? A proponent of the resolution voiced the anxieties prompting its introduction. Making Augsburg "a stepping stone" for university entrance might have considerable appeal, this speaker remarked, but whether such a step would produce "fortunate" consequences was "another matter." When the resolution came to a vote, it prevailed without audible opposition. The Augsburg constituency was not yet ready to sanction a transformation of the Greek department into a modern liberal arts college.[60]

Nevertheless, the future of Augsburg College was brighter than this attitude suggests. Although the 1909 conference manifested a deep distrust of American higher education, it endorsed two steps that demonstrated genuine concern for the school. One of these, the raising of an endowment fund of $100,000, eluded fulfillment. The other, authorizing installation of a central campus heating plant, was completed by the autumn of 1909. The era of the small wood-burning stove in every dormitory room, a source of nostalgic memories for several generations of Augsburg alumni, was gone forever.[61]

More important, the imbalance seemingly created by the decision to establish a theological instead of a college professorship was more apparent than real. Since the new theological professors were assigned teaching responsibilities in the college and academy as well as the seminary, their talents strengthened the institution's total program. In this respect, the role of Dr. Evjen became particularly significant. A graduate of Augsburg's college and seminary departments, he had studied for four years at the University of Leipzig, where he earned his Ph.D. degree in 1903 at the age of twenty-eight. Church history was his specialty as a theological professor, but his college classes provided an outlet for impressive capabilities in a number of other fields, including general history,

93

philosophy, philology, and political science. Although personal eccentricities complicated Evjen's relations with colleagues and administrative superiors, many of his students gratefully remember the intellectual stimulus generated by his teaching.[62]

The influence of George Sverdrup, Jr., also became a factor at the start of the 1909 school year. The LFC conference of 1908 first elected him to the theological professorship left vacant by his father's death, and he served on the academy-college faculty in 1907–08. In addition, Sverdrup was granted a one-year leave of absence with full pay to broaden his preparation in theology. Upon his return from a tour of study at the universities of Leipzig and Berlin in the summer of 1909, he was appointed vice-president of Augsburg Seminary, a post he held along with the theological professorship and miscellaneous teaching responsibilities in the academy and college departments.[63]

As vice-president, Sverdrup assumed much of the authority normally exercised by the president. The annual report describing Augsburg's academic activity was submitted in his name to the LFC conference of 1910. This document proposed a number of modest changes. It recommended permanent tenure for Mills, who had served under a second annual appointment in 1909–10, and advocated limited curricular expansion, including courses in botany and the history of philosophy, as well as a combined offering in sociology and political economy. Although one delegate argued that these additions endangered the status of Norse and religion in the college program, the delegates accepted them with apparent unanimity. This action was a first step in the slow evolution of the Greek department into Augsburg College, a process substantially completed by 1922.[64]

Sverdrup's expanded role reduced the participation of Oftedal in the administration of Augsburg, although he still retained the presidential title. Oftedal was more active as chairman of the board of trustees — a post he had filled with only minor interruption since 1874. However, his report as board chairman to the 1910 conference expressed a desire to retire completely from any position of leadership. Since this report turned out to be Oftedal's valedictory to the LFC, its general comments concerning Augsburg and his own plans are of particular interest.

"The Lord found it fitting," remarked Oftedal, "to take our old tried and true leader home to Himself; but He who wounds also heals; and He has in [Georg Sverdrup's] young son given us a new president who, superbly equipped as he is both by temperament and education, will direct the work of Augsburg with the same steady confidence as his father." In alluding to his own future, Oftedal assigned highest priority to his Greek studies to which he had devoted much of his time since retiring from seminary teaching in 1904. He estimated that if his health and energy remained at their present levels, at least ten years would be required to achieve the goals he had set for himself.[65]

Unfortunately, Oftedal had less than ten months to live. A gall bladder ailment which had troubled him for several years became so severe that hospitalization was required in the late winter of 1911. Surgery was performed on March 30 at Deaconess Hospital, but Oftedal failed to rally, and died the afternoon of the same day at the age of sixty-seven.

PATTERNS OF
STUDENT LIFE

WHEN SVEN OFTEDAL died in 1911 a distinctive style of student life that he had profoundly influenced was changing. Many of its essential features would remain vital for years to come, but pressures to conform to dominant trends in higher education were mounting. George Sverdrup, Jr., who was thirty-two years old in 1911, faced the difficult challenge of striking an acceptable balance between continuity and change.

A number of old values were worth preserving as adaptation to the 20th century proceeded. In addressing the college graduating class of 1884, Georg Sverdrup had defined the school's chief goal as being the encouragement of responsible personal individuality. There were schools, said Sverdrup, "where the aim appears to be the stuffing of knowledge into youth as one pours peas into an empty sack." Some educational leaders failed to recognize that "the cloth should be tailored to the man, not the man to the cloth." At many schools the governing rule was: "Never think! Learn instead to conform to the prevailing code, and you will succeed. . . . There are schools where the teachers are eloquent and the students inarticulate . . . where the students are daily overwhelmed with a flood of words even though they may be yawning with drowsiness. . . . where everything is communicated, but little or nothing is absorbed." Augsburg, the elder Sverdrup proclaimed, was not this kind of institution.

But why did the academic program require so many languages, he questioned. "Surely not to enable a young person to make himself ridiculous by parading a knowledge of Greek and Latin." The chief value of language study, according to Sverdrup, was that it removed the linguistic impediments blocking a broad view of the world. "It is possible to live in a remote shaded valley, particularly when one has known no other surroundings; but the young man who can escape to high plateaus and scan the horizon is doubly fortunate." Liberation from language barriers was comparable. A young person desiring a comprehension of what was stir-

96

ring in the world required a broader perspective than only one language could provide.[1]

According to Sverdrup, the non-curricular aspects of student life reinforced the academic program. Management by the students of their own boarding club and medical aid society encouraged the development of individual responsibility. So did the administration of discipline on campus. In reporting to the 1883 convention of the Conference, Sverdrup alluded to the question of student morality. City life, he remarked, "had its temptations," which a few Augsburg men found alluring. The only way to deal with the problem was to arouse the students' own sense of responsibility. Where this approach failed, he concluded, no amount of coercion by school authorities could achieve fruitful results.[2]

If these comments suggest a strain of liberalism — particularly when measured against 19th century denominational college standards — there were limits to Georg Sverdrup's permissiveness that became more narrow as he grew older. His 1884 commencement address underscored the institution's obligation to direct student intellectual development along proper paths. Augsburg, he said, was attempting "to focus attention away from the shifting cultural climate of our time to the simple truth that alone can give the heart peace and the spirit purpose." [3] Such a goal, coupled with Sverdrup's commanding physical presence, scarcely encouraged students to undertake a sympathetic examination of such theories as Naturalism or Darwinian Evolution.

On the more mundane level of daily routine, Sverdrup's forceful personality also circumscribed the exercise of student freedom. An alumnus who attended the academy in 1906–07 recalls that the president's appearance on campus shortly after supper unmistakably signaled the end of recreation and the beginning of evening study. Under such a dispensation the detailed prescription of hours for work and play was quite unnecessary.[4]

Nevertheless, Sverdrup's emphasis on student autonomy was more than rhetorical. The examination system established soon after he assumed leadership indicates how seriously he regarded the nurture of individuality. On the theory that education should prepare the student for life rather than examinations, this system dispensed with grades based on periodic tests. Faculty members could — and did — give tests at irregular intervals, but the results were not entered on a permanent record, and did not affect graduation. Eligibility for the B.A. degree depended entirely on performance in a series of written and oral comprehensive examinations administered during the last two weeks of the concluding college year.

The first week was set aside for the written portions of these examinations. In the early years the written tests covered four subject-matter areas: Norwegian, English, Greek, and Latin; German subsequently was added. The Norwegian and English examinations consisted of essays on problems designed to challenge the students to think. After being formulated by the Norwegian and English instructors and approved by the faculty, these problems were announced at the start of the five-hour examination periods. John Blegen recalls that in 1880 the Norwegian topic was: "The Relationship Between a People's History and Its Literature"; the English, "Singleness of Aim." English and Norwegian instructors shared responsibility for grading the essays in their respective fields, with one censor for each language appointed by the faculty. Final grades were determined by an average of the evaluations made by instructor and censor.

The Greek, Latin, and German written examinations measured the student's competence as a translator. At the start of the test, a proctor gave him a published excerpt from the language in question which had not been assigned or studied in the regular language course. No instructional aids, such as dictionaries, could be used. Following completion of the written portion, each student was subjected to an oral examination of from fifteen to twenty minutes which "covered subject matter previously studied in class, and might deal with any field covered in the four years."

So far as can be determined, the faculty never systematically evaluated the examination scheme. However, pressures for modification soon developed. Sverdrup frequently complained that too many young men arrived on campus late in the fall and departed early in the spring. To discourage such delinquency, the faculty in 1888 required all students to pass annual examinations administered early in May as a precondition for promotion to the next class. A decade later the institution shifted completely to conventional examination and grading procedures. H. N. Hendrickson, who regretted the change, attributed it "to the influence of surrounding colleges, especially the State University." Since many students, too, needed the discipline of periodic examinations, Hendrickson grudgingly admitted that "The . . . installment plan of getting a degree appeared easier." [5]

OTHER EFFORTS to institutionalize student initiative were more enduring. The Augsburg Seminary Boarding Club, an ambitious experiment in student self-government, was founded in 1872 and dissolved in 1924. Its establishment two years before Georg Sverdrup's arrival suggests that Weenaas deserves a share of credit for developing the tradition of student responsibility. The first president was so overburdened with work that his students were obliged to assume direction not only of housekeeping functions, but frequently also the conduct of their own classes. Since most of them were mature men eager to acquire an education, this arrangement proved satisfactory.[6]

The boarding club was a cooperative society completely under student jurisdiction. Its membership consisted of all students and others connected with the school who desired to belong and whose dues were not in arrears. With the assistance of a twelve-man council elected annually by the club, a student manager or "boarding boss" — also an elected official — supervised food service from initial purchase through preparation and serving. The membership established guidelines for operating the enterprise at monthly business meetings, and periodically a student committee audited the accounts. Faculty and administration involvement was limited to providing a campus dining area and equipment, but on at least one occasion club finances became so tangled that faculty intervention was legally necessary. These occurrences were rare, however; surviving records prove that student power governed the boarding club.

In addition to food service, the boarding club exercised authority in a number of other areas. It elected and supervised a campus postmaster. More important, it dealt with fuel administration. The "wood boss," who served *ex-officio* on the twelve-man council, was elected annually by the boarding club membership. His duties included procuring wood, supervising its storage, and determining the suitability of differing grades of wood for the various stoves in use. The fire hazard inherent in Augsburg's heating system made these responsibilities awesome, but the authority of the wood boss apparently matched them. He could commandeer the services of all students except the boarding club manager and those on kitchen duty. Refusal to obey his call for assistance was punishable by a fine of twenty-five cents for each offense.[7]

Unlike the boarding club, the Augsburg Medical Aid Society, founded in 1876, was governed by a joint student-faculty regime — its constitution specified that only theological professors were eligible for the presidency. All students residing on campus were required to affiliate, and others could belong. Society functions included recruiting physicians, negotiating with pharmacists for purchase of drugs at reduced prices, and supervising sanitary practices on campus. An insurance plan funded by modest premiums — about $1.50 per person each year — financed the operation. In any given year a student member could collect $15.00 in benefits to cover medical fees, drugs, and nursing care. Whenever heavy claims depleted insurance reserves, the society could levy an emergency assessment. Fortunately, it rarely was necessary to do so.[8]

The installation of modern plumbing when New Main was constructed burdened the medical society with additional responsibility. Since most Augsburg men were not familiar with the modern bathroom, a comprehensive code regulating use of the new facilities seemed wise. One rule stipulated that students holding membership in the society were entitled to "one bath a week (tub or shower), free of charge." Non-members and members delinquent in their dues had to "pay the sum of (10) ten cents for each bath." No one could "occupy a bathroom more than thirty minutes, nor remain under a shower more than ten minutes." Bathers were obliged to supply their own soap and towels, and "required to empty and carefully wipe the tub before leaving the room." A corps of sanitary inspectors appointed by the society's executive committee enforced these regulations.[9]

During the Georg Sverdrup era students also managed the library. When the institution moved from Marshall to Minneapolis in 1872, library holdings totaled 467 volumes, of which 238 were theological works. The accession rate of the next four years cannot be determined, but it is certain that by 1876 the collection exceeded 500 titles — a fairly respectable collection compared to 19th century denominational school norms.

Assistance came from a number of sources. A subscription of $217 by delegates to the Moline, Illinois, meeting of 1869 marked the first step. In addition, a hope cherished by Weenaas "that the Swedish brethren would willingly deliver to the new sister school their Norwegian and Danish works . . . in the library of . . . Augustana Seminary" was partially realized. According to Weenaas, "The Swedes did indeed fulfill this wish," but not entirely to his satisfaction. Instead of surrendering choice works in Norwegian and Danish literature, they delivered "duplicates and books of lesser value." Nevertheless, he added, "it is interesting to have some Swedish literature in the library, and we are very grateful to the Swedish brethren for obliging us." [10]

Meanwhile, Weenaas was acquiring a number of books, most of them basic theological works published in Europe, at his own expense and on his own personal credit. He formally donated these titles to the school at the Conference convention of 1872, asking in return that the church body assume an outstanding debt of $200 that he had contracted through book purchase. The convention accepted Weenaas' proposition, and acknowledged with "heartfelt thanks" contributions of books and a sum of $102 from supporters of the library.[11]

Following Augsburg's move to Minneapolis Gjermund Hoyme, a theological student, was appointed librarian, thus establishing a new area of student responsibility which the founding of the *Idun* society four years later broadened. Theoretically, *Idun*'s function was distinct from that of the seminary library. The latter's holdings were to consist of books required for class work, while *Idun* aspired to secure general reading material. In reality, however, the two collections became almost indistinguishable. A decision taken in 1881 placing the seminary holdings under the jurisdiction of librarians chosen by the society further blurred the distinction, although the two libraries continued to be cataloged separately.[12]

This innovation coincided with an *Idun* revival. In its first four years the society had accumulated only 110 volumes, many of them heavy German and Latin theological tomes. Responding to sharp student complaints that library resources were inadequate, *Idun* in 1881 organized a determined solicitation campaign aimed at securing contributions of both money and books. This drive yielded 157 volumes, an augmentation which more than doubled the *Idun* library.[13]

During the next decade a combination of *Idun* initiative and regular accessions to the seminary library expanded total holdings to 2,320 volumes, including both books and bound periodicals. Of these, 1,137 belonged to the *Idun* collection and 818 to the regular library. The remainder consisted of books contributed by the Norwegian Augustana Synod as part of the 1890 merger arrangement, and approximately 100 volumes bequeathed by the estate of Knut O. Lomen, a Norwegian Augustana Synod theological professor who died in 1890. These holdings included a preponderance of Scandinavian titles by such Norwegian authors as Henrik Ibsen, Bjørnstjerne Bjørnson, Jonas Lie, Alexander Kielland, and others. American writers, including Ralph Waldo Emerson, Mark Twain, Henry David Thoreau, and Edgar Allen Poe either were absent or present in only a volume or two. British literature fared somewhat better, although serious gaps also marked this area. The *Idun* library contained the complete works of Shakespeare, most of Charles Dickens and Sir Walter Scott, and a smattering of William M. Thackeray, Oliver Goldsmith, and Lord Byron.[14]

Due to a paucity of records, it is impossible to reconstruct library development during the 1890s, although clearly the turmoil of the decade diverted attention and resources away from library expansion needs. Also, the 1898 settlement ending the prolonged dispute between Augsburg and the United Church meant the loss of 700 volumes. While most of these titles were old, they included such indispensable volumes as Luther's Complete Works and valuable editions of the Church Fathers.

Shortly before negotiation of the 1898 settlement, a group of campus leaders founded another library society, The Students' Historical Association of Augsburg Seminary. Its announced goals included the acquisition of historical literature for the library, procurement of maps for classroom use, and promotion of student interest in history. A fear that an adverse decision in the litigation pending between Augsburg and the United Church might deprive the school of its library helped to encourage creation of the association. "Should the case have been decided in favor of the United Church," one of the founders pointed out later, "we would have lost, besides lots and buildings, the Seminary's library and perhaps 'Idun'." [15]

To finance its ventures the association sponsored a series of public lectures by faculty members for which it charged admission. In addition, it levied an annual membership fee of fifty cents, and offered life memberships at $2.50. Apparently this offer attracted few if any respondents, but student memberships for 1898–99 numbered 66, more than one-third of the entire student body. By November, 1900, the combined proceeds of membership fees and public lectures yielded sufficient revenue to purchase 102 volumes for the association library. Most of the titles acquired were standard historical works, and all were in English. [16]

Although association leaders were justifiably proud of the society's performance, the maintenance of three separate libraries raised many problems, including duplication of purchases, and the issue of who was entitled to use one or the other collection. To resolve these difficulties, officials of the three libraries in February, 1900 created a representative board made up of all three which they vested with authority to supervise the libraries "in general." The board was to be consulted with respect to book ordering, but ultimate authority to purchase continued to reside in the executive committee of each library. Unlike *Idun* and the historical association, the new board was provided with a faculty advisor, a post that Professor Wilhelm Pettersen accepted. [17]

In this capacity Pettersen "gradually became more prominent in the administration of the . . . libraries," and student power declined. The catalog of 1907 lists him as librarian, a responsibility that he combined with teaching until he resigned from the faculty in 1910. Two faculty members held the post part-time until Johannes Nydahl was appointed full-time in 1919: William Mills from 1910 to 1916, and John Evjen from 1916 until Nydahl's appointment. At the same time the historical association passed quietly from the scene; *Idun* formally dissolved in 1909.[18]

Several circumstances contributed to the transfer of library authority from students to faculty. One factor involved the changing character of the student body. The balance between relatively mature men of immigrant origin and younger American-born graduates of public high schools was shifting in favor of the latter, who were less capable of assuming managerial responsibilities. Library administration also was becoming more complicated. Expansion of holdings required more sophisticated cataloging techniques than those improvised by student librarians.[19]

Meanwhile, the library's capacity to serve college needs — as distinguished from those of the seminary department — advanced haltingly, although completion of New Main improved the physical setting. The area assigned for library use in the basement of the new facility (where language classrooms and laboratories would be located in the 1960s) was more spacious than the cramped quarters in Old Main. Whenever the seminary's chronically precarious finances permitted expenditure beyond bare necessities, funds from the general treasury for library expansion supplemented student efforts. In 1907–08, for example, the administration spent $468.79 for the library, compared to an annual average of less than $200 for the 1902–19 period. This allocation partially filled a serious gap by purchasing, among other titles, 91 volumes of British and American literary classics. At the start of the same school year the Minneapolis Public Library located a branch on campus alongside the school's regular library, an arrangement that permitted easy access by Augsburg students to the city library's growing resources for the next ten years.[20]

From 1902 to 1919, Augsburg's total library count increased from 3,000 to 12,000 volumes.[21] Although this growth may seem moderately impressive, many of the titles added were only marginally useful for the college department. They included 3,000 volumes of works in theology and church history acquired from H. C. Hegtveit, a Norwegian church historian. A collection of official Norwegian government reports procured by Oftedal accounted for another part of the increase. In addition, temperance and missionary societies both on and off campus donated an indeterminate number of books in their particular fields of interest. Following Sverdrup's death, a group of his admirers launched a campaign to augment the mission collection as a memorial to the departed president.[22]

Food service and medical aid were governed by student power for a longer period than was the library. The future of the boarding club seemed secure until coeducation was introduced in 1922. Arrival on campus of women students and their dean, Miss Gerda Mortensen, whose recent graduate training at Columbia University had included a study of student personnel services, sharpened an awareness of the society's shortcomings. Complaints that food preparation failed to meet acceptable standards mounted. The refusal by boarding club officials to sanction the purchase of such items as glass water tumblers and coffee cups with handles reinforced discontent. So did the general level of dining hall decorum, which seemed more like that practiced by a threshing crew than a collegiate community.[23]

In the autumn of 1924 the administration responded to these objections by assuming control of food service, retaining for a time the ancient twelve-man council as a student advisory body. Two years later student government abandoned the health insurance scheme on the theory that it could not adequately serve Augsburg's enlarged student body — a step that marked the demise of the medical aid society.[24]

EXTENSIVE STUDENT involvement in the management of campus life narrowed the scope of conventional extra-curricular activities during the first forty years of Augsburg's history. Young men whose daily routine included chopping wood to heat the entire campus had less need for an organized physical education and activity program than their 20th century counterparts. Moreover, prevailing standards frowned on team sports. Lawn croquet became an accepted and popular fair-weather pastime long before 1900, but until the 1920s some conservative Augsburg supporters raised strong moral objections to intercollegiate athletic competition. An even stronger bias interdicted drama.

Forensics, on the other hand, enjoyed privileged status from the beginning. The *Demosthenian* Society, founded September 25, 1872 — in the first month of Augsburg's operation in Minneapolis — apparently dominated the extra-curricular area for a few years. Its constitution defined *Demosthenian* goals as being "debate, declamation, composition, and parliamentary practice." Unlike later 19th century student organizations, the society conducted its meetings and kept minutes in English, a practice consistent with the mistaken expectation that Norse-Americans would soon abandon the Norwegian language.

Demosthenian sessions employed an established but flexible format. Following an invocation and other preliminaries — a "declamation," essay reading, original oration, or some combination of these — the debate proper began. Generally, one or two participants on each side presented their arguments. "Assistant disputants" then engaged in rebuttals, after which the membership was given an opportunity to discuss the

104

issues. Normally, but apparently not invariably, a judge or panel rendered a decision for either the negative or affirmative, the issue being which had developed the better case. If the scheduled debaters failed to appear or came unprepared, the announced topic might be explored in a general discussion from the floor.

Issues debated at biweekly *Demosthenian* sessions ranged over a wide area. On October 19, 1872, the appointed disputants argued the proposition: "Resolved, that a farmer is better off than a storekeeper." The judges ruled in favor of the affirmative. At its next meeting the society considered the topic: "Resolved, that a library is of more benefit to a community than a temperance lodge." Again the affirmative won. Subsequent debate sessions argued that: ". . . the co-education of the sexes is most recommendable and ought to be introduced into every institution of learning; . . . unlimited religious freedom as practiced in the United States is productive of religious revolution; . . . liberty of the press is productive of more good than evil; . . . capital punishment ought to be abolished; . . . Revolution is at all times against the spirit of Christianity; . . . the Indian politics [policy] of our present government is unjust; . . . the Scandinavian element in the United States ought as soon as possible to assimilate with the American element."

Frequently the "recording scribe" reconstructed the main argument in his minutes. For example, the record of a meeting held on May 8, 1875, includes the following summary of a confrontation on the question: "Have the savages any right to the land in which they live?" — a timely issue only thirteen years after the Minnesota Sioux war, and one year before Custer's Last Stand:

The aff. side . . . claimed that the savages have rights to the land in which they live. It is not civilization that makes a person superior to another from the creation. There is no caste that is superior to another, but there is a complete equality. Those who settled in a country first had also the right to it; the savages must have a home as well as the civilized. If the civilized wish to settle in the country of the savages, they must have permission from them; but they have no right to drive them away and take the land in possession. They have forms of governments as well as the civilized though perhaps not as good administered . . . it would be gross injustice if the civilized deprived them of their country and drove them into the most barren regions, where they would necessarily perish . . . the neg . . . claimed that the savages have no right to their land in which they live because they misuse the land or does [*sic*] not use it at all, and therefore can the civilized take it in possession, cultivate it and receive the crop of it and drive the savages away. The civilized have the real right to the land as God said to the children of Israel that they should be the owner of the land.[25]

Precisely when meetings of the *Demosthenian* Society ceased is uncertain; surviving records extend to 1876. However, an immediate successor, the *Athenaeum* Society of Augsburg Seminary, was in operation by 1882, and flourished until 1904. Like the earlier organization, *Athenaeum* concentrated on oral expression and conducted its deliberations exclusively in English. Meanwhile, a Norwegian-language forensic society known as *Den Nationale Øvelses Forening* had come into existence; its minutes begin in 1878. This organization, also known as *Norrøna Debatforening*, became bilingual in 1905, a step that apparently coincided with the end of *Athenaeum* as a separate society. For the next three years *Norrøna* was known as the *Alpha* and *Omega* debating society. In 1908 it became part of the Augsburg Oratorical Association, which under faculty supervision assumed jurisdiction over "all oratorical contests and debates." [26]

As was true of the *Demosthenian* Society in its day, later Augsburg forensic organizations, both Norwegian and English, challenged students to think about contemporary issues, thereby countering curricular emphasis on classical languages. Norrøna's agenda, to be sure, included debate topics that reflected and strengthened pernicious Scandinavian-American prejudices. For example, on December 16, 1892, the question of the day was: "Which is the more dangerous, Catholicism or alcoholism?" However, the next session discussed a more edifying topic: "Is socialism to be recommended?" On November 2, 1894, a few months after the famous Pullman Boycott had generated hysterical fear of trade unionism throughout the nation, *Norrøna* weighed the issue: "Do workers have the right to strike or not?" Two meetings later the basic right of revolution was debated. Following the Spanish-American war, the society considered several questions relating to "imperialism," one of the chief concerns of the day. The session of October 26, 1900, discussed the topic: "Resolved, that possessing overseas colonies would be harmful to the United States." [27]

THE ROLE OF MUSIC in Augsburg's earliest history was less impressive than that of forensics. In reporting to the Conference convention of 1873, President Weenaas noted that during the past year, Ole Paulson had "voluntarily" given vocal instruction on campus "twice weekly in the evening hours from seven to nine." [28] With some assistance from Oftedal, Paulson rendered the same service in 1873–74. Unfortunately, his permanent departure from Minneapolis in 1874, and Oftedal's preoccupation with other activities left a gap in Augsburg's embryonic music program that remained until 1877, when Oliver Larson, organist at the Swedish Augustana Lutheran Church in Minneapolis, accepted an appointment as part-time instructor in music. Larson soon organized a chorus from within the student body.[29]

Although he was an accomplished musician, Larson's contribution seemed inadequate to the supporting church body. The Conference convention of 1879 complained that there was "little or no opportunity to practice song or music" at Augsburg, and requested the board of directors to initiate corrective action.[30] Without referring specifically to a strengthened emphasis on conducting liturgy in the training of ministerial candidates, Sverdrup informed the next convention that the request for "more instruction in song and chanting [*Messe*] has been met to the fullest extent." [31] Subsequent presidential reports listed "instruction in song" as a subsidiary responsibility of individual teachers, but music did not acquire curricular status until 1920. In his accounting for 1882–83, Sverdrup regretted a reduction in music instruction, but hoped for immediate improvement. A number of circumstances, including a prolonged illness suffered by the music instructor in 1884, frustrated this hope.[32]

Augsburg's identification with the militant anti-liquor crusade that developed among Scandinavian-Americans in the 1880s elevated the significance of music on campus. Spurred by a conviction that "few nationalities . . . suffered more from drunkeness" than the Norse,[33] several Augsburg faculty members — notably Reimestad, Oftedal, Pettersen, and later Nydahl — became active participants in the movement to promote total abstinence among individuals and to outlaw the manufacture and sale of intoxicants in the larger community. Most students responded enthusiastically to the concern of their teachers. Before long Augsburg became known as an uncompromisingly dry institution. Although the editor of *Reform*, a leading Norwegian-language prohibition organ, affiliated with the United Church leadership during the Augsburg controversy, he lauded the school for unequivocally embracing the movement. An editorial of June 27, 1893, asserted:

Augsburg has been a mighty force in the promotion of total abstinence among our people. For several years all its professors have been practicing teetotalers, and this has left a mark on the students who in turn have carried the message into their congregations. But perhaps there is an Augsburg student who drinks? I doubt it, and if so, he must find his situation extremely lonely. I am prepared to sing Augsburg's praise for this. And whether or not Augsburg affiliates with the United Church, I hope that it can forever be said that the school stands in the front ranks of the Norwegian institutions of learning in our country so far as total abstinence is concerned.[34]

To some degree Augsburg's reputation as an unfailing bulwark of the dry cause was built by a faculty-student vocal group. Organized by Reimestad in 1885, the Students' Quartette (that became the Augsburg Quartette in 1893), was at first actually an octette. A favorable reaction by Minneapolis audiences to its appearances suggested to total abstinence leaders that this group might effectively supplement the spoken word at dry rallies. Accordingly, in the summer of 1888, Reimestad and three students embarked on their first Midwest tour as a formal quartette.

From the viewpoint of its sponsors, the venture "was a decided success." How many individual renunciations of strong drink were influenced by the vocalists cannot be determined, but rallies featuring their talent drew larger crowds than a single speaker or two could attract. Moreover, the free will offerings gathered at each rally not only financed the tour, but yielded sufficient revenue for participating students to remain in school. Encouraged by the 1888 response, the quartette again toured the Midwest region in 1890, 1892, and 1894, and again its audiences were appreciative. In 1895 it visited Norway, performing at more than fifty concerts sponsored by the Norwegian Total Abstinence Society.[35]

Whatever else might be said about the anti-liquor crusade, its cultural contributions were modest. Few critics would acclaim any of its tracts as literary masterpieces nor its verse as inspired poetry. Moreover, rigid total abstinence adherents avoided association with groups combining acceptance of convivial drinking with genuine appreciation of good music, drama, or fiction — a reality that for many decades reinforced Augsburg's cultural isolation even within the Scandinavian-American community. Nevertheless, the quartette's cultural impact was creditable. Its skilfully performed repertoire, consisting largely of "appropriate temperance texts, emotional and exhortatory" set to "old Scandinavian melodies" heightened musical interest among Norwegian-Americans residing in remote areas, and many rural churches organized choirs for the first time.[36] This, in turn, generated an enthusiastic response to the Norwegian Lutheran Choral Union, a federation of choirs organized under the leadership of Reimestad, M. Falk Gjertsen, and others on January 30, 1892. Before long more than seventy choirs affiliated. For several years music festivals (*sangerfester*) sponsored by the choral union ranked as a major cultural event in many Norwegian-American communities.[37]

The quartette also drew students to Augsburg. Its most famous recruit, Frederik Melius Christiansen, the future St. Olaf College choirmaster, was persuaded by Reimestad to enroll at the school following a concert at Marinette, Wisconsin, during the 1892 tour. Although Christiansen's career as an Augsburg student was brief, he later looked back on his experience at the institution "as a turning point in his life." [38] At the close of his first school year in 1893, he accepted Oftedal's advice "to continue his music rather than try for an academic career." [39] He graduated in May of the following year from Northwestern Conservatory of Music at Minneapolis. Nine years later his long term of service at St. Olaf began. In the intervening period he offered private lessons, accepted a variety of musical assignments, and studied for two years at the Royal Conservatory at Leipzig, Germany, where he received his diploma in the spring of 1899.

Before going to St. Olaf in 1903 — and to some extent thereafter — Christiansen maintained close ties with Augsburg, serving the school as part-time music instructor from 1893 through 1897. He joined the quartette for its 1894 tour, contributing his vocal talents as first bass, and enriching the program with violin solos. In collaboration with Hans Urseth, he published several song collections, the first appearing in 1894. Christiansen's biographer remarks that "The two formed a happy combination, Christiansen setting to music the poetry from Urseth's pen." [40] Notwithstanding a rather cool relationship between St. Olaf and Augsburg, Christiansen's friendship with Urseth, Hendrickson, and other Augsburg personalities remained warm and intimate after his move to Northfield. Henry P. Opseth, who had been one of Christiansen's pupils several years earlier, became music director at Augsburg in 1922. Given this continuous association, it is not surprising that the Christiansen tradition left a mark on music at Augsburg College.

While the quartette delivered musical exhortations against strong drink, agitation for prohibition developed into an organized extra-curricular activity. Beginning in 1881, a succession of lecturers representing the movement appeared on campus, prompting one student to ask: What is a prohibitionist? The issue he raised was neither total abstinence nor outlawing liquor — apparently both these propositions commanded universal assent — but whether membership in a campus prohibition society meant affiliation with the official Prohibition Party. Many drys hoped and believed that liquor could be defeated through a capture of the Republican Party, a possibility made more remote if third-party activity lured anti-liquor Republicans from their GOP allegiance. The propriety of maintaining a campus club formally or informally affiliated with a political party also generated doubts.

Before these troublesome questions could be settled, the rise of an intercollegiate movement in which Augsburg drys wished to participate resolved the issue in favor of a campus prohibition club. On January 15, 1887, the Students' Prohibition Club of the State University invited "the prohibitionists of Augsburg Seminary, Hamline University, and Carleton College" to consider "calling a state collegiate prohibition convention to be held here in Minneapolis sometime this winter." A meeting of "the prohibitionists of Augsburg Seminary" held ten days later deferred action on establishing a club on campus, but decided "in favor of a convention," and selected a committee of three to meet with spokesmen of the university club.

A series of conferences among representatives of the drys on the four campuses led to the calling of a convention on April 25 to organize a state intercollegiate association of prohibition clubs. Shortly before the convention met, and evidently to create a base for the Augsburg delegation to represent, campus drys formally organized the Prohibition Club of Augsburg Seminary. As anticipated, the April 25 convention established the Inter-Collegiate Prohibition Association of Minnesota, with the Augsburg affiliate holding full membership. So far as can be determined, this was Augsburg's first involvement in an intercollegiate enterprise.

When the prohibition club resumed activity in the autumn of 1887, a complication developed. Article II of a proposed constitution defined "the object of this club" as being threefold: "a) to work for total abstinence . . . b) to diffuse among the students a clearer conception of Prohibition as the leading political issue of to-day . . . c) to support *the* political party which adopts as its chief plank the prohibition of the manufacture and sale of intoxicating beverages." Because he objected to partisan political activity on campus, and since section c explicitly aligned the club with the Prohibition Party, Sverdrup vetoed this portion of Article II.

After some discussion, the club decided to exclude the objectionable section from the constitution without drafting a substitute. At the same time it maintained affiliation with the intercollegiate association and a thinly disguised relationship with the Prohibition Party. A meeting on February 17, 1888, went so far as "to recommend" the selection of Reimestad and Pettersen as delegates to the forthcoming national Prohibition Party convention.[41]

This course of action soon provoked dissent within the constituency.

On May 29, 1888, the board of directors passed a resolution counseling against the creation of "political clubs" on campus "under conditions now prevailing." [42] In response, club officials initiated a series of exchanges with the directors designed to clarify the resolution's implications: Were the directors instructing the prohibition club to disband? At a meeting held on June 5, 1889, the board defined as objectionable a campus organization "affiliated with or under the leadership of a particular political party." [43] The club interpreted this to mean that it could continue operation if it severed formal ties with the Prohibition Party and its subsidiaries, including the intercollegiate association. For more than a decade the prohibition club functioned as an Augsburg Seminary organization with no formal off-campus affiliation. Meanwhile, the total abstinence standard maintained its hold on the Augsburg community.

FROM THE BEGINNING of Augsburg's history, religion had been a central element in student life. A chapel service opened every school day, and students frequently assembled for prayer meetings either formally or informally. Particularly after Sverdrup became president, the administration strongly encouraged pre-theological students, and even those not preparing for the ministry, to volunteer for service in Lutheran congregations both during vacation periods and while school was in session. The institution's religious orientation was highly visible.

An increased emphasis on religious concerns accompanied the policy changes following Sverdrup's 1884 pronouncement that in the future more than in the past, Augsburg should seek to become "exclusively" a divinity school. Thereafter, presidential messages at commencement and on other occasions dealt less frequently with such issues as immigrant adjustment to American life and more often with topics like world missions. Official ideology still placed high value on student individuality and autonomy, but the obligation of the school to promote its own theological orientation was more strongly emphasized.

An historical sketch carried in the first catalog published in 1891 explicitly endorsed the maintenance of a closed religious-educational community. According to the sketch, in the first "ten or fifteen years" of Augsburg's existence, faculty recruitment had produced "many disappointments and bitter experiences." Available teachers were either incompetent or spiritually deficient (dels uduelige, dels aandløse), a combination that seriously distorted the religious life of many talented students. "It soon became apparent," continued the sketch, "that until teachers trained by the school itself and embued with the spirit of its founders were secured," Augsburg could not expect satisfactory return from its labors. Since 1885, when the policy of hiring alumni for the preparatory department's teaching force was formally instituted, harmony had "reigned in the faculty," with each instructor working "faithfully for those entrusted to him and in unison with his associates." At the same time applications for admission in the years immediately preceding 1891 had permitted an abundant selection of students "who were willing to enter the service of the Church, while . . . others were recommended to enter schools more suitable to their purpose." [44]

Student life soon reflected this reordering of priorities. The Mission Society of Augsburg Seminary, for many years the chief representative of religious activity on campus, was founded in 1885. According to its constitution, the society's goal was to familiarize Augsburg students with the missionary enterprise through lectures, reports, and literature, the acquisition of which was a responsibility of the society. Before long the scope of its activity went beyond these initial objectives. Early in 1888 the society, working cooperatively with local congregations — with Reverend Gjertsen's Trinity parish in the lead — organized an ambitious home mission program for the Twin City area. Specifics of the program included visiting the victims of illness and poverty; conducting evangelistic services and prayer meetings; participating in Sunday school work, and organizing this enterprise where needed; and distributing Christian literature. To some extent the mission society translated all of these plans into action. The Sunday school work was particularly important, leading to the organization of several Lutheran congregations. Meanwhile, overseas missions received their share of attention. In addition to publicizing work on the various fields, the society frequently contributed modest sums of money, especially to the Madagascar mission at which two Augsburg graduates, John P. Hogstad and Erik Tou, were stationed. [45]

The oversimplified dichotomy between Augsburg "piety" and St. Olaf "intellectualism" that emerged in 1891, together with Sverdrup's assault on "humanism," heightened religious concern at Augsburg. F. Melius Christiansen found the school in the grip of perpetual revival in the autumn of 1892, a discovery that caused him some discomfort. [46] Subsequent developments in the controversy with the United Church further strengthened the evangelistic spirit. Students who left Augsburg in September, 1893, to attend the United Church Seminary were as committed to the Christian faith as those who remained, but the latter regarded themselves as special heirs of the 19th century religious awakening in Norway. Peder Nilsen's campaign to rally support for Augsburg

112

succeeded in firmly identifying the school with revivalism, and encouraged an influx of new students associated with the same tradition.

THE MISSION SOCIETY and the concerns it represented continued to flourish after the turn of the century. In 1900 the society assumed responsibility for conducting two religious services a month at the Hennepin County Poor Farm. From time to time it cooperated with local churches in a ministry to disadvantaged residents of Minneapolis slum areas. The most ambitious effort of this kind was initiated in late 1915 when the society, assisted by several Lutheran Free Church congregations in Minneapolis, established a city mission on High Street. This project, later known as the Gateway Mission, continued for many years at several downtown locations. At the same time augmentation of the mission library, and the organization of rallies and meetings designed to build enthusiasm for propagating Christianity continued.

Although the mission society was reluctant to affiliate formally with such inter-synodical organizations as the Twin City Luther League, it served as a connecting link between Augsburg and religious groups outside the LFC by uniting with other Lutherans on behalf of foreign missions. In 1906 the society sent a delegation to a regular convention of the Students' Volunteer Movement, a federation of Protestant collegiate and seminary chapters working for an expansion of missionary activity. Contact maintained for many years with the volunteer movement had a significant side effect not directly related to the organization's main purpose: it placed Augsburg students in closer touch than ever before with life on other campuses.[47]

Several facets of extra-curricular activity expanded after 1900. Thanks largely to the efforts of gifted amateurs on the faculty, especially Hendrickson and Urseth, music made some progress. Soon after joining the teaching staff in 1900, Hendrickson reorganized the old Reimestad quartette, enlarging it into the Augsburg Glee Club three years later. Until 1933, when a merger of the glee club and the women's choral society created the Augsburg College Choir, the glee club ranked as the school's leading musical organization. Hendrickson, who also taught full-time and served as registrar after 1907, continued as director until 1914, when Harry Anderson replaced him. Anderson's period of service ended in 1919, whereupon Hendrickson resumed the directorship until the appointment of Opseth in 1922.

In 1908 Hendrickson organized another vocal group, the Augsburg Sextette, "from some of the best material in the Glee Club." The original sextette roster included Henry O. Hanson, J. Albin Winther, Theodore

113

C. Blegen, Lawrence B. Sateren, Thorvald O. Burntvedt, and Hendrickson. Unlike the glee club, it led an "intermittent existence," being reactivated for periodic tours during summer vacations. The first tour, involving more than 100 concerts, was taken in 1909. A second was organized in 1912, and a third in 1921. Hendrickson managed and directed all three.

Due to financial stringency and a weak tradition, the advance of instrumental music was less impressive than that of vocal. In the early 1880s student contributions provided the chapel with an organ which for some reason was never used during chapel hour. Students also purchased the school's first piano in 1901, and a few years later they financed another organ for the chapel in New Main. According to Hendrickson, "the school did not buy a single musical instrument till co-education had been introduced and a department of Music . . . organized."

Until 1904, when Urseth decided to initiate action, "no consistent effort was made to promote instrumental music" at Augsburg. Despite a lack of available talent and resources, Urseth organized a band that, in Hendrickson's opinion, "was on the high road to become a musical asset" by 1909, the year Urseth died. Thereafter, the band "fell on evil days, owing to frequent change of leaders and . . . personnel." Under the baton of Carl J. Petri in 1919–21, it experienced a brief revival that, unfortunately, withered when Petri left the school. Meanwhile, several small orchestras had been organized, all of which "led a brief, though enthusiastic existence." [48]

Journalistic activity was more rewarding. On December 15, 1898, the *Augsburg Echo* appeared for the first time. Bilingual until 1925, when it shifted from a magazine to a tabloid format, the *Echo* at first devoted more space to long feature articles on such subjects as "Funeral Customs Among the Ancient Egyptians," than to happenings at Augsburg. The latter were chronicled briefly in a column or two, somewhat like a small town newspaper records social life details. Nevertheless, the birth of the *Echo* was important. Earlier attempts to establish a student newspaper had failed, whereas the *Echo* possessed a strong determination to live.

Although not as central as in earlier years, forensics retained considerable extra-curricular significance after 1900. Campus debating societies continued to attract large memberships and to maintain full schedules. Sponsorship by the Lutheran Free Church Book Concern of an annual oratorical contest awarding cash prizes to winning participants helped to sustain interest in public speaking. Contest rules required entrants to write their own orations and limited eligibility to academy and college students. Administration of the event, including judging, was a responsibility of the Augsburg faculty. At the initial contest held on April 1, 1905, Arthur Markve won first place with an entry called "Mother Love." Two years later Theodore Blegen's appreciative evaluation of William E. Gladstone as "England's Grand Old Man," won him that honor.[49]

Meanwhile, oratory and the dry movement became more closely linked. The prohibition club was relatively inactive from 1891 until 1905, when it adopted a new name, The Prohibition League of Augsburg Seminary, and resumed affiliation with the Minnesota Intercollegiate Prohibition Association, the chief activity of which was an annual oratorical contest held at one of the member schools. The Augsburg league entered a participant in 1906, when the association met on the campus of Gustavus Adolphus at St. Peter, Minnesota. A year later the association met at Augsburg. Other institutions entering contestants included Gustavus, St. Olaf, and Red Wing Seminary. Prohibitionists at a number of schools, notably Hamline and the University of Minnesota, were represented only by observers.[50]

In addition to proselytizing on campus and working within the intercollegiate association, Augsburg prohibitionists participated directly in election campaigns. Fourteen persons served as precinct workers in the contest waged by Willis G. Calderwood, a front-rank leader of Minnesota's Prohibition Party, for a Hennepin County legislative seat in 1906. They also committed their slender financial resources to the cause. Early in 1906 the prohibition league established a fund based on pledges of one dollar a month from each participating student to finance organizational activity by a league member within legislative districts where Prohibition Party prospects seemed brightest. Since the counties of western Minnesota comprising the seventh congressional district appeared promising, the league chose this area, commissioning Markve, then a college department junior, as its organizer. Election returns that year registered an impressive rise in the Prohibition vote within the counties where he had campaigned.

The Markve project attracted interest and attention, some of it facetious, outside the Augsburg community. The *Minneapolis Journal* reported a shift of concern among Augsburg students from the Chinese mission field to the seventh congressional district. Such an interpretation may have embarrassed the administration, but Sverdrup did not restrain Prohibition Party activity on campus as he had done eighteen years earlier. By 1906 Norwegian-American tolerance of political action outside the Republican Party was higher than in 1888. So was support for the dry movement.[51]

AS THE FIRST Sverdrup era drew to a close, mild symptoms of discontent began to multiply. One complaint indicated that language transition was proceeding more slowly than many students thought appropriate. In 1891 English had been the official language of instruction in fourteen of the college department's twenty-five weekly class hours on the freshman, sophomore, and junior levels, and twelve hours on the senior level. The precise division ten years later is not clear, but catalog data suggests that Norse was abandoned in all college work except in the Norwegian offerings and some of the religion courses. Within the theological department Norse retained a firmer hold. Urseth's appointment in 1898 as "English Professor of Theology" marked the beginning of a shift, but until the 1920s, two of the four theological professors still lectured in Norwegian. Norse also displayed an amazing vitality elsewhere on campus; boarding club minutes were kept in that language until 1912, and mission society records until 1915.

Several factors helped perpetuate Norwegian longer than Weenaas had anticipated in 1873. The arrival in the 1880s and 1890s of thousands of additional immigrants who settled in communities where the mother tongue continued to be spoken, as well as a conviction held by many pious Norwegian-Americans that religious truth could not be safely communicated in English, readily accounts for a general delay.[52] More important, Norse remained overwhelmingly the language of the Lutheran Free Church. As late as 1926, these congregations conducted more Norwegian than English services, and Augsburg's president delivered his first English report to an annual conference as late as 1930.[53] Ministerial candidates and students accepting assignments to teach summer parochial school — the mainstay of Norse language instruction in the absence of a Norwegian Lutheran elementary educational system — were expected to maintain a firm command of the Norwegian language.

Maintaining Norse proficiency was not a problem when natives of Norway made up the bulk of Augsburg's student population. It became so after 1900 as the balance between immigrants and natives shifted in favor of the latter. Of the three young men receiving their B.A. degrees in 1905, all were born in the United States. The count in 1907 was five natives to four immigrants; in 1909, five to one; and in 1910 all six were American born.[54]

Inevitably, an Augsburg student born in the United States of Norwegian immigrant parents faced a language problem less formidable than

116

that confronting a young man of Norwegian birth, but nonetheless frustrating. Nearly always Norse was spoken in his home and neighborhood, but his first rudiments of formal education in the public schools tended to establish English as a more facile means of communication for him than Norwegian. Pressures to escape the immigrant ghetto by speaking "the language of the country" reinforced a preference for English. While attending Yale graduate school early in the century, George Sverdrup, Jr., always communicated with his father in English, while the elder Sverdrup consistently wrote to George in Norwegian.

Besides preferring English, an Augsburg student who had been partially "Americanized" by attending public schools and who was establishing contact with other campuses through the Students' Volunteer Movement and other intercollegiate activities wanted to feel that he was attending a college rather than the "Greek" department of a divinity school. A member of the college class of 1911 recalls that he and his fellow seniors decided to inscribe "Augsburg College" rather than "Augsburg Seminary" on their emblematic pin. The significance of this incident may have seemed minor, but it was a symbolic challenge to the ancient concept that Augsburg was an integrated divinity school rather than a college and seminary located on the same campus.[55]

In addition to the language question, student awareness of a growing gap between Augsburg's academic program and evolving standards in American higher education was growing. From 1898 through 1910 more than half of the college department's graduates chose fields other than the ministry, compared to one-fifth in the 1885–97 period. Several entered medicine and law, others became businessmen, farmers, and public school teachers. A small number gained admission to leading graduate schools: George Sverdrup, Jr., class of 1898, and Carl W. Blegen, '04, to Yale; Charles E. Stangeland, '98, Columbia; Oliver T. Lee, '01, University of Chicago; and Theodore Blegen, '10, University of Minnesota. While the study habits and language proficiency gained at Augsburg helped prepare these young men for advanced academic work, deficiencies in the college department's program along with the institution's unaccredited status obliged all of them to obtain additional undergraduate work before pursuing graduate study. A similar problem faced Augsburg graduates aspiring to qualify for secondary school teaching at a time when state departments of education were raising certification standards.

The place of athletics in student life also was becoming an issue. Early in 1906 a controversy concerning availability of the gymnasium in New Main for student use precipitated a minor rebellion on campus. Georg Sverdrup, whose office was immediately above the facility, and whose

117

aversion to gymnastic noise exceeded his enthusiasm for athletics, recently had imposed severe restrictions on gymnasium hours. On January 16 a group of thirty-four students presented to the board of trustees a communication demanding an open-door policy. Notwithstanding student participation in a fund drive to equip the gymnasium, and "without any reason being given," the petitioners charged, "students have been denied the right of the gymnasium and the use of . . . apparatus . . . purchased [with] students' money." Moreover, they continued, "we have begged and petitioned the president that a director be appointed . . . our begging has met rebuffs. . . . We have waited patiently . . . in vain." The board was asked "to see to it that a director is appointed who is willing and competent to lead the exercises, that the gymnasium is open . . . every day in the week . . . for not less than one hour and a half, of which one hour shall be devoted to physical exercise . . . and one half hour to basket ball." The petition closed with an ominous threat: Should the board fail to act, "we, the undersigned students, realizing the futility of any further attempts, will refuse to enter our respective classes."

Oftedal's immediate reaction to this manifesto is not on record. Neither is that of Sverdrup. However, the administration conceded the petitioners' key demand by opening the gymnasium for an hour and a half in the afternoon. In addition to a regular teaching load, S. O. Severson, English instructor in the college and academy, accepted the post of athletic director. Whether basketball immediately became part of the gymnastic routine is not clear, but the game did emerge as an informal activity two years later.[56]

Without courting the honor, Urseth became the hero of the innovative faction within Augsburg's student body, including the sports enthusiasts. His status as "English Professor in Theology," identification with the movement to accelerate Norwegian-American assimilation into the national mainstream, teaching effectiveness, and impressive poetic talents associated him with the forces working for change and academic improvement. Even the complaints of his critics, particularly the charge that his theology verged on modernism, enhanced his standing with campus reformers. At the same time, Urseth's loyalty and tact precluded his emergence as an anti-administration leader within the faculty.

However, Urseth could not always control his more exuberant followers. Within hours after Sverdrup's death a group of them circulated a petition, accompanied by an unknown number of signatures, calling for the election of Urseth as president of Augsburg Seminary. Concerned at what he considered the impropriety of this move, Urseth severely reprimanded its promoters.[57] Although the drive to make him president survived this episode, he was not chosen. Instead, an Oftedal-Helland-Urseth triumvirate was established, with Oftedal as acting president and the other two men as deans. That this interim regime failed to set the institution on a new course is understandable. Oftedal remained detached, Urseth was incapacitated by illness for nearly a year before his death in April, 1909, and conservatism retained a powerful hold on the constituency.

Nevertheless, the interim between the two Sverdrup eras did mark some changes in student life. One example was the institution's more explicit recognition of the claims of non-ministerial students. Even though the LFC conference of 1909 reaffirmed the old divinity school idea, endorsement of curriculum expanison by the faculty strengthened the drive for modernization. School catalogs before 1908 had noted that "Nearly all the graduates [college and seminary] are engaged in religious work in the Lutheran churches in America or in foreign mission fields." However, supplementing this statement in the 1908 catalog was another that reflected a change in Augsburg's self image: "Indeed, hundreds of young men have attended Augsburg and graduated from its college department who have not pursued theological studies afterward or ever intended to . . . the courses are not planned to make a necessary but a fitting road to theological studies." [58] The next edition softened the obvious contradiction between the two statements by changing the opening phrase of the first from "Nearly all . . ." to "A large majority . . .", and carrying the second statement intact.[59] Without repudiating the divinity school principle, Augsburg began to affirm that it positively welcomed students not aspiring to become clergymen.

Team sports also were winning acceptance. In the autumn of 1907 a group of students founded an athletic association for the purpose of promoting "athletics in general," and cooperating with the faculty in establishing a sports program. The birth of this organization, asserted the *Echo*, opened "a new epoch in the history of our school." Sports enthusiasts would agree. Basketball had been entirely intramural until 1907–08, when Augsburg entered outside competition for the first time.[60]

The initial encounter was a home game with a YMCA team on December 7. Augsburg triumphed by a score of 44–29. Subsequently it met St. Olaf twice, Hamline and Gustavus once, and played a return match with the YMCA team. It lost the latter, split honors with St. Olaf, and won over Hamline and Gustavus. Unlike the St. Olaf team, which was coached by faculty Athletic Director Irving E. Noakes, Augsburg's players managed their own enterprise both strategically and logistically. Albert Thorson, a college department junior who served as "Director of Gymnasium" under the supervision of a faculty committee, was one of the players. Other team members were John E. Blegen, Thorsten T. Roan, Joseph R. Michaelson, and James B. Larson. All except Roan, a third-year theological student, were enrolled in the college department. Henry O. Hanson, a college senior, was manager.[61]

In 1907–08 the athletic association placed Augsburg's first official baseball team on the field. However, basketball reverted to intramural status during the next two years. Although the reason for this step is not clear, perhaps a concession was being made to those Augsburg supporters who believed that competitive sports, particularly basketball, were incompatible with divinity school ideals.[62] In any case, outside competition was resumed in 1910–11, when the legendary team consisting of Peder Konsterlie, Bert Balerud, Harold Johnson, Henry Quanbeck, and James Gronseth established its reputation. Although several years elapsed before a complete athletic program became a reality, team sports and other standard collegiate activities had an assured place in student life. As the experience of the next decade would disclose, the choice open to Augsburg's college department was not between the *status quo* and "modernization," but between the latter and liquidation.

TOWN AND GOWN

 PARADOXICALLY, the relationship between Augsburg and Minneapolis was more intimate in the 1870s, when prairie and swamp separated campus and city, than thirty years later, when metropolitan growth brought the two into close physical proximity. The *Echo* for September–October, 1907 reported that several new students recently had been "two or three blocks" from the school without finding anyone who could direct them to the campus. By contrast, a stranger arriving in 1875 experienced no difficulty. Nearly every Minneapolis resident knew that by traveling the road southward along the Mississippi River's west bank, he would eventually see Old Main dominating the landscape. Compared to other structures in Minneapolis, Augsburg's building appeared imposing, an impression enhanced by its location on high ground.[1]

Its reputation as a cultural center reinforced community interest in Augsburg College. Programs on campus attracted not only Norwegian-American church people and members of the city's Scandinavian colony, but also "Yankees" and non-Lutherans. John Blegen, who was one of two class orators at the graduation exercises of 1880, recalls his performance before an overflow audience that included such celebrities as Judge Isaac Atwater, "the southtown's leading citizen," and John Arctander, prominent local attorney. "A commencement at Augsburg in those days," writes Blegen, "was a special event in south Minneapolis, since there were few gatherings like it."[2]

Oftedal and Sverdrup seemed to promise stronger bonds between Augsburg and the entire Midwest, including Minneapolis. Soon after becoming associated with the school both men explicitly attacked what they regarded as undesirable isolationist tendencies among Norwegian-Americans. In explaining his reasons for issuing the controversial "Public Declaration" of 1874, Oftedal insisted that his obligations extended beyond the theological classroom. He also felt impelled to assist his countrymen in gaining "a comprehension of their potentialities [*Folkegaver*] and duties to the American nation." Norwegian clergymen, who alone among the immigrants possessed the advantages of higher education, were by and large unfitted for this task, Oftedal charged. According to him, the typical pastor was "worm-eaten with classicism, bathed in monarchism and frozen stiff in orthodoxy," in addition to being "driven by a need for professional status, and nostalgic with thoughts of home." He implied that under such leadership, Norwegian-Americans would forever remain an unassimilated lump within the main body of American society.[3]

One issue directly related to Oftedal's generalized blast was whether public education should be supported by Norwegian-American Lutherans. Fearful that secular tendencies within American schools might subvert religious faith, the Norwegian Synod was attempting, with only limited success, to establish a separate Lutheran elementary system. A number of prominent Norwegians, some of whom were affiliated with the church, sharply challenged this project. Shortly after arriving in the United States, Georg Sverdrup became a participant in the dispute. In two articles published in 1876 and 1877 by *KvartalSkrift*, a quarterly journal edited by the Augsburg faculty, Sverdrup identified himself as an uncompromising supporter of the "American common school." [4]

Sverdrup's first article argued the superiority of American education over the European variety. Far from being undesirable, he asserted, interdiction of religious instruction in the former was appropriate, since the communication of Christian truth was a congregational rather than a state responsibility. Moreover, such interdiction was necessary. That Conference and Synod congregations could not cooperatively conduct religious schools was well known, he wrote: "How then can all the denominations existing in the United States agree on a program of religious instruction for the public schools?" [5] American public education also could claim other virtues. By admitting children from all ethnic groups and levels of society, it worked for preservation of democracy and against establishment of a social system based on class and caste. In addition, it operated directly under popular control; voters elected boards of education.

In the closing paragraphs of his second article, Sverdrup placed the school issue in a larger Norwegian Lutheran context. Norse immigrants, he wrote, had "gained nothing and lost much by refusing to learn what could be learned in the public schools." Emotionally and intellectually, they lacked a sense of identification with the United States. The consequences, according to Sverdrup, were lamentable. If anything, Norse-American proclivity to drunkeness exceeded that of so-called "pagan Americans," against whose influence the clergy claimed to be guarding the immigrant flock. Equally tragic, the refusal of Norwegians to equip themselves for citizenship in their new home had left them open to manipulation by unscrupulous machine politicians. Perhaps public education alone could not transform this demoralized group into self-respecting citizens, but its potentialities were impressive if properly utilized.[6]

Sverdrup concluded by rejecting contentions that public school education might undermine the commitment of young Norse-Americans to Lutheranism. "I do not believe," he wrote, "that the Lutheran church has to hide in a corner." If it possessed any vitality, it should welcome open confrontation with other groups within America's free society. Avoidance of such a challenge could only signify impotence and weakness.* [7]

A year after Sverdrup's articles appeared, Oftedal won election to the Minneapolis Board of Education, an office he held for ten years. Later claims by Augsburg partisans no doubt exaggerated his role in this post. One writer, for example, asserted that Oftedal "introduced the so-called High School System which is now common throughout the United States." [8] However, his service was creditable enough to win the respect and confidence of board colleagues; he served for a time as secretary, and was twice elected president. In 1886, two years before his school board tenure ended, he accepted membership on the Minneapolis Library Board and served until 1896. During that time he successfully advocated two policies: establishment of branch libraries, and acquisition of Scandinavian literature.[9]

While Oftedal's extensive civic involvement served as a link between Augsburg and Minneapolis, his journalistic activity maintained contact with a large group of Scandinavian-Americans outside of the school's supporting constituency. Several Oftedal critics respected his competence as a newspaperman. Commenting on the establishment of *Folkebladet* under the joint editorship of Oftedal and Sverdrup, Weenaas remarked that this venture placed Oftedal "in his proper niche" (*paa sin rette Hylde*).[10] According to Pastor Johan A. Bergh, a prominent Old School Conference leader, Oftedal was not well suited to fill the theological chair, adding that "If he had become a member of *Skandinaven's* editorial staff he could have gained entre into American politics and gone to Washington." Bergh believed Oftedal would have found an appropriate outlet for his abilities as an agrarian leader.[11]

*The original article reads: "*Har den [lutherske Kirke] nogen Kraft i sig, saa lad den komme ud, lad den vise sin Kraft i den aabne Brydning i det frie Folk; tør den ikke vaere med der, saa har den tabt sin Kraft og er som det saltløse Salt.*" Andreas Helland, ed., *Samlede Skrifter i Udvalg*, 1:383.

The early files of *Folkebladet* confirm these judgments. Adversaries of the Augsburg professors correctly represented the newspaper when they called it "secular" (*verdslige*), meaning that it was more than a synodical house organ. Its comprehensive news coverage embraced such diverse areas as Austro-German-Russian diplomacy, domestic politics within Scandinavia, France, Italy, and Britain, as well as the United States; Minnesota politics; and a wide range of Twin City political, economic, and social concerns. Few inhibitions restrained its left of center editorial policy. An article appearing on June 8, 1882, stoutly defended both trade unionism and the right to strike. The violence precipitated by disputes between labor and management was regrettable, but "given our country's lack of legal protection for workers, they are obliged to create unions, secret or open, to protect their interests."

Folkebladet's broad coverage and editorial militance attracted readers and subscribers not affiliated with the Conference, which in turn enhanced Oftedal's standing among Scandinavian-Americans and within the community generally. When the University of Minnesota established a chair in Scandinavian languages in 1883, he was regarded as a contender for the post.[12] His reputation as a colorful public speaker created a demand for his presence at such events as annual May 17 Norwegian festivals. Other groups came within the range of Oftedal's broad interests as well. Preoccupation with the study of modern Greek led him to contact Greek-Americans residing in Minneapolis, who accepted him as a trusted friend.[13]

For more than a decade after Oftedal's arrival, his gregarious nature helped to maintain the warm relationship between Augsburg and Minneapolis that was originally established by Ole Paulson with Judge Vanderburgh and other local citizens who assisted in the first building program. Like Paulson, Oftedal in 1882 persuaded a number of Minneapolis businessmen to participate in a fund drive that financed the purchase of four lots needed for building North Hall, a dormitory constructed in 1884. The sum involved was not large — approximately $3,700 — but Augsburg spokesmen interpreted it as an indication of good will.[14]

TWENTY YEARS LATER rapport between seminary and city was less evident. When construction of New Main encountered financial difficulty, Oftedal again sought community support. At first prospects seemed promising. An agreement negotiated with the Commercial Club of Minneapolis in June, 1901 exchanged reciprocal pledges designed to assure completion of New Main on a debt-free basis. In return for commitments that Augsburg would remain in Minneapolis and provide $19,000

124

for the building fund, the club promised a solicitation campaign with a goal of $10,000. Since the estimated cost of New Main was $37,000, and the building fund already possessed $8,000, the problem of financing the new facility apparently had been solved. It was ready for occupancy by the turn of the year.[15]

Unfortunately, the commercial club campaign fell $8,000 short of its projected $10,000 goal. To further complicate matters, a dispute developed as to whether the $2,000 actually raised should be credited to the club. In delivering his annual board of trustees report to the Augsburg Corporation on June 5, 1903, Oftedal remarked with sarcasm: "The splendid result of this effort . . . of Minneapolis' largest commercial organization is . . . $603.00 instead of $10,000 . . . in addition thereto was raised $1408 and placed to the credit of the club. But the last mentioned amount was raised by the undersigned almost exclusively outside of the club amongst businessmen and friends of Augsburg here in the city." Meanwhile, the Lutheran Free Church had no recourse but to assume responsibility for the remaining deficit.[16]

Commercial club officials defended themselves against charges of bad faith, arguing that their commitment was a promise to conduct a campaign designed to raise $10,000 rather than a firm guarantee to deliver this sum. They insisted that club members had made an intensive effort to secure contributions and pledges, and cited the Gjertsen affair as the main reason that many businessmen refused to participate.[17] Although this explanation no doubt had some validity, the Gjertsen storm would have inflicted less damage had Augsburg's relations with Minneapolis been more secure. A combination of circumstances that had occurred during the preceding twenty years had separated the institution from the city. Assignment of priority to these events is a matter of judgment, but some theories are possible.

First, Sven Oftedal's effectiveness as liaison man with the community presumably had faded since the 1880s. His eccentricities of personality and dress were more geared to the frontier society of earlier years than to the metropolitan setting being cultivated in Minneapolis by 1900. In describing contacts with potential "Yankee" contributors during the 1882 fund drive, Oftedal noted that most men who had "worked their way up to prosperous status from dire poverty" retained their "original crudeness." [18] Oftedal could not be called crude, but the experience of severing native ties and seeking a fresh start in a new environment created a bond between himself and these men. Twenty years later a more sophisticated generation was moving into the leadership of Minneapolis.

Possibly its representatives found Oftedal quaint, and tolerated his more serious endeavors with amused forbearance.

More important than any issue of personality was the general aim of Augsburg's development in relation to that of Minneapolis. From 1880 to 1890 the city's population more than tripled — from about 47,000 to over 164,000. Rapid growth accentuated old urban problems and created a host of new ones. It also placed a burden on existing educational agencies. However, Augsburg's modest capacity to help was further circumscribed by the mid-1880 policy decisions. The contribution that Augsburg was equipped to make — that of offering a general education program geared to Norwegian immigrant needs — was explicitly disclaimed by the administration during this period through its rule to restrict admission to applicants "with some thought of entering the ministry." Understandably, the possibility of maintaining a successful relationship with groups outside of the supporting church receded. *Menighedsmaessig Presteuddannelse* was a defensible commitment, but not one that could be expected to excite Minneapolis as a whole.

While community awareness of Augsburg declined, the school faced the challenge of adjusting its values to an urban setting that by 1890 had become dominant in its neighborhood. The tradition established by the 19th century religious awakening in Norway — which served as Augsburg's most significant guideline — underscored the civic responsibilities of committed Christians and called for full involvement in community life. The same tradition cherished the concept of converted Christians as a group apart, a redeemed flock obliged to distinguish itself from the "world." An approved mode of proclaiming Christian identity was to renounce "so-called innocent pleasures, dancing, card-playing, drama and the like." [19] Clearly, these two imperatives were in tension with one another. Members of the converted flock who assumed a civic responsibility courted the danger of becoming "worldly," of losing their special identity. In the face of this peril, a choice had to be made between retreat into the security of the redeemed flock, or acceptance of the risks posed by involvement in the wider world.

The transformation of Augsburg's locale into an urban area brought the school face-to-face with this dilemma. Without renouncing the doctrine of civic responsibility, it opted for withdrawal and separatism. As saloons multiplied on Cedar Avenue, the avoidance of worldly temptation became a major preoccupation. An Augsburg way of life emerged, marked by adherence to a moral code strictly proscribing drinking, dancing, card-playing, and the theater (but not necessarily tobacco), and a corresponding reluctance to associate with groups not sharing this code. Campus debating societies and *Folkebladet* continued to discuss a wide range of public issues, but the practice of civic responsibility came to be equated with the prohibition crusade.[20]

The persistence of an immigrant consciousness intensified Augsburg's isolationist impulse. Notwithstanding his advocacy of Norwegian-American assimilation, and perhaps because his activities kept him in frequent touch with leaders of the Minneapolis establishment, Oftedal retained a strong sense of the gap separating his people from descendants of elder American stock. "Let us in our school affairs not look to institutions of learning operated by Americans," he commented in his board of trustees report to the United Church convention of 1891. "They are in most cases built by rich men, supported by rich men, and rather lavishly conducted. Our schools are all built with our people's hard earned and small savings, supported by the same means, and intended for young men, who for the most part, must pay for their schooling with hard work." [21]

A conviction that Twin City Yankees despised Scandinavians encouraged the kind of attitude articulated by Oftedal. Throughout the 1880s and 1890s, *Folkebladet* complained of discrimination against both Norwegian and Swedish immigrants. It blamed Governor William R. Merriam for alleged tardiness in granting a hearing to one Norwegian-born Hennepin County official suspended on charges of embezzlement. Said the editor: "The United States Constitution affords an accused person the right to a speedy hearing, but apparently Governor Merriam does not perceive the need for speed when only a Norwegian is involved." [22]

In Minneapolis and throughout the state the Washburn-Nelson senatorial contest of 1895 aroused considerable ethnic sentiment. Knute Nelson, a native of Norway, had effected a Scandinavian breakthrough in 1892 by winning the Republican nomination for governor and triumphing in the fall election. Following his re-election in 1894, Nelson successfully challenged the return of William D. Washburn, Sr., to the United States Senate. * Since Washburn, a prominent industrialist and civic leader, symbolized Minneapolis "Yankeedom," and Nelson represented an aggressive Scandinavian-American drive for power, a nationality clash was imminent. On another level, the battle marked a contest between Minneapolis — the state's largest city — on the one hand, and a coalition of St. Paul and much of rural Minnesota on the other. This configuration perplexed Scandinavians residing in Minneapolis: Should

* Prior to enactment of the 17th Amendment to the Federal Constitution, United States senators were elected by state legislatures, rather than by a direct vote of the people.

they back Nelson out of ethnic loyalty, or demonstrate their Minneapolis patriotism by supporting Washburn? Pressure to follow the second course mounted as the race got underway.[23]

Several Norse-American spokesmen invited charges of disloyalty to their city by speaking out for Nelson. *Folkebladet*, often critical of him, now backed the Norwegian on purely ethnic grounds. It wondered how convincing "Yankee snobbery and New England cultivation" could be "in a state that Scandinavian workers both rural and urban deserve the most credit for having built up." The Washburn camp argued that their candidate "was the man because of his descent from those New England families that from time to time had given the country great leadership." *Folkebladet* refused to be impressed by this colonial contribution. "The nation had no place else to turn since there was no one else around," it retorted.[24]

Following Nelson's victory, Washburn supporters in Minneapolis ignored the canon of American electoral politics to graciously acknowledge defeat. Instead, they sustained a furious attack on Nelson, charging that he and his managers had resorted to every conceivable trick to win the election.[25] *Folkebladet* brushed aside the substance of these charges, choosing to interpret them as an attack on Scandinavian honor. It asserted that Minneapolis newspapers could not come to terms with the reality that a "Norwegian peasant lad" had triumphed over one of the nation's "bigwigs" (*Storkakse*). To this it added a suggestion that a Scandinavian mass meeting be called for the purpose of registering an effective protest against alleged treatment of Nelson by the press.[26]

Folkebladet oversimplified the 1895 senatorial campaign. To be sure, Nelson's Norwegian origins were humble, but he also was a highly skilled politician known to be on tolerable terms with James J. Hill and Governor Merriam's Republican machine. For this reason a number of reformers preferred Washburn, whose reputation for rectitude matched his incompetence as a political manager. Nor is it clear that attacks on Nelson in the Minneapolis press were manifestations of contempt for the Scandinavian "race." Rather, the newspapers were voicing genuine resentment at being deprived of representation in the United States Senate, an advantage they believed Minneapolis deserved.

Nevertheless, Scandinavians residing in Minneapolis during the late 19th and early 20th centuries felt the sting of non-acceptance more keenly than their grandchildren would realize. A *Fortune Magazine* survey of the Twin Cities published in 1936 noted a disparity between Yankee and Scandinavian status within Minneapolis society: ". . . in the more ostentatious but still Victorian dwellings that crown Lowry

Hill . . . few people of Scandinavian extraction will be found. Socially and financially Minneapolis is still dominated by the New England families that settled it, and with three or four exceptions, there are no Scandinavians in positions of importance outside politics." [27]

Convinced that it could never win the respect of the Minneapolis establishment, Augsburg withdrew to its own ethnic base. Here, unfortunately, the possibilities were largely confined to the immediate church constituency, that by 1900 included a relatively small proportion of the total Norwegian Lutheran flock. Even the Cedar-Riverside area, a major Norwegian population center, was controlled by hostile forces. Lars M. Rand, who served the area as alderman from 1890 to 1910 was "a man of the people," but in a very different sense than Oftedal.

Norwegian-born and a practicing attorney, Rand emerged as a dominant personality in Minneapolis Democratic politics soon after his first election to the city council. He was a machine politician to his fingertips — a professed and convincing friend of the "workingman," adept at securing positions for Norwegians within the police and fire departments, a resourceful manager of caucuses and conventions, solidly backed by Cedar-Riverside saloonkeepers whose interests he brazenly represented, unbeatable in the precincts of the sixth ward, and the despair of moral reformers, whether Yankee or Scandinavian. He personified the urban boss whose flexible ethical standards appalled clean government advocates but who, nonetheless, rendered indispensable help to foreign-born constituents at a time when the American welfare state was only a vague dream.[28]

One suspects that the responsiveness of Cedar-Riverside Scandinavians to Rand reinforced Augsburg's withdrawal tendencies and its anti-urban orientation. In any case, fraternization between the Augsburg circle and Rand's "saloon element" was unthinkable. Following the alderman's death on September 27, 1913, *Folkebladet* avoided characterizing him as a creative public official. He was, the paper observed, "an extraordinarily cunning politician" (*en ualmindelig slu Politiker*), a shrewdly accurate analyst of majority opinion in his ward — with which he invariably identified — and an unfailing friend of the saloon. On a more positive note, *Folkebladet* did acknowledge that Rand's compassion for people in distress was genuine, but his association with the liquor element negated this redeeming personal quality.[29]

Aside from work within Lutheran congregations, the Augsburg community related itself to south Minneapolis through total abstinence and prohibition activity. The first effort along this line was launched in 1883, when a number of individuals associated with the school, led by John J.

129

Skørdalsvold, established the Scandinavian Coffeehouse at 1215 Washington Avenue South. Conceived as a social center that would keep youth out of the saloons, the coffeehouse originally opened as a cooperative venture. It soon drifted into financial disaster, leaving a substantial debt for which Skørdalsvold assumed personal responsibility. Thereafter it functioned for a number of years under private ownership.[30]

A few months after establishing the coffeehouse, the Skørdalsvold circle, within which both Sverdrup and Oftedal were active members, founded the Scandinavian-Lutheran Total Abstinence Society. Unlike the other project, this organization achieved longevity under a number of name changes reflecting shifts in membership and tactics. Most important, the word "Lutheran" was soon deleted to underscore a conviction that "in such a movement, all friends of humanity, irrespective of denominational affiliation, should cooperate." Following a gradual loss of Swedish members, the word "Norwegian" was substituted for "Scandinavian," then dropped. Meanwhile, similar societies formed in other parts of Minneapolis left a membership largely confined to southside residents, and a logical name change occurred. It became the South Minneapolis Total Abstinence Society.[31]

This group worked for two objectives: persuading everyone to renounce strong drink; and securing the strongest possible statutory restrictions on the liquor trade, up to and including total prohibition. To accomplish these ends, it held frequent membership meetings, pressured legislators and councilmen, sponsored rallies and congresses, distributed literature, and encouraged the formation of a network of societies like itself. From the viewpoint of the dry cause, this crusade was rewarding. By the early 1890s a substantial segment of Norwegian Lutheranism had endorsed prohibition.[32]

Although held together by an implacable hostility to liquor, the total abstinence society and its fellow travelers divided on the question of how the prohibition goal could best be achieved. One faction contended for affiliation with the Prohibition Party; another argued for working within established political structures. This disagreement reflected not only divergence of opinion on tactics, but also degrees of reluctance to renounce the Republican Party which in the late 19th century held the allegiance of many Norwegians.[33]

The Augsburg professors leaned toward the third-party faction. At various times, Oftedal and Pettersen participated in Prohibition Party politics, both on the local and state levels, and Reimestad ranked as one of the party's top leaders, receiving the nomination for lieutenant-governor in 1888, and for fifth-district congressman in 1894. Two years later Reimestad became a member of the team supporting William Jennings Bryan for the presidency by running for the Minneapolis Library Board on a fusion ticket that combined the backing of Democrats, Republicans, and Prohibitionists committed to Free Silver with that of the Populist Party. Like Bryan, he lost.[34]

Identification with the dry movement's extreme wing contributed to Augsburg's isolation by preventing associations that might have been mutually rewarding. However, dry activism did maintain a link with other Norwegian Lutheran groups at a time when rapport between Augsburg and these groups was at a low ebb. Equally important, it placed the Augsburg community in touch with a large number of non-Scandinavians affiliated with mainline Protestant denominations. In the late 19th and early 20th centuries the dry movement was not identified with conservative fundamentalism as it was later. On the contrary, churchmen of liberal theological orientation, including many Unitarians, regarded prohibition as an integral part of a comprehensive social reform program that also demanded women's suffrage, elimination of child labor, effective factory inspection, and establishment of settlement houses.

Participation in such a movement contributed to the Americanization of Augsburg, and to a small degree countered the forces working for isolation. Nevertheless, Scandinavian Lutheran drys sometimes exasperated allies in the broader crusade for social reform by dogmatically assigning an absolute priority to the prohibition issue. A striking example of this developed in 1892, when a reform coalition attempted to elect two liberal jurists, Thomas Canty and Daniel Buck, to the Minnesota Supreme Court. Since adverse court decisions had weakened the effectiveness of trade-unionism, many critics of the *status quo* regarded the success of Buck and Canty as a prime goal of the campaign. Oftedal might have been expected to feel the same way. For years *Folkebladet*, whose editorial policy reflected his views, had deplored labor's invidious position before the law.

However, Oftedal's worry about the corrupting influence of saloons on Minneapolis wage earners exceeded his anxiety to improve the legal status of organized labor. Upon learning that either Canty or Buck, possibly both, at one time or other had served as legal counsel for liquor firms, he and a number of other Scandinavian church leaders publicly urged the re-election of Charles Vanderburgh and Daniel A. Dickinson, the conservative incumbents. The endorsement manifesto, titled "An Address to the Scandinavian Voters of the State," avoided direct reference to Canty and Buck, but unmistakably identified them by warning

131

against "casting . . . votes for men who have become the legal servants of the liquor traffic." In recommending Vanderburgh and Dickinson, the pastors said nothing about their judicial competence, apart from noting their zeal for liquor law enforcement. Of the two, Vanderburgh was singled out for praise. He had been "an active worker for those things that are so dear to us all — church, Sunday School, temperance and works of benevolence." [35]

The Progressive Age, a sophisticated reform weekly published in Minneapolis and edited by William R. Dobbyn, a Univeralist clergyman and staunch prohibitionist, responded with a well-founded criticism. What evidence supported the attack on Buck and Canty? Even if the two men had served as attorneys for liquor firms, this did not automatically transform them into moral derelicts under the absolute sway of a demoniac power. Dobbyn's journal also reproached the pastors for permitting themselves to be victimized by the agents of "corporate monopoly," who allegedly had planned the attack on Buck and Canty in the bar of the West Hotel in Minneapolis. Thus, *The Progressive Age* continued, signers of the address had lent "themselves to the manipulations of a class of men who crack glasses over their parvenuish co-operation, and plan between drinks how the people shall be crushed." [36]

Although colored with overstatement, this accusation made a point. Obsession with prohibition froze many Scandinavian Lutherans into a one-issue stance that not only rendered them vulnerable to demagogic deception, but also distorted reality by making the saloon responsible for all problems facing the United States. While it was sympathetic to Bryan's 1896 crusade for Free Silver and against Wall Street, *Folkebladet* reserved its warmest plaudits for Joshua Levering, presidential candidate of the Prohibition Party. Following Levering's appearance in Minneapolis during the campaign the newspaper commented: "His argument that the thousands of saloons in this country are more responsible than anything else for our depressed economic conditions is no doubt the strongest that can be presented in the political campaign." [37]

A similar point of view remained dominant at Augsburg for years to come. Beginning in 1908, annual conferences of the LFC consistently approved a "Temperance Resolution" without taking a position on the wide range of social issues engaging the attention of most major Protestant denominations. This is not surprising. Compared to the saloon question, other concerns seemed trivial. The resolution passed in 1913 affirmed: "We consider the liquor traffic the most dangerous enemy of our spiritual, moral, social and civic welfare." It apparently followed that if this "enemy" were defeated, the whole gamut of social problems challenging American society could easily be managed.[38]

AUGSBURG'S ISOLATION from the Minneapolis community continued for several decades after 1900. Although individual Minneapolis businessmen outside of the church constituency contributed financial support, many years would pass before the school attempted another venture like the unfortunate commercial club campaign. At the same time Augsburg spokesmen conveyed an impression of unhappiness with the city in general, and the Cedar-Riverside area in particular. Catalog statements interpreted the move to Minneapolis as a turning point in Augsburg's history, but omitted any reference to the cultural advantages available in an urban center.

An impulse to move the school out of Minneapolis — either to a suburban site or an even greater distance away — also developed. While relocation did not become a distinct possibility until the Augsburg Park scheme emerged in 1921, arguments favoring a move were voiced many years earlier. In May, 1912, a special committee of the Alumni Association appointed to investigate campus expansion recommended against acquiring "more land at the present location where . . . encroaching influences" threatened to hamper Augsburg's development. The committee advocated the need for "more room and more fresh air," adding that these were available "in the outskirts of the city." [39]

Among the "encroaching influences" deplored by the Alumni Association were several accompaniments of metropolitan growth that any educational institution would have regarded as antithetical — industrial smoke, commercial invasion of the campus neighborhood, and prospective residential blight in adjacent areas. However, the term also carried other implications. An argument for Augsburg Park published in 1922 candidly affirmed specific discontents with the existing campus: "The old neighbors, who were supporters of the school, have moved away to more desirable locations, and their place has been taken by a more or less undesirable class of people of varied race and color." Augsburg Park, the article continued, would be strikingly different. In suburban Richfield LFC members who presently were "scattered over the city" had an opportunity to acquire residential lots "in a congenial neighborhood of friends and acquaintances in the immediate vicinity of the school." [40]

This view, which would seem distinctly parochial 45 years later, correctly represented Augsburg's self-image in 1922. The school regarded itself as an educational arm of the LFC, rather than an institution with any particular obligations to the city. In 1874 it had nourished the aspi-

133

ration of becoming a Norwegian cultural center as well as a theological seminary. A decade later the administration redefined institutional goals more narrowly, affirming an "exclusive" or "essential" commitment to a special brand of ministerial education. The schism of 1893 reinforced this commitment, but drastically reduced the supporting base. Thereafter United Church and Norwegian Synod spokesmen often referred to Augsburg as *"Frikirkens Presteskole"* — the Free Church divinity school. To Augsburg supporters this term had descriptive validity, providing the word *Frikirken* was not pronounced with a sneer or enclosed in quotes.

A few students not affiliated with supporting congregations began to enroll at Augsburg in the 1920s, but official responsibility continued to be limited to the LFC. One searches George Sverdrup's messages in vain for any reference to the school as a Minneapolis institution, unless praise for slum mission activity can be so regarded. This did not mean abandonment of concern for that large portion of humanity outside of the Augsburg constituency. The Guiding Principles of the Lutheran Free Church and Augsburg's values hopefully were radiating a redemptive influence, especially on Norwegian Lutherans of every synodical persuasion, but also on American society as a whole.

Within this context Sverdrup found room for a new departure: transforming the Greek department into an accredited American college designed primarily to serve LFC youth. Precisely when this goal became explicit is unclear, but its fulfillment — short of full accreditation — ranks as the most important achievement of the George Sverdrup administration.

THE EMERGENCE OF
AUGSBURG COLLEGE

 GEORGE SVERDRUP moved into the presidency of Augsburg Seminary, not in a single leap, but by stages. During the academic year following Georg Sverdrup's death (1907–08), he served on the preparatory-college faculty as a temporary professor. His election to his father's theological professorship by the 1908 LFC conference, which also granted him a year's study leave, assured the younger Sverdrup's candidacy for the full succession. After returning from Germany in the summer of 1909, Sverdrup accepted the seminary vice-presidency and became *de facto* chief administrator in addition to his teaching duties. Oftedal's death on March 30, 1911, elevated Sverdrup to acting president, and on July 11 the board of trustees formally elected him to the presidency.

Several circumstances dictated that George Sverdrup's rise to power be gradual. From his point of view, accepting the Augsburg appointment meant abandoning a promising career, and he wanted to be certain of his decision. Assuming Georg Sverdrup's responsibilities apparently required a higher level of training and experience than the son possessed in 1907. Most important, George Sverdrup needed to establish closer rapport with the Lutheran Free Church. Even though he had been born and reared on the campus, conservative supporters of the school felt that his identification with the Augsburg tradition was not sufficiently close.[1]

To a large extent this distrust was based on knowledge that George Sverdrup had been exposed to non-Augsburg influences. Instead of the Augsburg preparatory department, he had attended South High School in Minneapolis, graduating in 1894 at the age of fifteen. After receiving his B.A. degree from Augsburg's college department in 1898, he continued his studies at the University of Minnesota, where he broadened his undergraduate background in mathematics, Greek, and Latin. With a teaching career in mind — not necessarily at Augsburg — he gained admission to the Yale University Graduate School in 1901. Here he pursued Semitic languages (Hebrew and Arabic), Biblical studies, Greek, and philosophy. His academic performance was sufficiently outstanding to complete the M.A. degree in a single year — an achievement that impressed his father — and to win the respect of his professors who urged him to seek his doctorate degree.[2]

Unfortunately, finances were a problem. The graduate school offered remission of tuition for 1902–03, but Sverdrup found it expedient to accept a reasonably lucrative tutoring assignment lasting through the academic year. His students were three young men whose qualifications as Yale undergraduates needed reinforcement. One of them was a son of David R. Francis, a Democratic politician from Missouri who would be American ambassador to Russia in 1917 when the Bolshevik Revolution erupted. The group pursued its studies at a summer resort on the Canadian side of Lake Ontario, rather than at New Haven.

Slightly more affluent than a year earlier, and with the help of a small fellowship voted by the LFC, Sverdrup resumed his work at Yale in 1903. His program, that now pointed toward a career in Biblical archaeology, included more work in Semitic languages, Old Testament history, general archaeology, and epigraphy. After two years of study, the second on a Yale scholarship, he won a fellowship to the American Institute of Archaeology at Jerusalem. Here he spent 1905–06, dividing his time between study and field research. The following year he accepted a teaching position in the Syrian Protestant College — later American University — at Beirut. While at this post he was appointed American Vice-Consul to Syria, a position that Georg Sverdrup feared might lead to a political career.[3] After his father's death, George resigned as viceconsul and returned to Minneapolis, but did not immediately abandon hope that he might complete the work required for his Ph.D. This hope failed to materialize; responsibilities at Augsburg over the next years demanded his full attention.[4]

THE FIRST DECADE of George Sverdrup's administration was not a resounding success. Enrollment declined to a dangerous low. In 1911–12 the college department had 53 students, and the trend during the next seven years was consistently downward: 52, 37, 37, 31, 28, 25, 23. Curricular development, although a major concern, proceeded slowly. No visible building and ground improvements graced the campus, and the budgetary situation remained precarious. Odds were against survival of the college department — if not the entire institution.

Whether a president endowed with more experience and aggressiveness than Sverdrup could have reversed this unfavorable tide sooner is problematic. In any case, his style of leadership was not calculated to produce immediate results. His profound respect for personal individuality prevented the kind of manipulation that might have manufactured annual conference majorities for a controversial program. Nor was he able to use flamboyant rhetoric as a tool. His reverence for language inhibited him from using evocative cliches for popular effect. "Many other men," writes Nils N. Rønning, the Norwegian-American editor and author, "would have tried to win . . . confidence and good will . . . by using the old slogans. . . . He did his own thinking and gave expression in his own way to his thoughts. . . ." [5] At first this unorthodox approach to executive responsibility created an impression of weakness and indecisiveness. However, prolonged exposure to Sverdrup won him the respect and admiration of the constituency, and this in turn reinforced his own self-confidence. Meanwhile, his administration faced a troublesome educational policy issue, and a number of related problems.

The educational policy issue was in fact a dilemma: How could the Greek department be transformed into an accredited American college without compromising the concept that Augsburg was a divinity school organized into three departments? Conservatives opposed to modernization could and did invoke the legacy of Georg Sverdrup, particularly the recommendation made in 1884 that Augsburg more than "hitherto" should seek to become "exclusively" a divinity school. On the other hand, Augsburg had never achieved this goal. Near the end of his tenure the elder Sverdrup had vaguely suggested a need to move toward accreditation of Augsburg's academic program. Following his death pressures to renovate the college curriculum increased without achieving any measure of success. Many young people in the LFC not aspiring to become ministers desired college training under church auspices. It also seemed obvious to some advocates of reform that a broader college program would improve preparation for theological study.

Although he refrained from delivering ringing pronouncements on the subject, it is evident that George Sverdrup thoroughly agreed with the faction favoring modernization. But he did not relish a brutal confrontation on the issue. In addition, he was determined to maintain his father's legacy as intact as possible. A carefully written section in the closing chapter of Helland's *Augsburg Seminar Gjennem Femti Aar* presumably defined administration thinking on the problem:

One of the most difficult problems facing the school has been and continues to be the status of the preparatory departments.

That the school's first and foremost responsibility is ministerial education, and that this involves not only the theological but also the preparatory departments, must never be lost sight of if the institution is to remain faithful to its mission. No other consideration must be permitted to interfere with or limit fulfillment of this responsibility. The question then arises if it is possible and desirable to organize the preparatory departments in such a way that at the same time and in an effective manner they can offer academic training to young men not planning to study theology or to engage in pastoral activity. The school believes this to be both possible and desirable, and that as now organized, it provides a good opportunity for such an education at the same time that it offers an appropriate preparation for theological study. Whether additional resources and a more generous endowment would enable the school to achieve its goals more effectively deserves to be considered by its friends.[6]

Helland might have added that more friends with affluent status could have eased tension between Augsburg's two main goals by providing resources to sustain both. Under the direction first of Fred Paulson and later Miss Ragna Sverdrup, the treasurer's office operated with admirable efficiency, but this could not compensate for a severely limited financial base. Moreover, within the overwhelmingly rural Lutheran Free Church there was a dearth of talent to staff the board of trustees. Following Oftedal's death in 1911, Knute B. Birkeland, a former pastor who, for a number of years had engaged in a variety of enterprises, became chairman of the board, a post he surrendered in June, 1925, shortly before his tragic and mysterious death.[7]

Although loyal to Augsburg, Birkeland was not an ideal board chairman. He broad view of trustee prerogatives — which is amply documented by his reports to annual LFC conferences and frequent *Folkebladet* articles — generated friction between the chairman and other trustees, as well as members of the faculty. The absence of visible tension between Birkeland and Sverdrup was probably due more to Sverdrup's diplomacy than to the other man's restraint.

Nevertheless, Birkeland served Augsburg well during the first half of his tenure as chairman of the board. With the help of Endre E. Gynild, who functioned as liaison between the school and its supporting congregations, the Birkeland board persuaded the LFC to increase its level of financial support. By 1919 the outstanding debt, which in 1915 had totaled more than $29,000, was liquidated, an achievement that brightened commemoration of the school's fiftieth anniversary. Plans to collect an endowment fund of $100,000 remained unfulfilled, however; in November, 1919 it was estimated at $55,182.[8]

Within these financial limits, the Sverdrup administration attempted to win accreditation for the college and preparatory departments while maintaining the seminary. The first step was taken in 1909–10, when the faculty requested an evaluation of the college department by the Board of Examiners of the Minnesota Department of Education to determine whether Augsburg college graduates could qualify for certification as high school teachers.[9]

Professor Arthur E. Haynes of the University of Minnesota, who conducted the examination, discovered a number of deficiencies precluding immediate accreditation. The school, he pointed out, needed "an endowment of at least $250,000." In addition, Haynes recommended enriching "the curricula of all . . . departments (including the preparatory) by taking out some of the so-called culture studies like history and language, and supplying their place by such sciences as chemistry, astronomy, zoology, etc." Effective instruction in these disciplines required "a building, properly constructed for teaching the natural sciences and provided with well-equipped laboratories." He noted that the school had "no equipment for teaching either zoology or chemistry," neither of which was offered. Although physics was taught in the preparatory department, "the equipment for this subject" was "inferior to that of our own state high school."

In the concluding section of his report, Haynes left some basis for hope. Augsburg was educating "boys and young men from the farms," whose limited financial resources ruled out attendance at more expensive colleges. This being so, the school seemed "to be making an effort to solve a most important problem and therefore deserve[d] encouragement." He suggested instead "that when the graduates ask for professional certificates" they be required "to pass examinations in, at least, educational psychology, history of education, pedagogy, and school organization and law, until these subjects are taught in the college."[10]

Although the Sverdrup administration assigned high priority to winning accreditation, other concerns worked against an energetic response to the Haynes report. In the spring of 1911 the president devoted much of his energy to formulating plans for a pastoral summer school that would feature a well-known Norwegian theologian as its principal lecturer. Significantly, too, he made no allusion to accreditation or innovation in reporting to the LFC conference of 1911. Instead, he discussed such traditional themes as the need for rapport between Augsburg and the congregations, and the institution's role as a training center for congregational servants.

The president also called attention to the urgency of strengthening instruction in Norwegian. He predicted that "for some generations" (*endnu i nogen slegtled*) Norse would remain the language of the LFC even though it was becoming more difficult to maintain proficiency in it. To meet the problem, he recommended authorization of a stipend for training a competent teacher of Norwegian language and culture. The conference responded affirmatively, delegating to the faculty and board of directors the responsibility of selecting a recipient. Adolph Furre, a member of the college class of 1912, was chosen with the understanding that he would pursue work at the University of Christiania long enough to earn the degree in historical and language studies — roughly the equivalent of an M.A. degree. Furre's death in the spring of 1913 abruptly ended the hopes associated with him and, for reasons that are not clear, the issue of a Norwegian professorship was left unresolved.[11]

Meanwhile, Sverdrup and his associates were quietly seeking to comply with the recommendations of the Haynes report. Shortly after receiving the document, the faculty requested and received an annual board of trustees appropriation of $150 for laboratory equipment.[12] Gradual curriculum expansion that had begun a few years earlier also continued. Botany had been introduced in 1910; chemistry was added in 1913. A number of professional education courses, including school administration, history of education, and philosophy of education were offered for the first time. The addition of these courses fell far short of revolutionizing the curriculum, although it became less rigid by providing for a few electives.

These meager innovations did not go far enough to achieve accreditation either by the state department of education, the University of Minnesota, or the North Central Association. For a time hopes seemed plausible that the university might extend recognition. An investigation by the Education Committee of the University Senate in the spring of 1915 produced a report that "in the main . . . was favorable" to the school. However, on May 6, 1915, the senate postponed action on the report until a new and permanent committee appointed to determine the relations of the university to the schools of the state had probed all institutions of higher learning in Minnesota.[13]

This new committee evidently employed more rigorous norms than its predecessor. In March, 1916 most of the examiners returned highly adverse assessments of Augsburg. The man responsible for chemistry reported: "The equipment is very meagre, and the classroom instruction, in my judgment, would not meet the University requirements." Although complimentary to Professor Peter A. Sveeggen, who had joined the faculty in September, 1915, the English examiners pointed to three serious shortcomings in their field: inadequate faculty, a "practically nonexistent library," and insufficient course offerings. Representatives evaluating Greek instruction found the beginning course in that language satisfactory, but did "not think that credit should be given en bloc for work done at this school . . . the teachers are overworked . . . and library facilities in much of the work is [sic] utterly inadequate." [14]

On the basis of these findings, the Committee on Relations of the University to Other Institutions of Learning recommended to the University Senate "that two years of collegiate work at Augsburg Seminary be recognized, and that specially recognized students in classical languages, Norwegian and English be permitted to register provisionally in the Graduate School." [15] Senate ratification of this resolution established the university's basic accreditation policy vis a vis Augsburg for many years to come. Understandably, Sverdrup and his associates were deeply disappointed, even though the possibility of broader accreditation short of full recognition remained open.[16] After 1920 "specially recognized students" in disciplines other than classical languages, Norwegian, and English gained admission to the graduate school as their instruction moved closer to university standards.

Nevertheless, Augsburg faced a serious crisis. Its accreditation status was lower than that of such institutions as Hamline and St. Olaf, and the possibility of immediate improvement was limited, since its small, largely rural constituency tended to distrust American higher education. Perhaps this explains why Sverdrup again avoided the accreditation issue in reporting to the conferences of 1916 and 1917. On both occasions he mildly deplored the declining enrollment pattern, but conveyed the impression that more vigorous recruitment would overcome the problem. In 1918 he remarked that no increase in enrollment could be expected until after the war, adding that, in any case, Augsburg must continue its mission.[17]

In 1918–19, when college enrollment dropped to 23, a sense of alarm became evident on campus. Articles and letters advocating coeducation and other innovations appeared in the Echo. A member of the college class of 1917 stated the issue bluntly:

In spite of all the good things that one might say of Augsburg, something is wrong. For years the attendance has steadily been on the decline. Especially has our college department suffered. Conditions must be remedied at once. People have blamed the war, but even before the United States entered the war the enrollment in the college department was steadily declining. . . . Augsburg does not measure up to requirements at present. To be sure, some strides have been taken in recent years to raise the standard, and some sciences have been added. But more must be done, so that it will appeal to the boys in our congregations.[18]

Although such statements could be interpreted as critical of the administration, Sverdrup probably welcomed pressures on behalf of change. His conference report of 1919 dealt extensively with Augsburg's responsibility to non-ministerial students. Conference members responded to the president's concern with a resolution authorizing the faculty, board of trustees, and school directors to investigate the enrollment problem and "in this connection" to consider whether "a more practical academic program in the preparatory departments" could be developed.[19]

In accordance with this resolution, both the faculty and board of trustees went to work on the curriculum problem during the summer of 1919. A special faculty meeting held on August 6 delegated to a curriculum committee the responsibility of formulating a new program both for the academy and college departments. A month later the faculty adopted a series of recommendations presented by the committee. Although the changes were modest, they did enrich the college program. English offerings were expanded significantly, and the chemistry curriculum was increased from two to four courses. Greek, heretofore a graduation requirement, was designated as an elective for students not planning to study theology.[20]

THE ACADEMIC YEAR 1919–20 marked an upturn in Augsburg's fortune. Along with the newly revised program, several circumstances were encouraging innovation. The composition of the faculty had changed since the start of Sverdrup's presidency. Wilhelm Pettersen had resigned in 1910 to enter the ministry; his chair was not immediately filled. In 1915 Samuel Severson became a public school principal; Peter Sveeggen succeeded him. A year later John Blegen retired. R. Boyd Nell, Augsburg's first specialist in natural science, joined the faculty in the autumn of 1916. Disagreement with the administration led to Evjen's dismissal in June, 1919.[21] Two new teachers accepted appointments in the same year: Lars L. Lillehei succeeded Evjen, and Elmer D. Busby became responsible for mathematics. At the same time, Nydahl left his classroom to assume the post of full-time librarian at the school.

Although Evjen's departure removed a source of intellectual stimulation from the campus, the overall shift in personnel from 1915 through 1919 brought new influences to Augsburg. Of the four men joining the teaching force during this period only Lillehei was an alumnus of the school. Sveeggen, who had attended Red Wing Seminary, and held both a B.A. and M.A. degree from the University of Minnesota, was thoroughly trained in both literature and rhetoric. Nell had served for three years as professor of natural science in Wartburg College at Waverly, Iowa, and had taken advanced work in Columbia University. Busby's experience included service at several denominational colleges, including Concordia at Moorhead. Like Sveeggen, Lillehei had earned an M.A. degree in the University of Minnesota. His specialties were church history, religion, Norse and, subsequently, Greek.

The ferment of the post-war period also was pushing the school toward change. In addition, commemoration of Augsburg's fiftieth anniversary in the autumn of 1919 promoted institutional self-examination. Most of the festival rhetoric, to be sure, pointed backward rather than forward, but inevitably the present and future intruded on the celebration.[22] A lively meeting of the Alumni Association aired a wide range of problems relating to the school. No clear guidelines emerged, but the association appointed a committee of seven members under the chairmanship of Pastor John A. Houkom to investigate and recommend new departures in educational policy for both Augsburg and for the Lutheran Free Church.[23]

In early 1920 Houkom's committee conducted a survey designed to discover what opinions the Augsburg community had on the issues facing the school. Responses to a questionnaire disclosed a divergency of view. One item probed sentiment on coeducation. Of 149 respondents, 102 favored admitting women to the college, 40 took the opposite view, and seven were non-committal. Eighty voted for coeducation in the academy, 53 voted against, and 13 declined to state a position. Opponents of coeducation advanced several arguments: "Contrary to the principles upon which Augsburg was founded: . . . . Augsburg is our 'presteskole'; . . . . We have not the equipment or . . . location for a co-educational school; . . . . Co-education offers too many temptations toward frivolity and play; . . . . Would be detrimental to the spiritual life of the school."

A second controversial item was whether the campus should be relocated. Eighty-two respondents favored moving, 55 voted to remain on the seminary block, and 11 were noncommittal. Of those specifying a new site, the greater number preferred suburban Minneapolis. "Scattered suggestions" named Fergus Falls, Rochester, and Thief River Falls in Minnesota, and Glacier Park, Montana. The committee also surveyed alumni opinion with respect to establishing a Bible school on campus, a proposal that had won substantial support within the LFC. Again, the response was divided, 61 voting yes, 71 no, and 18 refusing commitment.

In order to gain an impression of Augsburg's image among its graduates, the committee formulated a fourth question: Is Augsburg a divinity school? Forty-six replied yes, 44 no, 38 returned qualified answers, and 20 were noncommittal. Houkom interpreted the response to this question:

What we must do . . . is to emphasize, that henceforth there is conducted, in close harmony with a school in theology, a first class and standard college department, where young people may acquire a splendid education under Christian leadership.[24]

After appraising the findings of its survey, the committee developed four policy recommendations that it hoped would benefit Augsburg without fomenting discord within the LFC. The first proposed establishment of a Bible school on the Pacific coast. This recommendation had a double purpose: to compensate for the closing of Bethany College in 1917, a step that had deprived the West Coast of an educational institution; and to meet the Bible school demand without imposing the responsibility for such an enterprise on Augsburg. The second recommendation suggested adoption of coeducation at Oak Grove Ladies Seminary, but not at Augsburg Academy. The third called for coeducation at Augsburg College. Finally, the committee "resolved . . . that the Board of Trustees of Augsburg Seminary be instructed to look about for a better location for Augsburg Seminary, and that the Augsburg Academy be moved there first with the view that the college and theological departments shall be moved there also as soon as practicable." [25]

At its regular annual meeting, held on May 27, 1920, the Alumni Association voted to submit the report to the spring conference of the LFC with a recommendation that the four proposals be adopted. Houkom anticipated "quite a debate" at the conference, a possibility that he welcomed, since discussion would disclose Augsburg's "true needs" and point the way to "proper correctives." [26]

However, compromise and accommodation rather than heated confrontation characterized the 1920 LFC conference. A decision on coeducation at Augsburg College was postponed until 1921. The conference did approve two proposals advanced jointly by the faculty, directors, and board of trustees. The first authorized the trustees to seek a new site for Augsburg Academy "in the neighborhood of Minneapolis." The second recommended the addition of "at least one new member . . . to the present faculty," and encouraged steps "to improve . . . laboratory . . . library . . . and other necessary equipment." To the first proposal the conference appended a suggestion that coeducation be instituted at Augsburg Academy after its relocation. It also endorsed immediate establishment of a Bible school, leaving the issues of location and organization to a committee of nine members.[27]

Impatient Augsburg reformers no doubt were disappointed at the failure of the conference to act decisively on coeducation. Nevertheless, the general mood of the proceedings marked a break with the immediate past. In describing conference "sidelights," *The Lutheran Free Church Messenger* remarked: "Co-education was finally mentioned and none fainted. While there will be no change in our schools for the time being, it is easy to read the signs of the times that co-education is coming. . . ."[28]

The *Messenger* spoke prophetically; coeducation would soon be a reality at Augsburg College. However, in the summer of 1920 no one could predict when women would gain admission. At that time the only certainty was that the decisions taken by the 1920 conference had generated debate not only on coeducation, but also on a variety of related issues: Was the conference resolution authorizing relocation of the academy and coeducation therein wise? Should the entire institution be moved to a new site, or did the old block still serve adequately? Should a separate Bible school be established, and if so, where? Did the concept of a "Greater Augsburg" imperil the institution's sacred mission? Should either coeducation or a college program be established at Oak Grove? [29]

Views on this complex of issues followed no definite pattern. Gynild, a member of the board of trustees, favored relocation of the academy, but stoutly opposed admitting women to the college.[30] Pastor Christopher Ytrehus, a graduate of the theological class of 1888, objected with equal fervor to moving the academy and adopting coeducation either there or at the college.[31] Carl J. Nestvold, a younger pastor, disliked the academy proposal, but supported college coeducation.[32] Other participants in the discussion wanted women at the college, but not men at Oak Grove. Some advocates of coeducation favored the Bible school, others took a negative stand.[33]

The tone of most communications to *Folkebladet* and the *Messenger* left an impression of formidable opposition to any innovation that might compromise Augsburg's program of ministerial education. Apparently these polemics did not unduly worry the proponents of change, most of whom expected victory in the near future. Nevertheless, the entanglement of Oak Grove, the Bible school, and Augsburg Academy with issues relating to Augsburg College threatened to delay resolution of the coeducation question. Realizing that priorities had to be drawn, the board of trustees took no action on the academy resolution. In reporting to the 1921 conference, Birkeland disclosed that a survey of congregational opinion had given the board neither the encouragement nor the promise of financial assistance needed to put the resolution into effect. Consequently, he recommended postponement of action on relocation until economic conditions improved.[34]

Although Gynild's opposition inhibited the trustees from officially recommending admission of women to the college, Birkeland personally argued for coeducation in his report.[35] Sverdrup did likewise. In presenting his case, the president contended that the Lutheran Free Church was obliged to train women as well as men for congregational service, a proposition explicitly affirmed in the "Guiding Principles" of the church. Modern conditions demanded college training for women if they were to achieve their full potential. He added that the church had to take one of two steps: permit women to attend Augsburg College, or establish a separate college for women. Since the latter was financially unrealistic, coeducation was the only reasonable alternative.[36]

In deference to conservative opinion, members of Committee No. 2, who were responsible for framing proposals relating to Augsburg Seminary, hesitated to endorse immediate adoption of coeducation. Instead they suggested a congregational referendum on the question. When this recommendation reached the floor on Friday, June 10, delegates decided to consider it in conjunction with a resolution formally introduced by Sverdrup and Birkeland. The intent of the latter was clear enough, but since its authors sought to argue a case as well as present a recommendation, the wording was awkward. It read: "Since the Lutheran Free Church has accepted responsibility for training men and women to work within and for the congregation, the annual conference cannot recommend that women seeking admission to Augsburg be denied access to college instruction if they meet prevailing entrance requirements."

Presentation of the Committee No. 2 report precipitated a debate that continued through the afternoon of June 11. Several participants attacked both the wisdom and constitutionality of the referendum. Speaking for the opponents, Gynild asserted that admission of women inevitably would lead to Augsburg's complete transformation into an American college. Another delegate argued that coeducation would augment enrollment, thereby widening the base for an expanded academic program. Jens E. Fossum, president of Oak Grove, disclaimed any intention of establishing coeducation, adding that Oak Grove would be happy to send its graduates to Augsburg if women were admitted to the college. Fossum had eliminated one problem: supporters of Oak Grove could now back coeducation at Augsburg without fearing that such a stand compromised the interests of their school.

On the afternoon of the second day Sverdrup entered the discussion. His intervention led straight to a resolution of the immediate issue, and succeeded in elevating his stature as a Lutheran Free Church leader. After a move to defer voting on coeducation until the next conference was defeated, he introduced a resolution placing the church on record as favoring coeducation, but postponing final action until 1922 in order "to provide the time needed for the Lutheran Free Church to understand and approve this step." In speaking for his resolution Sverdrup asserted that while he opposed the referendum idea, his proposal created an opportunity for congregational action if this was desired. For him the question was a practical one. "We must have the people with us," he said, "and they will support us when they understand that [coeducation] is necessary."

At this point Sverdrup went further than ever before in defining his concept of the college department's role: "It has been said that co-education will lead to Augsburg becoming a full-fledged American college — but is not this what we want? For that matter, Augsburg has been a college for many years." To support this contention, he cited the paragraph from his father's 1906 conference report calling for improvement of the school's academic program — a passage that had been quoted before by advocates of reform and would be used again by George Sverdrup to quiet doubts about his continuing the earlier policies established by the elder Sverdrup.

George Sverdrup won an impressive victory; the conference approved his motion by a margin of 256 to 11. Encouraging as this outcome was to the friends of coeducation, the preponderance of affirmative votes was not a true measure of sentiment on the central issue. Many delegates who deplored the thought of women students at Augsburg supported the motion because it appeared to yield a point where concession was not absolutely necessary, the probability being that coeducation commanded a majority within the assembly. Just prior to the vote Pastor Hans J. Urdahl remarked: I thank God for Sverdrup's resolution. Augsburg is the congregation's school; but attempts by some individuals to force things [forcere ting] create an impression that the congregations belong to Augsburg." Following announcement of the results, the session adjourned in a spirit of harmony.[37]

A few weeks later Sverdrup drew on the reserve of good will created by his stance at the conference. In a signed communication printed in *Folkebladet* on August 17, 1921, he indicated that coeducation might be provisionally adopted at the start of the 1921–22 school year. According to Sverdrup, several young women were applying for admission without being encouraged to do so by anyone at Augsburg. How should such a problem be handled? To deny young women educational opportunity would "afford us no happiness," he wrote. Fortunately, another solution was available. "We cannot make special preparations this year to accept women students," he pointed out. "But . . . if there are young women who apply for admission to college under conditions as they are — we cannot say no." Sverdrup emphasized that a final decision on coeducation remained in the hands of the Lutheran Free Church: "If the next annual conference says that Augsburg shall not open its doors to women, that will settle the question."

Five young women — Hilda L. Ostlie, a sophomore, and Katherine V. Kleven, Clara A. Nybroten, Lillian V. Olson, and Anna Oudal, all freshmen — were admitted in September on the terms defined by Sverdrup. Their impact on school life was less revolutionary than expected. The first issue of the *Echo* for 1921–22 commented: "Some people had thought that the appearance of coeds in the halls of Augsburg would arouse some stir, but other than the first surprise . . . we are now accustomed to it as though we have always had coeducation." Curiously, although the *Messenger* carried a brief story on Augsburg's new departure, *Folkebladet* omitted any reference to it. This may have been a prudent oversight, calculated to still controversy.[38]

Admission of the five young women had a mixed effect on the deliberations of the 1922 conference which, in accordance with the Sverdrup motion of a year earlier, was responsible for a final resolution on coeducation. The administration was confronting the church with an accomplished fact that shifted the burden of proof from the advocates to the opponents of the change. Some delegates resented what they regarded as an unwarranted exercise of presidential power. Whichever consideration carried the greater weight, debate on the issue was both prolonged and warm. The final vote registered 141 in favor of coeducation and 81 against. A number of conservatives remained convinced that Augsburg had embarked on a disastrous course, but the issue of whether women should be admitted to the college was definitely settled.[39]

The next problem was a practical one — additional dormitory facilities on a crowded campus. Old Main housed the theological students and college men; North Hall was reserved for boys enrolled in the academy. To accommodate the women, the Nydahl and Helland families were requested to vacate West Hall, the residence built in 1874. An expenditure of $1,147.58 converted it into a dormitory facility capable of housing approximately twenty-five girls. A year later the other professors' residence, a two-family structure that later became known as Morton Hall, also was appropriated for women's housing. This step obliged the Harbo and Lillehei families to secure living quarters elsewhere.[40]

To some extent, the hope that Augsburg soon would relocate compensated for the inadequacy of these housing arrangements and generally cramped campus situation. The Augsburg Park project, which envisaged an idyllic site for the school in suburban Richfield, had taken shape in the fall of 1921. Although the desirability of moving had been discussed for several years, no specific proposals had evolved. On the contrary, in early 1921 the board of trustees made preparations to renovate existing facilities. It established Augsburg's ownership of the entire seminary block by purchasing a small lot near the corner of 7th Street and 22nd Avenue that had eluded acquisition for many years. The board also proposed a reconstruction of Old Main designed to extend the life of that wooden facility by at least fifty years. This plan was authorized by the LFC conference of 1921.[41]

Preliminary efforts to renovate Old Main brought a difficult problem to light. Minneapolis building codes required that dormitories of more than two stories be fireproof. Since Old Main was a five-story structure, city authorities ruled against major improvements, but did allow minor repairs so that the building could be utilized for a few years.

This development encouraged the board to investigate the relocation alternative. Birkeland, whose business acquaintances included several real-estate dealers, learned of an available plot in Richfield which he felt would serve as an admirable campus site. His first published reference to the project, carried by *Folkebladet* on August 24, 1921, enthusiastically described the tract's advantages: "It is located less than two miles from the [Minneapolis] city limits. An electric tram line runs through the land. A major highway providing access to the heart of Minneapolis is in the vicinity, and a beautiful oak grove extends to a lake with high banks and a sandy beach." Readers of *Folkebladet* and the *Messenger* shortly became thoroughly familiar with this promotional line.

Birkeland soon persuaded influential Augsburg people that the Richfield tract would be an ideal location for the school. A conducted tour of the area converted Sverdrup. Said he, "When Birkeland telephoned me and asked if I wanted to accompany him on an inspection of a piece of land that would be appropriate for Augsburg, it was not difficult to say yes. Soon after our arrival . . . Birkeland said, 'here is the site for Augsburg,' and again I replied yes, this time with my whole heart."

149

Birkeland's fellow trustees, leading clergymen, and senior faculty members such as Helland and Hendrickson, responded similarly.[42]

Unfortunately, a wide gap separated Birkeland's dream from its fulfillment. The plot commanded a price of more than $100,000, a sum far in excess of the Augsburg board's available resources. Conceivably the LFC might have assumed responsibility, but this was by no means certain. Moreover, the next annual conference would not meet until June, 1922, and it seemed doubtful that the land would remain available.

Birkeland's ingenuity formulated a solution to the difficulty. On January 24, 1922, he and a group of men incorporated the Augsburg Park Association, an organization legally separate from Augsburg Seminary and the LFC, but controlled by persons closely identified with both. The association negotiated purchase of the tract, divided it into residential and campus sections, and proceeded to sell lots within the former. Lots were to be priced high enough to subsidize purchase of the entire tract. Thus, an individual buying a lot was securing ground for his own home in a desirable area, and also was contributing to the acquisition of a campus which the association would transfer free of encumbrance to Augsburg Seminary after all payments had been made. Association sponsors meanwhile encouraged Augsburg to seek a buyer of the old campus. Hopefully, the sale of this property would yield sufficient revenue to finance a building program on the new site. Within a few years the school would be operating in a new plant on a spacious campus surrounded by congenial Scandinavian neighbors, and including a substantial contingent of LFC adherents.[43]

A proposition that involved no financial risk and at the same time promised the school rich benefits could scarcely be rejected by the Lutheran Free Church. A few dissenters registered complaints, but the conference of 1922 endorsed the park project.[44] Four years later the church authorized a $500,000 fund drive to finance new buildings on the site.[45] A number of circumstances combined to destroy the realization of this ambitious project. The fund drive failed, association finances fell into disarray, the Great Depression forced rigid curtailment, and the advantages of remaining on the seminary block became more apparent. Nevertheless, the possibility of moving to Richfield as a solution of Augsburg's space problem persisted until 1949.[46]

AUGSBURG PARK was an unfortunate venture in several respects. Not only did it ultimately fail, but it also fostered the dream of a suburban campus separated from the grim realities of the inner city, a vision obscuring Augsburg's potentialities as an urban institution. On the other hand, the

150

project reinforced the drive for change. Activity on behalf of relocation pointed up the school's weaknesses, and shifted attention from the past to the future. An article by Hendrickson recommending Augsburg Park asserted that "We have been too inclined to look backward. . . . Augsburg must grow if it is to become a power among our people." [47]

Coeducation, too, spurred expansion and change. Enrollment trends after 1922 undermined what remained of the old integrated three-department divinity school. Although official homage was paid to this concept, the college clearly was becoming an institution in its own right. Measured in percentage terms, college enrollment increased tenfold in the 1918–28 decade. During the same time seminary attendance remained stable; that of the academy declined.

A significant expansion and reorganization of course offerings accompanied this enrollment increase. The first academic major — in English — had been introduced in 1917. Education was added in 1920; history in 1921; ancient languages, Norse, social science (including philosophy), natural science, chemistry, and religion in 1922; music in 1923; physical education in 1926; and French in 1927. By 1928 thirteen academic departments were in operation. The unique curriculum of earlier days had given way completely to one based on modern American college standards.

General education requirements also conformed to prevailing norms. Compulsory religion courses — one two-credit course per term — demanded more of the students' time than at many church-related institutions, but Norse, the other traditional mainstay, was dropped in 1921. Entering students with no foreign language prepartation were required to complete 20 credits in one language; in 1931 this was reduced to 12 credits, the equivalent of one year. It should be noted that these were quarter credits. Until 1899, when it adopted the semester system, the school had operated on the basis of an undivided school year. It shifted to the quarter system in 1920, but restored the semester pattern in 1936. A modified quarter system was re-established in 1966. [48]

More students and a broader curriculum required a substantial increase of the teaching force. In 1920–21 the combined college-academy faculty consisted of eight full-time professors (four of whom also taught in the seminary), and nine temporary or part-time instructors. Ten years later the number had doubled to sixteen in the first category and nineteen in the second. Several new teachers served only briefly; however, a number of key people among the newcomers devoted the remainder of their professional careers to Augsburg, contributing much to the development of the college.

John Sigurd Melby joined the faculty in 1920. A graduate of the college in 1911 and the seminary in 1914, Melby had taught in Bethany College at Everett, Washington, before accepting the Augsburg appointment. His initial assignment was a double one: academy instructor and "Head Master of the Academy Dormitory." During his first year Melby assumed two additional responsibilities. Together with Harold A. Johnson, he coached basketball, and participated actively in the school's religious program. Before long these divergent roles expanded. The head master position evolved into that of Dean of Men, informal supervision of basketball into a role as director of the athletic program, and identification with religious activities into a professorship in the department of Christianity. In 1923 Melby was appointed chairman of the latter. He continued as Dean of Men until 1941, and as professor of Christianity until his death in January, 1944.[49]

Melby was a reluctant candidate for these varied responsibilities. "Augsburg will never permit me to specialize," he complained on one occasion. "I have to be a jack of all trades." [50] Personally he assigned highest priority to his religion assignments. However, some of his students placed a greater value on his performance as coach and Dean of Men. Before his time physical education and team sports were peripheral activities under the supervision of student directors, with occasional assistance (unpaid) from interested faculty members. For more than a decade basketball and baseball teams manned by Augsburg students had engaged in outside competition, but intercollegiate athletics were not officially recognized.

The record of the 1920–21 academy basketball team, which Melby directed, established his reputation as a coach. During the following year he served as head coach, assuming personal responsibility for college basketball. Again his team had a successful season, winning eight games out of ten. Its performance in the next two years also was creditable — six out of nine in 1922–23, and 14 out of 16 in 1923–24.[51]

Undoubtedly the phenomenon of a religion teacher thoroughly identified with Lutheran Free Church pietism doubling as a successful coach raised the prestige of sports at Augsburg. It also weakened, but by no means eliminated, opposition to an intercollegiate athletic program. In the autumn of 1924, the administration applied for admission to the Minnesota College Conference. A meeting of the governing board of that organization held on December 6, 1924, unanimously voted to accept Augsburg's bid for membership. The *Echo* rejoiced, as did a number of younger alumni, one of whom wrote to Melby: "Cy, you don't realize how glad I was to read the headlines telling the good news that places Augsburg College among the other colleges of the state." [52]

Statistically the basketball team's record in 1924–25, its first season of conference play, was not spectacular; it won only two games out of nine. However, the experience gained and the return of key players, especially Oswald Oudal and Lyle Crose, placed Augsburg within bidding range of the conference championship. The team failed to achieve this goal in 1925–26, but did so the following year. Oudal and Crose graduated in 1927, a loss repaired in part by the rise of John Kolesar, who subsequently became the most decorated athlete in the school's history. Although a number of other first-rate players, including Luther Sletten, were on hand in 1927–28, the team finished third instead of first. The next year was a stand-off. In conference play, Augsburg won four and lost the same number.[53]

Meanwhile, Augsburg's intercollegiate program had extended to other sports. A baseball team entered conference competition in the spring of 1926, and a football team in the autumn of that year. In 1927 the football team tied with Macalester for second place, and the next year ranked as co-champion. Due primarily to the talents of five Hanson brothers from Camrose, Alberta, Canada, the school also emerged briefly as a powerful contender in hockey. The sport did not enjoy official conference status in 1927, but the team's performance earned an unofficial championship designation. When hockey was placed on a conference basis in 1928, Augsburg won the title.[54]

In the same year, the team's spectacular performance attracted national attention. The United States Amateur Hockey Association extended it an invitation to participate in the winter Olympics at St. Moritz, Switzerland. Aided by friends of the school and Minneapolis' Southside Commercial Club, Melby easily raised $4,500 to finance the trip to Europe. Unfortunately, a decision by the Olympic Hockey Committee to withdraw from competition cancelled the venture.[55]

Augsburg's meteoric rise to athletic fame, although ephemeral, reinforced student morale and heightened public awareness of the college's existence. Melby's reputation also rose. In addition to developing a basketball team of championship caliber, he was directing an athletic program that achieved success despite grossly inadequate facilities. His staff, too, was essentially part-time. Dr. Conrad L. Ecklund, a practicing dentist, coached football. Herman Ascher, a former University of Minnesota star athlete and professional baseball player, assisted Ecklund and had charge of baseball. The physical education program was under the supervision of Magne Skurdalsvold, who also coached a gymnastic team. Although Melby was formally in charge of the hockey team, it directed itself for the most part.

153

As Dean of Men, Melby largely ignored modern concepts of student personnel administration, but he possessed an intuitive understanding of youth that served him well. Among the problems he faced in administering discipline was a wide gap between Augsburg's strict code governing student conduct and the tendency of some young men to rebel against standards that not only outlawed dancing, drinking, and card-playing, but even viewed the theater and cinema with suspicion. Tension within the student body between "pietists," who regarded observance of the code as a mark of Christian commitment and the "worldly set," a few of whom were known to patronize bootlegging establishments in the Cedar-Riverside area, augmented the problem.

In dealing with this difficulty Melby did not practice undue permissiveness; on the other hand, his enforcement of the more stringent rules was judicious. More important, he cultivated a warm relationship with all students, most of whom responded favorably to his kindliness and the impression of sturdy manliness projected by his personality. On the theory that responsibility can be an effective antidote to rebellion, he occasionally appointed non-conformist students to serve as dormitory proctors.

The problems facing Gerda Mortensen when she joined the faculty as Dean of Women in 1923 were more complex than those confronting the Dean of Men. The task of guiding the integration of women into a student body with firmly entrenched masculine traditions was a delicate one. Moreover, Miss Mortensen soon became convinced that an effort to cultivate a more collegiate way of life on campus, a goal requiring modification of rural immigrant values with respect to dress, manners, and social graces, had to accompany the integration process. Such an effort required considerable diplomatic skill. Not all members of the Augsburg community agreed that social refinement was an appropriate educational goal, and most of Miss Mortensen's colleagues were unaccustomed to leadership by women faculty members.[56] Other difficulties also intruded. The campus was physically dilapidated, a tight budget demanded austerity, and the Dean of Women was obliged to divide her time between teaching American history and the duties of her office.

Miss Mortensen's performance soon demonstrated that her appointment was to the school's advantage. As the daughter of Jacob Mortensen, a prominent LFC clergyman who had served on the Augsburg staff, she knew both the school and its constituency intimately. Her professional training, particularly the work she pursued in student personnel at Columbia University, where she earned the M.A. degree in 1928, put her in touch with modern counseling theory and practice, an interest she enthusiastically maintained throughout her career. Miss Mortensen's personal qualities also meshed with the requirements of her position. Above all, she was endowed with an openness and flexibility that facilitated adaptation to the revolutionary changes marking Augsburg's development during the forty-one years she served on the faculty.

Henry Opseth, a St. Olaf alumnus and a protege of F. Melius Christiansen, came to Augsburg in 1922. He enjoyed the distinction of being the first full-time musician on the teaching force. Before his time music was an important extra-curricular activity, but offered no academic credit. As chairman of the new department of music, Opseth soon discharged his initial responsibility — the organization of a curriculum in his area. At the start of 1922–23, a full complement of theory courses and opportunities for individual instruction in vocal and instrumental music were available. Establishment of this broad program required augmentation of the staff. In 1922 Miss Belle Mehus accepted an appointment as instructor in piano and theory, and Miss Jenny Skurdalsvold as teacher of voice. Two small rooms in West Hall were converted into studios.

Following Opseth's arrival, the extra-curricular as well as the academic significance of music expanded. In addition to continuing the men's Glee Club, which had functioned for many years, he organized a ladies' glee club. In 1923–24 this venture gave way to a coeducational choir that was soon abandoned. Two years later Opseth established the Augsburg Choral Society, another women's group that maintained an independent existence until it merged with the Glee Club in 1933 to form the Augsburg College Choir. Meanwhile, male gospel quartettes continued to tour the constituency.[57]

Efforts to place instrumental music on a permanent basis were less successful, largely because there were insufficient funds for instruments and uniforms. Under Carl R. Youngdahl (1917–18), and Carl J. Petri (1919–22), an Augsburg Seminary band had achieved sufficient stature and self-confidence to organize tours. On his arrival Opseth assumed the leadership of this group, but failed to enhance its importance. Four years later he described the band's function as being to enliven "our athletic contests," and to put "pep into our gatherings." [58] An orchestra organized in 1926 under the guidance of Miss Emma Gaarde met its demise five years later, a victim of the Great Depression.

The role of music in Augsburg's program was multiple to a greater extent than that of most other activities. Opseth often stressed the cultural enrichment offered by his department both to students enrolled in music courses and the institution generally.[59] In addition the Glee Club,

155

Choral Society, and gospel quartettes regularly toured the LFC circuit, thereby perpetuating a tradition dating back to the 1880s. Undoubtedly these tours, like those of earlier years, helped to elevate musical taste and appreciation throughout the constituency. They also maintained a link between Augsburg and the congregations that facilitated both fund raising and recruitment of new students.

Opseth continued as chairman of the department of music until his death in late 1950. He trained a large number of students, many of whom became excellent teachers of music in the public schools, and a few who achieved distinction as professional musicians — Leland Sateren and Norman Myrvik are outstanding examples. Opseth's contribution to the institution both as a musician and a man whose personality encouraged the rise of a legend is impressive. While he does not rank as the founder of Augsburg's musical heritage — that had been established earlier by Reimestad, Urseth and Hendrickson, with significant help from F. Melius Christiansen — Opseth broadened the tradition and incorporated it into the school's music department.[60]

Carl Fosse became a member of the faculty in 1923, and remained at Augsburg until his death in 1942. An alumnus of Dakota Wesleyan College at Mitchell, South Dakota, where he took his B.A. degree, he held an M.S. from the University of Chicago. He pursued further graduate work in the University of Minnesota without fully completing the work for the doctorate. In addition to teaching all the chemistry offerings and at times the physics courses, he headed the department of natural science until 1930, when biology acquired separate status. Thereafter he served as chairman of the department of physical sciences. A self-effacing man who won the esteem of his students, Fosse was a competent teacher and department chairman who, with extremely limited resources, built an academically respectable chemistry program. Nor was he a narrow specialist. He had read widely in the history and philosophy of science, being concerned with the relationship between science and religion. He encouraged his students to investigate both areas with an open mind.[61]

Immediately following his graduation from Augsburg College in 1922, Arthur Nash accepted an appointment as instructor of natural science in the academy. He remained identified with this branch of the school for eight years, serving as its principal from 1926 to 1930. Meanwhile, he was pursuing graduate work in biology in the University of Minnesota where he took the Ph.D. degree in 1938. In 1924 he began teaching biology courses in the college, a responsibility that expanded as additional offerings in the discipline were introduced. This process culminated in 1930 with the establishment of a biology major and creation of a separate department, of which Nash was appointed chairman. With the exception of four years in military service during World War II and several semesters of leave, he remained at Augsburg until his retirement in 1966. He continued to teach for two additional years on a special appointment. The biology program, which he effectively adapted to an accelerating proliferation of knowledge in the field, was his basic preoccupation throughout this long period of service. Nash also accepted other responsibilities, serving as Dean of the College and Director of Veterans' Affairs from 1946 to 1950, and as chairman of the division of natural sciences for fourteen years.[62]

One day in June, 1926, a young woman named Marion Helen Wilson — later Mrs. Ervin H. Lindemann — who recently had earned an M.A. degree in the University of Minnesota, appeared on the Augsburg campus to be interviewed by Sverdrup as a candidate for a part-time teaching position in French. As she recalls the episode, Mrs. Lindemann approached the president's office with limited expectations. She had resided in the Twin City area for several years without learning of Augsburg's existence. Inquiries disclosed either a lack of information about the school, or that it was a center of narrow pietism where an outsider could not survive for more than a year. Since Mrs. Lindemann was of British ancestry, and Episcopalian rather than a Scandinavian Lutheran, she did not anticipate a rewarding interview.

She soon changed her mind. Sverdrup simply did not fit the Augsburg stereotype that had been described to her. On the contrary, he created the impression of an erudite scholar with broad cultural interests, a sophisticated sense of humor, and not a trace of Scandinavian provincialism. It was unnecessary, he remarked, for her to provide his office with credentials; he already possessed sufficient data to offer her the position. However, a formal contract seemed inappropriate, he thought, since the position was part-time and the remuneration small. He advised her to accept a more lucrative position if one became available; otherwise she was welcome to begin teaching when school opened. After spending the summer in Europe, she reported for duty in the fall.

This casually negotiated arrangement — so typical of Sverdrup's style — marked the beginning of a 25-year association between Mrs. Lindemann and Augsburg. She soon became convinced that acceptance of the post was a wise decision. From her point of view, Sverdrup was an ideal college president. He never undertook to guide classroom instruction along "proper" theological lines, but fostered an atmosphere of genuine academic freedom. Mrs. Lindemann also discovered that the strong sense of Scandinavian Lutheran identity characterizing most of the faculty did not preclude warm relationships with a colleague belonging to a different tradition. Above all, she was moved and impressed by the determination of the Augsburg community to keep the school operating, and by a corresponding willingness to sacrifice personal security and professional advancement for the achievement of that end.[63]

In some respects the students in Mrs. Lindemann's classes were unlike those she had encountered in earlier teaching situations. Their accents were heavily Scandinavian, a trait that Sveeggen energetically sought to eliminate. To some extent, a piety verging on anti-intellectualism was a problem. One young man objected to classroom treatment of the Greek gods in a classical literature course on the grounds that he had come to Augsburg to learn about the Triune God, not pagan deities. Fortunately, most students held a less jaundiced viewpoint. As the years passed an increasing number of them gained a clearer appreciation of the academic side of college life, a development that owed a great deal to the influence of faculty members like Mrs. Lindemann.

The simultaneous establishment of a French department and major in 1927 expanded Mrs. Lindemann's position to full-time status. With a few interruptions, she remained at Augsburg until 1953. Besides French language and literature, she occasionally taught Latin and Spanish, and conducted an outstanding general education course in world literature.

Several faculty members whose initial appointments antedated 1920 remained influential during the modernization period. Sveeggen continued as professor of English and chairman of his department. Along with seminary responsibilities, Lillehei taught Greek and headed the department of ancient languages. Helland, the oldest theological professor in terms of service, chaired the Scandinavian department and offered courses in Norwegian language and literature. Since Helland was primarily a theologian and involved in the seminary, the latter was an improvised arrangement negotiated after the administration failed to recruit a first-rate specialist in Scandinavian culture. Carl E. Nordberg, who had taken extensive graduate work in Scandinavian languages, history, and literature, accepted an appointment in 1920 but resigned three years later to join the St. Olaf College faculty.

Hendrickson, who had spread his energies over many areas since coming to Augsburg in 1900, embarked on a new career during the 1920s. He continued as registrar and taught a course in Latin, but his main preoccupation shifted to the history program. Determined to acquire competence in the discipline, he pursued graduate study in the University of Minnesota, completing the M.A. degree in history in 1931 at the age of sixty-two. He never completed the doctorate, but attained a level of scholarship commanding the respect of historians who knew him. In addition to serving as department chairman, Hendrickson taught all the offerings in European and English history, along with a course in historiography that provided excellent preparation for graduate work.[64]

A number of academic areas failed to achieve stability in the 1920s, primarily because permanent faculty was not immediately available. Early in the decade speech and debate commanded only minimal student interest. The appointment in 1927 of Sigurd B. Severson, an able educator whose talents Augsburg already had utilized in several fields, as instructor in public speaking promised to raise the prestige of forensics. Unfortunately, other responsibilities precluded Severson's full-time commitment to the speech program, and he resigned his Augsburg position in 1932.

The same difficulty plagued the department of Education which conducted one of Augsburg's most important programs, the training of secondary teachers. From 1920 to 1930 a succession of individuals headed this department — Nell, Severson, Lars P. Qualben, Ruth Atkins, and A. V. Overn. Mathematics, too, was handicapped by discontinuity. In 1923 Busby, who had taught both mathematics and social science, became chairman of the department of philosophy, economics, and sociology, a change that relieved him of further responsibility for mathematics. Miss Anna Gjesdahl was appointed to the vacancy. She served for two years, whereupon Louis J. Schnell, a University of Minnesota graduate student specializing in electrical engineering, assumed the instructorship. With the exception of 1926–27, when Herman W. Skon held the post, Schnell taught mathematics until 1931. He was succeeded by George Soberg who, since graduating from Augsburg College in 1926, had served as an academy teacher. The situation with respect to German instruction was similar to that of mathematics. Before 1929, the year that Karl Ermisch accepted a full-time position at Augsburg, graduate students on temporary appointment staffed the German department.

NOTWITHSTANDING these shortcomings, an exuberant mood dominated the Augsburg community as 1927–28 came to a close. The prospect of a spacious campus in Richfield reduced the problem of cramped facilities on the seminary block to a manageable annoyance. Since 1922, college enrollment had increased from 44 to 248. In the same period Augsburg moved from non-participation in intercollegiate sports to championship status in basketball and hockey, and a position of strength in football. Full accreditation had not yet been achieved, but with annual curricular

159

improvements, most friends of the school believed it to be possible in the near future.

Responsible spokesmen for the school confidently articulated the optimism felt on campus. Sverdrup's article in the 1928 *Augsburgian* was titled "Progress." "Augsburg is alive," proclaimed the president. Writing for the same publication, Samuel O. Severson peered confidently into the future. "On the basis of the progress made in the last few years," said Severson, "it is easy to predict that the next decade will witness a grander era than ever before." [65]

DEPRESSION DECADE

 THERE IS A striking parallel between the climate of opinion on the Augsburg campus in 1928 and the national mood preceding the stock market crash of October, 1929. In both cases an excessively optimistic view of the future obscured realities that should have been plainly visible. For example, official reports detailing Augsburg's financial situation submitted to the LFC conference of 1928 were far from encouraging. A combination of circumstances worked against an early move to Augsburg Park. Recurring deficits had accumulated a debt that the board of trustees was determined to liquidate before launching the fund drive for construction of a new plant. The diminishing sale of lots by the park association dimmed the hope of acquiring a new campus in the near future. Meanwhile, physical deterioration on the seminary block forced emergency improvements out of a treasury that was unable to finance the library expansion needed to win accreditation. In short, Augsburg was unprepared for the shock of depression following the stock market catastrophe.[1]

Affluence for Augsburg was out of the question considering the school's small constituency, much of it suffering from the chronic depression that had afflicted agriculture since 1921. However, a more enthusiastic acceptance of the "greater Augsburg" goal by the Lutheran Free Church in the 1920s could have meant a less desperate situation than developed during the depression of 1929. While Free Church members cherished Augsburg, several factors inhibited united effort on behalf of the college. One faction feared that pursuit of the American college goal was diverting Augsburg from its proper mission, while another deplored the slow pace of modernization. To some extent, the claims of Oak Grove and Willmar Bible School competed with those of Augsburg. Finally, the issue of whether the LFC should explore merger with the Norwegian Lutheran Church of America, an organization created in 1917 by the union of three Norwegian Lutheran synods, became entangled with Augsburg's identity.

All of these complications had become visible during the LFC conference of 1923. The report of Pastor Olai H. Sletten, president of the church and a staunch friend of Oak Grove, noted a "deep disquiet within the Lutheran Free Church with respect to Augsburg Seminary." According to Sletten, many people feared that the institution's effort to become a modern college was undermining its historic function, that of training clergymen. The church, Sletten continued, was obliged to provide opportunities for higher education, but Augsburg was not its only school. Impressive advances at Oak Grove suggested the possibility of adopting coeducation there, and expanding it into a college. If this were done, the seminary at Augsburg would retain its dominance within the school's structure.[2]

Sverdrup's conference report took sharp issue with a point of view that was gaining support among members favoring merger with the Norwegian Lutheran Church of America. A basic merger premise was that the LFC had been founded to uphold Augsburg's unique system of ministerial education. Recent policy changes had transformed the college department from an integral branch of the old divinity school into a separate institution. Unlike old-line conservatives, merger proponents did not regard this as an unfortunate transformation, but they did contend that it removed any justification for maintaining the LFC as a separate entity.

Sverdrup rejected this premise, arguing that the Lutheran Free Church was founded to protect the congregation from unwarranted synodical domination (a threat that still existed), as well as to sponsor Augsburg's educational principles. Moreover, he affirmed the compatibility of a modern college program with the ideals of his father and Oftedal. Except in its first two or three years, he insisted, Augsburg had never operated "exclusively" as a divinity school.[3]

A report by the LFC board of education, created in 1922, deplored current Augsburg policy along the same lines as Sletten, without suggesting the elevation of Oak Grove to a college. It acknowledged the need for higher education directed toward the sciences for students hoping to enter certain professions, but insisted that Augsburg's "program and Christian character as a divinity school must be maintained at all costs." According to the board, "Up to now Augsburg has exercised its greatest and most beneficent influence through the clergymen it has sent out." In addition, resources were insufficient "to build a college measuring up to accredited standards." The most Augsburg could hope to achieve was "accredited junior college" status. The report added a plea for restoration of Norse as a "leading discipline" in the college program.[4]

After hearing from Sletten, Sverdrup, the board of education, and others, the various recommendations committees sought to develop a consensus out of the diverse viewpoints presented. Basically, the resolutions presented combined support of Sverdrup's position with rhetorical concessions to the delegates who feared that the school was becoming dangerously secular. One resolution reaffirmed that Augsburg was "first and foremost a divinity school," adding: "We are grateful that an increasing number of our youth are seeking admission to our college, but progress in the preparatory departments must not be at the expense of the theological department." Another denied that Augsburg had "changed front" with respect to its historic goals. Several voiced confidence in Sverdrup's leadership. Expansion of Oak Grove's program beyond the secondary level was explicitly opposed, but the Fargo school was encouraged to work toward full recognition as an "accredited academy." Following a perfunctory debate, the resolutions were adopted.[5]

No stand was taken on the board of education's recommendation against seeking full accreditation for Augsburg College, yet it sparked a debate that impeded harmony within the Lutheran Free Church. Beginning on April 2, 1924, Carl M. Roan, a prominent Minneapolis physician, Augsburg alumnus, and member of the board of trustees, contributed a series of articles to *Folkebladet* entitled "Augsburg's Academic Future." The first instalment attacked the 1923 conference for failing to deal with an issue of such importance as that raised by the education board. Subsequent articles argued for accelerating Augsburg's improvements. Roan insisted on the necessity of winning full accreditation from the University of Minnesota as well as the North Central Association, whose standards he had thoroughly investigated.[6]

Had Roan employed a more restrained tone, Sverdrup may have found his crusade helpful; the articles urged Augsburg's administration to increase the pursuit of its established goals rather than to change course. However, Roan's blunt questions threatened the precarious unity of Augsburg's constituency. On April 30 Sverdrup asked *Folkebladet* to suspend the series, contending that Roan was presenting one side of a complex set of issues previously delegated to the Augsburg faculty.

Hans C. Caspersen, editor of *Folkebladet* and a believer in freedom of the press, declined Sverdrup's request, and the debate continued. Caspersen also sought Evjen's counsel on the NCA issue. Evjen responded with an argument against the perils of excessive standardization inherent in any effort to meet accreditation requirements.[7] The growing dispute led Sverdrup to comment publicly on the issue raised by Roan. In a signed statement published by *Folkebladet* on June 4, the Augsburg president indicated partial agreement with Evjen, but asserted that the former Augsburg professor was "going as far in one direction as Dr. Roan in the other." Accreditation by the NCA, continued Sverdrup, was not a matter of "life or death" (*livsbetingelse*) for Augsburg. On the other hand, conformity to the academic system "within which we find ourselves" was necessary. Augsburg's basic function, the training of ministers and "other laborers for the Lord's vineyard," could not be considered by the NCA. Nevertheless, the school was earnestly seeking to achieve standards meriting and capable of winning accreditation "where it was needed."

Folkebladet interpreted Sverdrup's position as "middle of the road," an accurate assessment. Although his statement implied a disparity between NCA demands and Augsburg's mission, it did not reject a quest for future accreditation. The meager resources available scarcely permitted improvement of facilities and augmentation of the library — both necessary before bidding for recognition. The president also may have calculated that an immediate fund drive to meet NCA standards was practically impossible.

Although neither Sverdrup nor Birkeland mentioned the Roan controversy in their reports to the 1924 LFC conference, it did influence the members' deliberations. On June 16 two delegates introduced a motion calling for appointment of a seven-man committee to investigate "the relationship between the school's president and one member of the board of trustees (namely, Dr. Roan)." [8] Such a definition of the issue worked to Sverdrup's advantage, for the propriety of a trustee publicly opposing the president of Augsburg was considerably more dubious than Roan's views on NCA accreditation. Following approval of the motion, an *ad hoc* committee conducted the investigation. Its report reprimanded Roan for taking a position against Sverdrup that endangered "harmony" within the Augsburg community. [9]

Unfortunately, unity continued to be elusive. During the LFC conference of 1925, the entire board of trustees resigned as a result of dissension between Birkeland and Roan on several issues. Upon request, two of the five — Pastors Asmund Oftedal and Michael B. Michaelson — consented to resume their posts; Roan and Birkeland were not recalled. Edward G. Hammer of Zumbrota, Minnesota, wealthy owner of a dairy and ice-cream business, succeeded Birkeland as chairman. [10]

Financial reports of the various branches of LFC activity also alarmed 1925 conference delegates; immediate consolidation was necessary to avoid economic disaster. The conference responded by creating a special commission of seven men to investigate the status of the schools and their relationship to one another. [11] With Ole O. Sageng as chairman, the commission published a report that was widely discussed in advance of the next conference. Four of the commission's 16 recommendations were fundamental: coeducation at Oak Grove; liquidation of Augsburg Academy; abandonment of Willmar Bible School; and appointment of a full-time financial secretary to supervise joint fund raising for Augsburg and Oak Grove.[12] Most of the other recommendations also noted the primacy of Augsburg College which, in turn, encouraged further initiatives by college partisans. The Alumni Association proposed to launch a $50,000 campaign to assist the Augsburg Park building program, and other proponents of an early move to Richfield resolved to seek conference approval of a $500,000 fund drive for the same purpose.[13]

The 1926 conference disappointed those who hoped for adoption of the entire education report. Coeducation at Oak Grove and the joint fund-raising plan were accepted, but delegates rejected disposing of the academy, in spite of Sverdrup's explicit recommendation. The proposal to close Willmar Bible School also was defeated — the next conference would vote its consolidation with Oak Grove. Conference members expressed thanks for the Alumni Association drive, but hesitated to approve the $500,000 project. A motion by Sverdrup requesting "the Board of Trustees . . . to take the necessary preliminaries to prepare for the gathering of $500,000 to move Augsburg Seminary to Augsburg Park" compromised the issue. The assembly approved Sverdrup's resolution, but the trustees declined to put it into effect. In their judgment the outstanding debt, which was increasing at an average yearly rate of $4,500, had to be eliminated before a campaign of such proportions could be considered.[14]

Augsburg's Statement of Operating Income and Expense, issued on April 30, 1927, suggested that debt liquidation might be possible; it registered a surplus of approximately $1,000. A year later, however, reduced contributions from the LFC, together with increased expenses, left a deficit of more than $14,000.[15]

A report submitted to the 1928 conference by a Committee on Efficiency and Economy attempted to uncover the reasons for the dismal economic status of most activities. According to the committee, "Hard Times" were a factor, but not the only one. The church was supporting "too many activities in proportion to its size." Its financial structure lacked order and system. Within the congregations "Spiritual Life" was "Waning." Annual conferences, "when swayed by pious enthusiasm," often authorized new ventures without calculating the capacity of the church to bear the added cost. Finally, "Disharmony in the Ranks" was fostering a spirit of "non-cooperation and non-support" on the part of too many Lutheran Free Church members.[16]

The report might have added that disharmony within the faculty created further difficulties. In 1926 Lars Qualben, a graduate of Augsburg Academy, College, and Seminary joined the teaching force as professor of New Testament in the seminary, and as chairman of the college Education department. Such a combination of responsibilities was unusual, but not out of line with Qualben's preparation. He had received his Ph.D. degree from Hartford Theological Seminary in 1923, and his M.A. from Teachers College, Columbia University, in 1924. Soon after returning to Augsburg as a teacher, he gained the respect of both students and colleagues. Sverdrup recommended his appointment as a permanent faculty member to the conference of 1927, a recommendation that gained approval.[17]

In January, 1928 Qualben emerged as a spokesman for merger negotiations with the Norwegian Lutheran Church of America. His argument, as presented in a pamphlet and several *Folkebladet* articles, elaborated an interpretation of Augsburg and LCF history that had been advanced and briefly debated in 1923. According to this view, a determination to maintain Augsburg as a divinity school consisting of three closely integrated departments was primarily responsible for the existence of the Lutheran Free Church. Beginning in 1922 the school, with the approbation of annual conferences, had moved rapidly away from the divinity school ideal. Specifically, it had adopted coeducation, represented itself as aiming to become "a strong American college," attempted to win full accreditation, participated in intercollegiate athletics, and signified an intent to close Augsburg Academy, a step that Georg Sverdrup would have refused to consider. Qualben contended that this pattern of development had fundamentally transformed Augsburg, thereby undermining the Lutheran Free Church's original reason for being. Since he perceived no essential difference in theological outlook between the two church groups, he concluded that merger merited exploration.[18]

Financial considerations, Qualben added, served to favor merger. The LFC was unable to support its existing programs; how, then, could it contemplate the expenditures needed to establish Augsburg as "a modern American College." Assuming the move to Augsburg Park, a building program on that site would require at least a million dollars. In addition, an endowment fund of from $500,000 to $750,000 had to be raised. The question was: Could a church group of 27,000 confirmed members carry burdens of such magnitude? Qualben believed not. In his opinion realization of the "greater Augsburg" goal depended on a substantial increase in the school's constituency.[19]

From the viewpoint of economic realism, history, and the image Augsburg College sought to cultivate, Qualben's case was persuasive.

166

New Main, dedicated in 1902, improved Augsburg's image both on and off campus.

Sivertsen Hall, acquired in 1939, became a girls' dormitory.

Gerda Mortensen Hall (below), built in 1955 as a women's residence, was converted to a men's dormitory in 1967.

Miss Gerda Mortensen was appointed Dean of Women in 1923, one year after coeducation was adopted. Although officially retired in 1964, she continued to serve Augsburg in a variety of areas.

Augsburg's first courageous coeds in 1921 were (from left): Katherine V. Kleven, Anne Oudal, Hilda L. Ostlie, Lillian V. Olson, and Clara A. Nybroten.

Theodore C. Blegen, who graduated from Augsburg in 1910, an author, historian, and educator. He retired in 1960 after more than 20 years as dean of the University of Minnesota's graduate school.

Charles E. Stangeland graduated in the class of 1898 with George Sverdrup, and served for many years as professor of political economy in the University of Berlin.

Carl W. Blegen, an Augsburg graduate in 1904, won world recognition in the field of classical archaeology.

Coach Anderson led his basketball team to their third straight MIAC championship in 1965. Shown are (seated): Roy Halvorson, Richard W. Kelley, Daniel K. Meyers, Steve T. Strommen, Jerry D. Hokkanen, Robert L. Kelly (standing): Howard E. Pearson, Assistant Coach, Allan J. Berg, Edward J. Nixon, Dan Anderson, Ronald A. Hanson, Ronald G. Nelson, Head Coach Ernest W. Anderson.

Members of Augsburg's first intercollegiate basketball squad of 1907–08 were (top): Thorsten T. Roan, Albert Thorson, Joseph R. Michaelson (center): John E. Blegen, Henry O. Hanson (seated): James B. Larson.

Si Melby Hall, completed in 1961, provided facilities for health and physical education, chapel services, and general auditorium purposes.

The Augsburg College Choir, directed by Leland B. Sateren, earned an international reputation. Members are shown here performing in St. John's Abbey, Collegeville, Minnesota, in 1967.

The Music Hall looked like this when it was purchased from the Tabernacle Baptist Church in 1947. Its steeple was removed a short time later.

Regular nationwide tours were conducted by the Augsburg College Concert Band. Director Mayo A. Savold is shown at center right.

Science Hall (1949) and the George Sverdrup Library (1955) are shown above. The Lisa Odland Observatory was added to the roof of Science Hall (left) in 1960.

Arthur Nash began teaching natural science and biology in 1922 and continued in that capacity until his retirement in 1968. He was Dean of the College from 1946 to 1950.

Martin Quanbeck served as registrar, director of teacher placement, professor of Education, and chairman of the Education department. He was Dean of the College from 1942 until 1946 and again from 1950 to 1965.

Sverdrup-Oftedal Memorial Hall (above), built in 1939, combined boys' dormitory space, dining facilities, and an office area for mission activities. Part of the building was converted to additional office space in 1967. The Studio (below), dedicated in 1964, served as a temporary student center until 1967, when it became home to the art department.

The College Center and Urness Tower for women (background) were completed in 1967. A proposed twin tower for men will share main floor lounge and conference facilities.

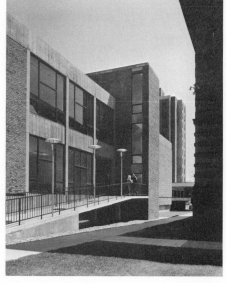

Kenneth C. Bailey, who became Dean of the College in 1965, also served as professor in the Department of Philosophy.

The College Center lounge is a popular area for non-academic student activities.

His contention that the school transfer question underlay the schism of 1893 was valid. It was equally clear that, with an enrollment ten times greater than the seminary, Augsburg College had become more than a branch of an integrated divinity school, and that Augsburg Academy would soon expire. To interpret these facts as anything less than a significant alteration of the college's relationship to the other two departments was questionable, and not consistent with efforts to identify Augsburg College as a liberal arts institution.

Nevertheless, the Qualben crusade aroused a storm. Melby published a widely circulated rebuttal, and Sverdrup responded with uncharacteristic vehemence. Both pursued essentially the same line of argument. For one thing, they challenged Qualben's version of the history of Augsburg, maintaining that the institution had never operated "exclusively" as a divinity school in the sense that Qualben was using the term, and issues other than the "transfer question" had contributed to the rise of the Lutheran Free Church. For another, they deplored the probable consequences of merger agitation. Melby predicted that the "first effect" of the Qualben pamphlet would be "to cripple" fund solicitation both for Augsburg and Oak Grove. "Its second result," continued Melby, "will be to widen the breach already existing within . . . the Lutheran Free Church." [20] Sverdrup, too, worried about the financial impact of merger agitation. Qualben recalled the president's initial reaction as being: "I am afraid that this movement is going to knock the bottom out of the drive for our schools." [21]

Sverdrup's vigorous opposition to Qualben at the 1928 conference also suggests a deep sensitivity to intimations that Augsburg was following a course different from that charted by the elder Sverdrup; his report explicitly denied any break in continuity between the two administrations. A brief reference to Qualben's comment that liquidation of Augsburg Academy would have been unthinkable in Georg Sverdrup's time bristled with indignation. Such a remark, said Sverdrup, dealt "with a possibility that no one has a right to raise publicly, and in view of its obvious intent, it deserves no further reply." As on earlier occasions, he quoted the passage from his father's 1906 report calling for standardization of Augsburg's program, representing it as a major guideline for his own administration. [22]

Since anti-merger sentiment and Sverdrup's prestige were dominant forces at the 1928 conference, no one seriously believed that Qualben would prevail. However, a respected minority led by such influential Minneapolis clergymen as Olai Sletten and Claus Morgan publicly backed the young professor and leaned toward merger. [23] To mollify this group, the conference approved a more moderate statement against church union than the one originally proposed; in commenting on the latter, President Gynild said it clearly had not been drafted by "diplomats." [24] Investigation of the Sverdrup-Qualben controversy produced a report vindicating Sverdrup, but the other man's future status at Augsburg was left to the board of trustees.[25] Following adjournment of the conference a series of negotiations between Qualben and the trustees failed to establish agreement, whereupon the young professor accepted an invitation to join the St. Olaf College faculty.[26]

WHILE ECHOES OF the Qualben affair reverberated throughout the Lutheran Free Church, Augsburg continued its battle with poverty. Viewed superficially the financial reports for 1929, issued too early to reflect the impact of the Great Depression, appeared more encouraging than those of the preceding year. Congregational contributions exceeded those of 1928 by nearly $9,000, and the deficit totaled only $4,000, rather than the $14,000 registered a year earlier. Nevertheless, the board of trustees interpreted Augsburg's financial situation as "very pressing, indeed more serious than in several years." As if sensing the imminence of economic collapse, the board earnestly requested the conference to act decisively with respect to Augsburg's fiscal problems.[27]

The conference responded by approving a $200,000 "Jubilee Campaign" designed to liberate Augsburg and Oak Grove from debt, a project recommended by a special committee that had been appointed in 1928 to plan an appropriate commemoration of the Augsburg Confession's four-hundredth anniversary.[28] Under the direction of Professor Hendrickson, who was granted a leave from his teaching duties, the drive raised $104,396, a sum substantially short of the goal but nonetheless creditable in view of the deteriorating economic conditions that followed the stock market crash. Augsburg's share, $63,755.11, cushioned the first blow of the Great Depression. Although debt liquidation remained an unrealized dream, the statement of income and expenditure for April 30, 1930, showed a surplus rather than the usual deficit.[29]

A year later the situation was considerably worse. Instead of $50,000, a figure regarded by the board of trustees as minimal, the joint school fund drive yielded Augsburg less than $30,000.[30] Since contributions from the church normally provided the school with about 60 per cent of its income, this sum left it in desperate straits. From June 1, 1930, to May 31, 1931, a deficit of more than $16,000 was incurred. "At the present moment," noted Hammer in his report to the 1931 conference, "teachers have not been paid their May salaries and they have been notified by the Board that it will probably not be able to pay any salaries during the summer months." Under such circumstances, no one could predict a resumption of classes in the fall.[31]

However, evidences of a grim determination to save the college already were visible. In the spring of 1931 the faculty and staff pledged ten per cent of their salaries for the upcoming year to the 1932 fund drive, an offer gratefully accepted by the board of trustees.[32] A poll conducted by Melby among LFC clergymen prior to the 1931 conference also encouraged those who assigned highest priority to the maintenance of Augsburg College. Although Melby's respondents felt that the Lutheran Free Church was carrying an excessive financial burden, 99 of them wanted Augsburg to remain a four-year college, while only 15 favored reducing it to a junior college.[33]

Subsequent developments confirmed Melby's findings. The conference of 1931 rejected a recommendation that Oak Grove be abandoned so that a total commitment could be made to Augsburg, but in allocating the proceeds of the next joint fund drive, it raised Augsburg's share from 80 to 85 per cent.[34] The board of trustees authorized a special summer campaign aimed at replenishing the school's empty treasury. Returns were modest — $5,363 — but sufficient to settle the issue of whether Augsburg should begin classes in September.[35]

A combination of austerity, faculty privation, faith, improvisation, Hammer's credit rating, and the generosity of supporters still having financial resources kept the school open through 1931–32. The joint school fund yielded Augsburg $33,746, a larger sum than a year earlier, although far below the established norm. Since college enrollment remained nearly as high as in 1930–31, tuition income theoretically did not decline. Unfortunately, students also were victims of the depression, and many of them paid their fees in a variety of promissory notes. Nevertheless, a slash of approximately $5,000 in operating costs held the budget roughly in balance, thus averting another increase in the outstanding debt.[36]

The depth of the Great Depression in 1932–33 demanded additional sacrifice. Augsburg's share of the joint fund drive sank to a discouraging low: less than $20,000 as of April 30, 1933. A deficit of $9,252.72 raised the total indebtedness of the institution to more than $74,000.[37] Only two alternatives appeared open: a reduction of the teaching force or a decrease in salaries. When confronted with this choice, the faculty opted for the latter. It submitted to the board of trustees a resolution proposing "that for the school year of 1933–34 the faculty be offered no stated salary, but that it be given its share of school income to be prorated over the payroll according to the now prevailing scale." The board accepted this arrangement, thereby avoiding a sharp curtailment of the college program. It also voted to discontinue the academy, a step approved by the conference of 1933.[38]

In reporting to the 1934 conference, Hammer remarked that "the situation is considerably better than it was a year ago." Joint school fund contributions exceeded those of 1933 by nearly $5,000, and the prorated scheme had reduced faculty salary expense by approximately $4,000. Even so, the accounts registered a deficit of almost $2,500. In addition, Hammer had negotiated an agreement with a group of creditors holding $27,500 worth of bonds issued by Augsburg several years earlier that obligated the school to retire ten per cent of the principal each year until the bonds were redeemed, the first instalment being due on October 1, 1934. Along with this arrangement the board was establishing a tidier management of finances. Fiscal reports submitted to the 1934 conference were more sophisticated than those of earlier years, and the trustees presented an estimate of income and expenditure for the upcoming year. Now that Augsburg's survival seemed assured, emphasis shifted to bringing indebtedness under control.[39]

Austerity continued. Liquidating the debt was in itself a formidable problem, and the persistence of depression, compounded by the disastrous drought of 1934, made it more so. To forestall a cut in the college program the faculty volunteered one more sacrifice: a 25 per cent payroll reduction for 1934–35. The board adopted this suggestion, specifying that the reduction should be less than 25 per cent for personnel in the lower salary scales and more for those drawing higher pay. A board-faculty committee consisting of Hammer, Hendrickson, and Ragna Sverdrup applied the board decision to individual salaries. Theological professors were reduced from $1,980 to $1,445; the two highest paid college professors from $2,160 to $1,555; and the lowest paid instructor from $1,620 to $1,215.[40]

The qualified optimism of 1934 became more confident a year later. By June, 1935 the joint fund drive was approaching its goal, and the board chairman's report to the annual conference noted slight progress in debt retirement, a gain attributable to "the severe reduction in salaries." However, restoration of pre-depression wage levels was not an immediate prospect. "It must be our aim," said Hammer, "to continue year by year to reduce the indebtedness of the school until all debt has been paid." [41] The conference endorsed this suggestion by approving a policy declaration that required all LFC boards to apply "not less than 10% of their income from the congregations" to debt retirement until all outstanding obligations were liquidated.[42] Adherence to this priority moved Augsburg toward solvency. A 10.5 per cent reduction in the debt was achieved in 1935–36, and an even larger one the following year.[43]

Salaries recovered more slowly. In 1937 the board granted the faculty a raise of five per cent, its first post-depression adjustment. Although this established a trend, several years passed before the salary cuts of the early 1930s were restored. Notwithstanding a larger teaching force and student body, Augsburg's total academic salary expense in 1940–41 was smaller than it had been ten years earlier.[44]

THE GREAT DEPRESSION forced a number of adjustments on Augsburg College, some harmful, others advantageous. While stubborn Augsburg Park enthusiasts refused to surrender completely their dream of a suburban campus, the possibility of moving to Richfield faded. A joint meeting of the school directors and trustees held early in 1931 recommended to the forthcoming LFC conference "that the thought of moving the school out to Augsburg Park be abandoned and that plans for the future be made accordingly." The trustees and directors advanced two arguments in support of this recommendation: "moving . . . involves a sum of money too large for the Lutheran Free Church under . . . present circumstances to raise," and the desirability of maintaining an arrangement "whereby students attending Augsburg College may take subjects at the University of Minnesota that are not offered at Augsburg." Impressed with this reasoning, the 1931 conference adopted the recommendation, thereby rescinding the resolution of 1926 calling for an early move to Richfield.[45]

Unfortunately, one aspect of the Augsburg Park problem remained unresolved. In 1927 the Augsburg Corporation had loaned to the Augsburg Park Association $37,000 of the school's endowment fund, accepting as security a first mortgage on all uncontracted land held by the association. The soundness of this investment became questionable after 1929, when a moribund real estate market left the association without income. As Professor Hendrickson, who served as park association secretary, tersely remarked, "There was not even enough money for taxes and interest, let alone principal." Augsburg's return on the mortgage nearly vanished, and tax delinquency threatened its $37,000 investment.[46]

To avert total loss, the Augsburg board of trustees in 1936 negotiated an agreement with the association that gave Augsburg Seminary clear title to forty acres — the designated campus area — in return for release of the association from the mortgage and payment by Augsburg of back taxes on the forty acres. The school now possessed a suburban campus site free of encumbrance, but the struggle for solvency discouraged relocation.[47]

Although the faculty was willing to accept a salary reduction, the crisis necessitated retreat on several fronts. A drastic curtailment of the athletic program mocked the dreams of Augsburg sports enthusiasts. The financial statements disclose a cut in athletic expense from $1,333.20 in 1930–31 to $259.93 a year later, a saving made possible by transferring to the athletic director full responsibility for coaching football and basketball.[48] James Pederson, a former distinguished Augsburg athlete, accepted this combined post in 1933. The restricted situation within which Pederson was obliged to operate — the over-extension inherent in his triple role, hopelessly inadequate facilities, and severely limited equipment budgets — worked against success. Outstanding athletes like Ernest W. Anderson and Hoyt C. Messerer helped to maintain the basketball team as a competitive force, but the record in football was disastrous.

In 1935 the school withdrew from conference participation in the latter sport, launching instead an intramural program that theoretically provided "playing experience to a greater number of students than was possible under the old system." [49] Such a claim was defensible, but confirmed sports lovers preferred the glories of the golden twenties. Augsburg's self-image with respect to athletics had undergone a radical transformation since 1928, when the campus resounded with "On to the Olympics." By contrast the 1935 *Augsburgian* introduced its athletic section with the quotation:

> The brave man seeks not popular applause
> Nor, overpower'd with arms, deserts his cause.

Although music, like athletics, suffered budgetary curtailment in 1931–32, the long-range effect was less traumatic. It is true that instrumental music went into eclipse: serious efforts to maintain a band or orchestra failed until the Great Depression ended. Vocal music, on the other hand, advanced impressively. Since arriving at Augsburg in 1922, Opseth had cherished the "choir idea," but insufficient talent had defeated several attempts to realize this goal. In the autumn of 1933, however, more than 60 students sought admission to the music organizations, a "wealth of material" by the standards of the time. A merger of the men's Glee Club and women's Choral Society on November 8 created the Augsburg College Choir.[50] Following four months of rehearsal, the new singing group departed on an extended Midwest tour. It encountered enthusiastic audience response, received favorable reviews, and

172

even demonstrated a capacity to earn its own way — at the tour's conclusion the books registered a balance "of some $250 above expenses.[51] The success of this venture not only established the annual tour as a regular event, but also generated wider opportunities for the choir. In 1934–35 it gained an expanded following by performing a series of Sunday evening concerts on radio station WCCO, while an increasing number of choir appearances in the Twin Cities called attention to the existence of Augsburg College, countering the isolation that separated the institution from its metropolitan neighbors.

Despite the determination of both administration and faculty to maintain the curricular program intact, some retrenchment was inevitable. A number of departments, including German, French, Latin, and social science, reduced their majors to minors. In 1932 the department of mathematics increased the requirements for a major without expanding its offerings. Instead, mathematics majors were obliged to take solid analytical geometry at the University of Minnesota in accordance with an arrangement between the two schools.[52]

That more severe cutbacks were avoided is remarkable. Even more remarkable is that Augsburg College emerged from the Great Depression with as strong a faculty as had staffed its classrooms in 1928. Nearly all the people who had accepted appointments in the 1920s and earlier remained, some increasing their effectiveness by pursuing further graduate work. In addition, several persons joined the faculty during the depression years.

Following the death of Professor Nydahl in 1928, Miss Selma Storien was appointed Augsburg's first professionally trained librarian. An austere budget imposed restrictions on library improvements, but within limits Miss Storien accomplished a great deal. She modernized the classification of holdings according to the Dewey Decimal plan, discarding the unique system inherited from her predecessors. She also supervised major library expansion in the basement area. Since there were no funds for such renovation, Miss Storien persuaded faculty members skilled in carpentry — chiefly Fosse, Helland, and Lillehei — to tear out walls that had separated Augsburg's various libraries, and to build many feet of shelf space.[53]

When Bernhard M. Christensen became a permanent member of the faculty in 1930, he already was associated with Augsburg and the Lutheran Free Church. Born at Porterfield, Wisconsin in 1901, he graduated from Augsburg College in 1922. For the next three years he attended the seminary, serving also as English instructor in the academy. After graduation he taught one year at Oak Grove High School. In the autumn of 1926 he was admitted to Princeton Theological Seminary, completing the work for both the B.D. and M.A. degrees in theology in one academic year. Following a summer of study at Columbia University in philosophy, he spent 1927–28 at the German universities of Berlin and Gottingen on a Princeton fellowship. Upon returning to the United States he attended Hartford Theological Seminary, receiving his Ph.D. in 1929. While studying at Hartford, and for a few months thereafter, he served on the pastoral staff of Trinity Lutheran Church, Brooklyn, New York.

Christensen's years as a graduate student were marked by considerable inner turmoil as he groped with the problem of relating the Christian faith as interpreted by his own religious tradition to the realities of 20th century life. Princeton, where he specialized in apologetics and systematic theology, he enjoyed "very much," but he mildly deplored its "strong tendency to stress the absolute correctness of the Calvinistic position." [54] At Columbia he became "more convinced than ever of the essentially anti-Christian character of present-day secular education." Unfortunately, no promising corrective to secularism seemed available: "That Fundamentalism is to be vindicated seems an impossible conjecture . . . where lies the line that *can* be successfully defended? If one could be certain that he had discovered not merely the Truth, but also its implications, nothing else in life would matter." [55]

At the University of Berlin, where he investigated the "philosophical background of Systematics," Christensen discovered an environment conducive to study "such as I have longed for all my life." In contrast to Princeton's "system oppression," a freer climate prevailed, although the professors at Berlin were less "liberal" than Christensen "had really expected. . . ." [56] Nevertheless, he felt unprepared to teach systematic theology, since he lacked a "system" of his own.[57] Prior to sailing home, he spent several weeks in Scandinavia, engaging in profitable conversation with Professor Eduard Geismar, the noted Søren Kierkegaard scholar.[58]

After his return from Europe Christensen's relationship with Augsburg passed through a brief but decisive crisis. The board of trustees had voted him a stipend to facilitate completion of his work at Hartford, with the understanding that he would shortly join the Augsburg faculty. Before these arrangements were completed, sharp disagreement developed between Christensen and Sven Oftedal's son, Asmund, a member of Augsburg's board of trustees, and associate pastor of Trinity Church, Brooklyn, where Christensen also was serving.

The younger Oftedal regarded rejection of "verbal inspiration [of the

Scriptures] as the first step toward 'modernism' " and the subversion of traditional Christianity. Christensen strongly dissented.[59] He argued that Lutheranism had "a definite and mighty message for the bewildered theological America of to-day, not least with regard to the central place of the Divine Message in the Scripture. But," he continued, "as long as Lutherans simply are content to be classed as Fundamentalists, that message will never be heard — and countless thinking young people will in helpless despair make the wrong choice because the alternatives have been falsely presented to them." [60]

The controversy soon shifted to Christensen's future relationship with the LFC and Augsburg Seminary. Since Asmund Oftedal was convinced that Christensen was "not an acceptable candidate for ordination," the latter surmised his own unfitness "to teach theology in a Lutheran Seminary." Believing there could be "no hope that the other members of the Board would be more kindly inclined," Christensen suggested to Sverdrup that the stipend be withdrawn.[61] Sverdrup declined, requesting instead that Christensen submit a statement of his position to the Augsburg theological faculty. Christensen complied with a one-paragraph communication:

I believe that the Bible contains the record of the historical revelation of God to the people of Israel, culminating in the perfect revelation in his Son. I believe that this record is so clear that for the purposes of the practical Christian life it constitutes a sufficient guide in all matters of faith and conduct. But in the scientific study of theology I do not believe that we can avoid a consideration of the historico-critical research that has been carried out in the last hundred years. These critical studies I do not look upon as hindrances, but rather as helps, to the true understanding of the Scripture. In general — though by no means in detail — I believe that the methods and results of historical criticism must be accepted if we are to have a theological message for those of our people who think earnestly and deeply. As a fair example of the general implications of these premises I should mention A. B. Bruce's "Apologetics." [62]

The theological professors judged this statement to be "in harmony with the position of the faculty." They also advised Christensen "to accept the stipend offered . . . by the Board . . . with the view toward teaching at Augsburg." [63] This action did not immediately resolve the issue of Christensen's future; he felt impelled to enter the parish ministry, at least temporarily. Continuation of the argument with Oftedal, who disagreed with the theological faculty's decision, reinforced his hesitation.[64] Ultimately, however, Christensen decided in favor of the Augsburg appointment, taking up his duties in 1930–31.

Like all permanent Augsburg Seminary faculty members, Christensen was assigned a major role in the college. As a theological professor, he taught church history during his first year, and practical theology thereafter; within the college he headed a new department of philosophy and psychology. Its curriculum included a required freshman course called "Man and His World"; general psychology, a sophomore offering; and — for the first time in Augsburg history — a full complement of philosophy courses.

The new department raised the validity of Augsburg's representation as a Christian liberal arts college. A course entitled "Man and His World" may suggest innocuous content, but many freshmen were challenged to reconsider a Fundamentalist point of view they expected a school like Augsburg to uphold. Kristofer Hagen, who taught general psychology, approached issues colored with delicate theological implications honestly and openly — the "Christian psychology" vogue that still enjoyed some standing in Norwegian-American Lutheran circles was not for him. Christensen's philosophy students and others who met him in non-curricular relationships were influenced by the degree to which he combined Christian piety with intellectual flexibility, and a profound respect for the world's great cultural traditions.

Anne Pederson, whose influence also helped to strengthen liberal education at Augsburg, began her long and productive career as an instructor and professor of English immediately after graduating from the college in 1932. For several years Miss Pederson taught part-time, an arrangement permitting her to take graduate work at the University of Minnesota. Like Miss Pederson, Bernhardt J. Kleven served on part-time appointments during the 1930s as a social science instructor. A member of the college class of 1922, Kleven had taught earlier in the public schools and Augsburg Academy. He received his Ph.D. degree in American history from the University of Minnesota in 1941, then was appointed as a full-time teacher at Augsburg.

Under Soberg and Ermisch, mathematics and German instruction achieved greater continuity than in the 1920s, but Education and social science were less fortunate. In 1932 Adolph Paulson, who had served for two years as academy principal and college social science instructor, accepted responsibility for both the social science and Education programs. Unfortunately, illness forced Paulson's leave of absence in 1933–34, requiring the employment of interim instructors in both areas. The next year Gordon C. Hanson was appointed to the Education position and Paulson, still in precarious health, taught the beginning courses in sociology and economics. Following Paulson's death in March, 1935 the social science program was directed by a succession of temporary instructors; it became an academic stepchild and remained so for several years. Hanson managed the Education program, including teacher placement, until 1938, when he accepted a more lucrative post in the University of Kansas at Wichita. He was succeeded by Martin Quanbeck.

Although the era's austere budgets precluded library, faculty, and plant improvement needed to win full accreditation, the limited gains of earlier years were preserved and even expanded. In the spring of 1930 the University of Minnesota Senate Committee on Relations to Other Institutions officially certified Augsburg's accreditation as a junior college. The committee also formalized an agreement made two years earlier, admitting Augsburg students to "the Graduate School when the major work . . . has been in one of the following fields, and when especially recommended for graduate work: English, psychology and education, classical languages, Norse, history and chemistry." [65]

This arrangement was not new, having prevailed since 1916. Now, however, it included additional majors, and was "permanent," rather than "tentative" — instead of being subject to immediate revocation, university accreditation of a major would be withdrawn only after a year's notice.[66] In 1933 biology was "tentatively" added to the list of approved fields. Whether this discipline achieved "permanent" status previous to full university accreditation of Augsburg on February 15, 1951, is not clear, nor important. According to Martin Quanbeck, Augsburg "graduates were treated somewhat more generously by the University's Graduate School than might be indicated by the [institutional relations] committee's action." [67] Meanwhile, Education graduates wishing to teach in Minnesota high schools were eligible for certification, the State Department of Education having recognized Augsburg's teacher training program since 1920.[68]

Nevertheless, lack of full accreditation seriously handicapped the school. When an Augsburg alumnus applied for admission to a graduate program in an institution other than the University of Minnesota, lengthy correspondence often was required to establish the college's status.[69] Certification of Education graduates outside of Minnesota was also a problem — North Dakota authorities withheld recognition until 1931.[70] Occasionally, student recruiters from rival colleges raised uncomfortable questions concerning the value of an Augsburg degree.

During the Great Depression, Augsburg College enrollment followed an erratic pattern. In 1928–29 and the next year it declined, then reached a record high of 249 in 1933–34. It fell slightly during the next two years, then resumed an upward course that accelerated significantly in the late 1930s. By contrast both St. Olaf and Carleton experienced a heavy loss of students. However, national college enrollment remained fairly stable through the depression years.

Basic reasons for the Augsburg trend are fairly clear. Tuition was low: $75 per year compared to $150 at St. Olaf. In 1929 it had been raised from $60, the rate since 1923. When authorizing this increase, the board of trustees had considered setting tuition even higher, but a tradition of accommodating the less affluent levels of Norwegian-American society prevailed. In the early and middle 1930s many young people desiring to attend a Lutheran college (in some cases, any college) discovered Augsburg to be within their financial reach. The school, moreover, maintained a generous policy with respect to scholarships. Rather than remitting half of the first year's tuition to the highest ranking young man and woman from a high school graduating class as did St. Olaf, Augsburg granted a full year tuition scholarship to such students.

Part-time jobs within walking distance of the campus also attracted indigent youths to Augsburg. In 1932 the board of trustees authorized Sverdrup "to establish an Employment Service for students at an expense not to exceed $50." [71] Under the competent direction of Abner B. Batalden, class of 1935, this agency secured board and room situations for a number of needy students. The opportunities made available by Batalden were not lucrative — most of them involved three hours of restaurant labor in return for three meals of varying quality — but during this period even menial jobs were scarce. While statistics are not available, it is safe to assume that more than three-fourths of Augsburg's students worked part-time. The school also took advantage of federal and state aid programs. In 1935–36 the National Youth Administration provided $4,030, which the school distributed to 34 students as compensation for productive work both on and off campus.[72]

Preoccupation with class work and employment limited social and extra-curricular activity, as did the persistence of a legalistic stance toward "worldly" pleasure. The *Augsburg Student Hand-Book and Directory* for 1933–34 prescribed a rigorous code of conduct:

"Attendance at dances either as participant, spectator, musician or usher will lead to expulsion.

Every student is earnestly urged to refrain from indiscriminate attendance at 'Movies.'

Drinking intoxicating liquors or patronizing pool halls will lead to expulsion.

Objectionable card playing is prohibited." [73]

A year later the handbook defined the same expectations in a less imperative tone: "The high aims and Christian ideals of Augsburg give no room for such demoralizing amusements as drinking, dancing, indecent movies, and objectionable card playing. Students who cannot live without these should not enroll at Augsburg." However, "the student's need for some kind of relaxation and amusement" was recognized. In an effort "to meet this legitimate need," the school maintained an athletic program and encouraged campus societies to organize "social activities." The Twin Cities also provided many cultural opportunities — "popular symphonies . . . Art Galleries, State Historical Library and . . . lectures and exhibits at the University of Minnesota." [74]

The second handbook more nearly reflected campus reality than the first. Although moral pressures against drinking and dancing persisted, violators rarely were expelled. Melby and Miss Mortensen were moving toward more enlightened student personnel management during the 1930s, the former pragmatically, and the Dean of Women in accordance with modern theory. Nevertheless, a substantial number of students felt restricted. Drama, for example, did not appear to have won respectability. Occasionally a society or class presented an innocuous skit, but establishment of a regular drama program seemed a remote possibility.

Devotional activities continued to dominate campus life. Attendance at daily chapel was compulsory, although after 1920 services were conducted in mid-morning, rather than before the first hour class, an arrangement that had prevailed since Weenaas' time. While students accepted this requirement in principle, complete observance never was achieved. In addition to daily chapel, the religious program included weekly prayer meetings and frequent evangelistic services. The Mission Society, whose membership included both collegians and seminarians, sponsored annual mission festivals, conducted religious services in the Minneapolis Gateway neighborhood, and distributed tracts on and off campus.

While some Mission Society members regarded their organization as the queen of extra-curricular life, many students achieved self-fulfillment in other activities. Debate and forensics were less important than in previous years, but under the direction of John S. Acker, who served as part-time speech instructor from 1934 to 1942, Augsburg debate teams participated regularly in forensic meets. Admission to the Writers' Club, a creative writing group that published the *Dial*, an annual literary magazine, was a coveted honor. An International Relations Club, organized in 1934, attracted a substantial membership and remained active for several years. The Aristotelian Society, also an active group, represented the natural sciences.

Although these campus activities provided some diversion, many students sought challenge and relaxation off campus. Future seminarians perpetuated the Augsburg tradition of working within local congregations as Sunday school teachers and parish assistants. Others engaged in politics: in 1936 a small disciplined group of conspirators temporarily seized control of the Junior Farmer-Labor Association of Hennepin County. Some students discovered unfamiliar facets of Scandinavian-American culture on Cedar Avenue, where such folk musicians as "Slim Jim" Iverson and the "Vagabond Kid" were featured attractions. Augsburg student life was indeed more pluralistic than the school's official image might have suggested.

INDICATIONS that Augsburg College was entering a new era began to multiply in 1936–37. Thanks to improved economic conditions and the efficient student recruitment drive directed by Batalden, 147 freshmen enrolled in the fall, compared to 83 a year earlier. As the year advanced campus life assumed new vitality. Many upper classmen responded enthusiastically to the teaching of Dr. Sverre Norborg, a European theologian-philosopher, who joined the faculty in September. Enough students reported for vocal auditions to organize a second choir, as well as a male chorus, and the orchestra reappeared. Coach Carl Swanson's basketball team achieved fourth place in conference play. Under the vigorous leadership of John Stensvaag, president of the Student Society, students displayed more initiative than they had for many years. In reporting to the 1937 LFC conference, Sverdrup remarked: "Seldom has such . . . enthusiasm of a quiet but determined kind existed at Augsburg. . . . the conviction that Augsburg has a mission and an important contribution to make has gripped the young folks at school." [75]

Although the new climate stimulated all areas of student life, two objectives emerged: a larger student body, and new facilities. Batalden, who since graduation had served in a number of capacities, successfully mobilized a student campaign to build enrollment from 278 to 400. Such a goal pointed to an urgent need for more dormitory space. On January 20, 1937, *Folkebladet* printed a brief communication from Paul Winther, a retired LFC pastor, deploring the crowded situation on campus, and suggesting that a decision to construct additional facilities would be an appropriate New Year's resolution.

Sverdrup and John Houkom, who had succeeded Hammer as chairman of the board of trustees a year earlier, agreed with Winther's proposal. Since both men previously had considered initiating action with respect to building, they welcomed this recommendation by a respected church father. In planning the Augsburg Corporation's annual meeting scheduled for March 10, Sverdrup suggested that Winther present his proposal to the group. Norborg also joined the new dormitory crusade through *Messenger* articles, from pulpits throughout the constituency, and in contacts with students. "There is," Sverdrup reported to Houkom, "a great deal of enthusiasm amongst the student body . . . and that is largely due, I believe, to Dr. Norborg's inexhaustible enthusiasm." [76]

The corporation meeting rewarded these preliminaries. By a unanimous vote, the session went "on record as being in favor of the erection of a dormitory," and recommended that the board "take preparatory steps as soon as possible for the realization of this plan." These steps included drafting a proposal for presentation to the 1937 LFC conference; publicizing the dormitory project; and securing as many pledges of financial support as possible. Legally, the power to authorize and direct a building program resided in the board of trustees and the corporation; however, a decision of such magnitude reasonably required approval by the Lutheran Free Church. [77]

Augsburg spokesmen presented their case to the 1937 LFC conference. Consistent with his usual style, Sverdrup employed a restrained approach. "We are not many relatively speaking, nor are we strong," he acknowledged. "But there are many enough and we are strong enough if we are on the errand of our Lord and Master." [78] Houkom was more direct. "To anyone acquainted with conditions on the old Augsburg Block," he pointed out, "it is evident beyond contradiction that there is much to be desired. . . . no educational institution of comparable size, standing and consequence in the country has been compelled to operate with such meager equipment . . . as Augsburg." [79] The report of Thorvald Burntvedt, president of the Lutheran Free Church, whose leadership had helped establish a united fellowship, alluded to the dormitory venture without specifically recommending it. Later in the deliberations, however, Burntvedt warmly endorsed the project.

Following a full and amicable discussion, the conference approved the building program as recommended by the board of trustees. A dormitory accommodating approximately 100 men and including a kitchen, dining room, parlor, and office space for missions was to be erected "at a cost, fully equipped, not to exceed $125,000." Construction could begin when $80,000 had been gathered, and hopefully would be completed by the fall of 1938. Work on the project was to be "immediately inaugurated under the personal direction of . . . Sverdrup, aided by such outside volunteer help and advisers as he may propose to the Board of Trustees for endorsement." [80]

Sverdrup, who earlier had suggested that Norborg might be an admirable director, reluctantly accepted the responsibility. On July 13 the board of trustees approved his project design, and voted to relieve him "from as much class work . . . as may be found necessary." Thereafter, the venture evolved rapidly. By the time classes opened in September, publicity, finance, and building committees were in active operation; $25,000 had been contributed or pledged; and the projected dormitory had been named "Sverdrup-Oftedal Memorial Hall." No one could seriously doubt that the facility would be constructed, a novel reality for a school that had not added a new building in 37 years. Meanwhile, another rise in enrollment reinforced optimism with respect to Augsburg's future. Although Batalden failed to reach his goal of 400 students, an increase of 23 per cent reflected credit on his recruitment campaign.[81]

News of the president's illness a month after school opened depressed campus morale. Members of the Sverdrup family had been aware that a heart condition threatened his well-being, but he refused to curtail his schedule until he collapsed on October 26. Two days later hospitalization was required. Although he received expert medical attention, Sverdrup failed to rally, and died on November 11. He was fifty-eight years old, the same age as was attained by his father.

Sverdrup's death inflicted an understandable sense of loss on the Augsburg community. His passing was abrupt, the respect and affection he commanded was genuine, and the future of Augsburg under a non-Sverdrup seemed unreal. A few months later Anne Pederson articulated the prevailing mood: "Who among us can forget that long, gloomy day in November . . . when the halls of New Main were crowded with silence [and] the flag on Old Main continued to fly at half-mast even after the noon whistles blew?" [82]

Fortunately, the school and its leadership rallied to cope with the new situation. By late November Sverdrup's tasks had been distributed among a number of individuals. Hendrickson was appointed to serve as interim president; Joel S. Torstenson, a college senior, partially relieved Hendrickson in the academic area by teaching the Freshman offering in European history. Helland was chosen dean of the seminary and Norborg taught Sverdrup's Old Testament courses. With the help of a special assistant, Burntvedt became director of the building program. Hendrickson's report to the 1938 LFC conference indicated that these arrangements worked reasonably well. "By making some necessary adjustments," said the acting president, "we have managed to carry on without any marked break in the continuity of the work or undue loss of teaching efficiency." [83]

This performance belied the notion that Augsburg depended on the Sverdrup dynasty. It also was a tribute to George Sverdrup's enduring influence. Although the functions of his office not only had included the responsibilities attached to a college presidency, but also those usually exercised by the dean, the business manager and, to a large extent, the department chairmen, he encouraged rather than stifled the initiative of subordinates. He once remarked: "It seems that the only thing worth doing in our world is to contribute something toward the liberation of individuals. All systems degenerate . . . even at their best they tend to repress and coerce. Let us do what we can to help individual personalities develop and grow." [84] Many staff and faculty members believed that this guideline directed Sverdrup's administration. According to Christensen, "it was evident to those who worked with [Sverdrup] that even his administrative work was largely a matter of teaching. . . . If he could not win men to see the truth inherent in a given situation he had no desire to control their conduct." [85]

Such an approach to college administration could not guarantee rapid institutional growth, but to many loyal friends it embodied the vital core of Augsburg's tradition.

"THE COLONIAL PERIOD
IS...PRACTICALLY PAST"

 WHEN AUGSBURG'S LEADERS took up the problem of choosing a successor to President Sverdrup, uncertainty with respect to procedure developed. The 1902 agreement between Augsburg and the Lutheran Free Church empowered the annual conference to elect professors in both the seminary and college departments, but omitted any reference to the presidency. An investigation of precedents disclosed that the election of Oftedal in 1907, and of George Sverdrup four years later had been by the board of trustees. It appeared that final authority rested with that group.

The trustees, however, hesitated to exercise such a responsibility entirely on their own. Early in 1938 they designed a method to secure broad participation in selecting the new president. The plan established a four-stage process: an informal but secret ballot within the Augsburg Corporation; a recommendation by the board of trustees to the annual conference, conference action on this recommendation; and a final decision by the board of trustees which presumably would be a ratification of conference action. At the same time Houkom privately canvassed faculty opinion, although no committee representing the teachers was appointed. Student participation in the decision also had been ignored, but a group of collegians and seminarians led by Abner Batalden became conspicuously involved.[1]

While the board refined selection arrangements two major candidates, neither one self-proclaimed, emerged: Bernhard Christensen and Sverre Norborg. Other possibilities also were discussed, but failed to generate enthusiastic backing. As between Christensen and Norborg, the former held a clear advantage. He had been associated with Augsburg longer than Norborg, enjoyed the confidence of LFC leaders to a greater extent, and was more identifiably "American" — although fluent in the language, Norborg spoke English with a pronounced Scandinavian accent. However, Norborg's following, with the Batalden brigade operating as a vanguard, was zealous and aggressive.

An issue that promised to broaden the Norborg appeal became evident in February. For some time LFC spokesmen had been discussing the problem of how closely they should relate themselves to the American Lutheran Conference, an inter-synodical organization with which the LFC affiliated. Since Christensen was strongly committed to cooperation, the question of where the other man stood had a possible bearing on the presidency. A series of Norborg articles carried by *The Lutheran Messenger* in January and February appeared to define his position. While not dogmatically opposed to inter-Lutheran cooperation, these articles were distinctly "anti-merger" in tone. Such statements as, "May the Lutheran Free Church never bow to any *Lutheran Imperialism, which wants to force unification upon Lutheran groups*," were more reassuring to uncompromising separatists within the fellowship than to those who wanted closer ties with the American Lutheran Conference.[2]

Comments in the *Messenger*, most of them written by Melby who, in addition to other responsibilities was editing the paper, pointed up the relevance of Norborg's position to the presidential question without explicitly advocating his election. On February 15 the lead editorial argued for maintenance of a strengthened LFC, and rejection of "the Road of Compromise" that would terminate "in the City of Duplication. . . ." According to the *Messenger*, this road was sometimes misnamed "the Way of Christian Fellowship and Love." Melby then shifted to the central concern of the moment: "Our choice of paths as a Church may be made when we select a new president. . . . It came as a severe shock to this writer that he does not know the real convictions of most of the nine men who have been suggested to him as successors of Dr. Sverdrup. . . ." This complaint evidently did not apply to Norborg, since he had made his position clear.

Although Melby's editorial disturbed the trustees, it failed to alter their planned course with respect to the presidency. A meeting of the Augsburg Corporation held on March 9 approved the selection procedure formulated by the board. As specified by this procedure the corporation members then participated in an informal preference poll. Of the 19 votes cast Christensen received eight, Burntvedt four, Pastor Clarence Carlsen four, Norborg two, and Hendrickson one. Following disclosure of these results to the board, the trustees unanimously adopted a resolution nominating Christensen for endorsement by the annual conference.[3]

The board decided against immediate announcement of its action and, so far as can be determined, the outcome of the corporation poll was never made public. Two considerations, one openly avowed and the other shared privately among LFC leaders, dictated silence on the board's decision. Houkom succinctly defined the latter in writing to Burntvedt: "It would not be at all desirable to give snipers too much time to start their work." [4] The other reason for delay was more compelling: if Christensen declined the board's nomination, announcement of it would prejudice the search for another candidate.[5]

Christensen hesitated before accepting, a stance reinforced by the problem of Norborg's future role at the school.[6] The same board meeting that nominated Christensen instructed Houkom and Burntvedt to "contact . . . Norborg with respect to retaining his services at Augsburg. . . ." In response to a communication from Houkom conveying the board's wish that he remain on the faculty, Norborg professed dissatisfaction with the turn of events since Sverdrup's death. "If the future belongs to the co-operation ideology," he wrote, "then Augsburg has lost *meaning* to me . . . the last few days it has dawned upon me that my service is not *vital* but merely technical. . . ." He acknowledged that such an evaluation might be erroneous, but if experience confirmed it, he would "bow before the majority and yet feel *free* to remain a Lutheran in strictly *theological* terms, apart from Augsburg." [7]

Although the reasons for Norborg's pique mystified LFC leaders — it was not clear whether he knew that the board had endorsed Christensen — the effort to retain him as a theological professor continued.[8] Meanwhile, pressures on the board of trustees to announce its presidential candidate — or candidates — began mounting. On April 13 *Folkebladet* commented that it would be unfortunate if the board nominees were simply "dumped" on the annual conference with no prior opportunity to discuss their qualifications. A southern Minnesota clergyman wondered "why . . . we pastors out in the field must wait for information until we meet with some one from Minneapolis who might be willing to tell us something about the subject, as discussed by those who might have the responsibility for filling the vacancy." [9]

In mid-May, less than a month before the annual conference, Houkom released a statement dated April 30 announcing the board's action and Christensen's affirmative response. "Quite contrary to appearances," the statement explained, "there has been no disposition to withhold this announcement unduly. Dr. Christensen . . . requested time to consider whether or not to consent to the use of his name as a candidate. . . . The Board indicated its desire to have his reply . . . by May 1. . . . This consent . . . has now been given by Dr. Christensen." [10]

This explanation quieted argument over the board's delay in publicizing its decision, but two potentially explosive issues remained. Should the trustees have submitted more than one candidate's name to the annual conference? And where did Christensen stand on such questions as the future of the LFC and its relationship to the American Lutheran Conference? Christensen declined specific commitment when asked for a clear statement on the second issue. His position was editorially defended by *Folkebladet*.[11]

A mood of excitement pervaded Thief River Falls, Minnesota, as the LFC gathered there on June 7 for its 1938 conference. Endorsement of Christensen appeared probable, but the Norborg camp's youthful wing worked zealously to secure support for their man. Along with other recommendations by the board of trustees, the Christensen nomination was referred to Committee No. 2. K. Berner Dahlen, who served as secretary of this committee, recalls agitation by Norborg spokesmen on behalf of a minority report calling for two presidential nominations, rather than one. Although such a course seemed reasonable to Dahlen and some of his colleagues, the committee approved the single nomination presented by the board of trustees.[12]

Following presentation of the Committee No. 2 report on the afternoon of Friday, June 10 conference proceedings moved toward a climax. The visible activism of Norborg's backers, both on the floor and in the gallery, heightened tension. So did a suspicion, shared by some Christensen supporters, that the conference was being called upon "to sign on the dotted line," rather than to participate in the selection of Augsburg's president. The situation taxed Burntvedt's skill as a presiding officer. On one occasion he reminded a group of students who were chanting "We want Norborg," that church conferences and athletic events did not operate under identical rules.[13]

Meanwhile, a complex parliamentary situation was unfolding. With Christensen's nomination the order of business, Pastor John Quanbeck presented a substitute motion proposing that "Prof. H. N. Hendrickson be retained as acting president for one year and Dr. B. M. Christensen be made dean of the college department and Dr. Sverre Norborg, dean of the theological department." Before discussion began, the conference secretary read a letter from Norborg stating that he would "refuse nomination to the office of president of Augsburg Seminary." The substitute motion was then debated, with eleven speakers participating — six for, and five against. Further deliberation on the Quanbeck proposal was interrupted at this point when the conference resolved to consider Norborg's nomination as theological professor. The assembly endorsed this nomination — which Norborg ultimately declined — whereupon discussion of the substitute resolution resumed and continued until a motion to table it prevailed by a vote of 146 to 79.

The Christensen nomination was again before the house. After five speakers had presented their views a motion to delay the election of a president for one year was tabled by a vote of 138 to 57. By this time tempers were frayed, and many delegates had left the church auditorium. Those who remained agreed to recess briefly for "the singing of a hymn and a season of prayer for the guidance of God's spirit in this important matter," then proceeded to ballot on the Christensen nomination. Of the 300 votes counted, 214 favored, and 70 opposed the nomination, 13 were marked "not voting," and 3 were cast for Norborg.[14] On Monday, June 13 the board of trustees completed the selection process by formally electing Christensen president.[15]

Shortly after his election Christensen commented: "The vote recorded at the Annual Conference did not reveal the unanimity of judgment which would seem to have been essential in so important a decision." [16] The point was well taken. If the more than 100 delegates who failed to cast ballots are added to the 86 who registered displeasure with the nomination, Christensen's majority was not particularly impressive. On the other hand objection to the selection method, rather than the candidate, placed many delegates in opposition. A few confirmed LFC separatists may have disliked Christensen's ecumenism but, on the whole, he commanded unreserved admiration and respect both within the constituency and the Augsburg community.

AN AUSPICIOUS BEGINNING soon established full confidence in Augsburg's new administration, healing whatever wounds may have been opened at the 1938 conference. September brought another substantial rise in enrollment — from 367 to 413. On October 28 an inaugural ceremony installed Christensen as president, the first occasion of its kind in Augsburg's history.[17] When the new year began Memorial Hall was ready for occupancy. Its curious interior arrangement failed to win the admiration of later generations but students, accustomed to North Hall's austerity and the dilapidated dining hall on the third floor of Old Main, regarded the move into the new building as a step toward luxury. The financial reports also disclosed that Memorial Hall had not undermined Augsburg's solvency, nor even significantly delayed debt retirement. Before long the possibility of additional construction was being discussed.[18]

During this time Christensen publicly advocated continuity with the past, rather than any pronounced departure from tradition. His report to the 1939 LFC conference defined "some of the goals" that he believed appropriate for the school as it moved forward. Augsburg, he said, should "provide full opportunity to the Spirit of God to do His creative and quickening work among members of the student body." It should "maintain and deepen . . . devotion to the . . . 'free and living congregation' " and "cultivate even more intimate relations with the congregations and people of our Church." Academic standards needed to be elevated through a "gradual enrichment of the curriculum and . . . building up of the Faculty. . . ." The administration was obliged "To build ever greater efficiency and deeper confidence in the business management of the institution. . . ." Finally, Christensen proposed to emphasize "Christian service as a definite part of Augsburg's program," adding that "A Christian school is more than an educational institution. It is a creative center of life and activity." [19]

As Christensen acknowledged, these goals were "by no means new. . . ." Nor did they fully interpret Augsburg's changing role as an educational institution. By 1939 the college had become considerably more than a branch of LFC activity. Lutheranism remained the denominational preference on campus, but as enrollment increased, the proportion of students from LFC congregations declined. This unplanned trend was due to the Minneapolis location, a comparatively low tuition rate, an efficient student employment service, and Christensen's prominence as a churchman and educator.

Such an extension was consistent with the new president's ecumenical outlook. Shortly before assuming office he commented: "It may well be true — I believe it is — that Augsburg's life will have to be lived in a larger arena than was the case a generation ago." [20] Nevertheless, the situation created a dilemma. How could Christensen and other Augsburg spokesmen encourage closer rapport between the school and "our" congregations when a dwindling proportion of students affiliated with the LFC? "While it is a cause for gratitude that Augsburg is able to serve a widening circle of Lutheran young people," he informed the LFC conference of 1940, "the large number of students from other synods may also tend to create a problem. . . ." [21] Subsequent paragraphs of Christensen's report analyzed the nature of this problem:

. . . if Augsburg is to fulfill its God-given calling, there must be a conscious return to an aim that was much emphasized in the early history of the school: that Augsburg was built to serve the Congregation. . . . In the struggle to meet . . . rising educational standards . . . it has not been easy always to relate the total program of the school to the conscious service of the Congregations as the living center of church life. Not that Augsburg has ever for one moment been unclear as to her calling to build Christian character and foster Christian thinking. But a strong re-emphasis upon these goals as subsidiary to the building of *the congregation* would, I believe, be salutary at the present time. . . . It is true that the congregations to which . . . graduates . . . now go forth will very often not be congregations affiliated with the Lutheran Free Church. Nevertheless the principle so often enunciated when Augsburg was almost exclusively a school of theology still holds true.

. . . the fact that many of our college students now come from Lutheran groups other than our own . . . while it has helped to swell . . . enrollment and has increased our income from tuition fees . . . also involved certain problems of educational adjustment if we are effectively to carry out the basic aims of our school . . . we do not believe . . . that the solution lies in discouraging students from other church groups from coming to Augsburg. . . . We need, however, if we are to serve the highest interests of our Church, to put forth a more definite . . . effort to secure a larger representation of young people from the congregations throughout our own Lutheran Free Church.[22]

While these observations were more than a nostalgic gesture to the past, they did not foreshadow a reversal, or even a slowing, of the trend in question. For the next 20 years Augsburg Seminary remained a virile if small branch of the school, and relations with the LFC continued amicably. However, neither of these realities impeded the college's development as a liberal arts institution serving a much broader community than the LFC. At the same time Christensen's rhetoric continued to reflect tension between fidelity to traditional goals and acceptance of an expanded role for the college with emphasis moving to the latter as one year succeeded another.

In reporting to the 1940 conference, Houkom and Christensen called attention to another pattern of change: a shift in the base of financial support. Due to higher enrollment, a slight tuition increase, and a concentration of LFC resources on the effort to pay for Memorial Hall, the proportion of operating income provided by the congregations was rapidly shrinking. In 1935 contributions had accounted for 55.29 per cent of total receipts, and tuition, 41.88 per cent. By 1940 contributions furnished only 29.95 per cent; tuition increased to 63.61 per cent. After calling attention to these statistics, Houkom raised several questions: "Are the congregations retiring more and more from their responsibilities . . . compelling Augsburg increasingly to depend on . . . tuition and fees for its living? Is the Lutheran Free Church forcing Augsburg gradually to seek to become independent of the Churches?"[23] Christensen also expressed concern. He said: "The work is bound to suffer if there is too great a disparity between the amounts received through tuition and the amounts received from other sources."[24] These exhortations failed to restore the desired balance. During the next 25 years the percentage of total income derived from church contributions steadily declined, falling to less than ten per cent in the 1960s. And, since other sources of support were difficult to cultivate, the administration had no recourse but to raise tuition.

Although Christensen placed a high value on the concept that Augsburg operated like an intimate family, he soon discovered that the informal administrative style of his predecessor was rapidly becoming obsolete. The call for a more systematic management of financial resources in his 1939 report has been noted. A year later Pastor Olaf Rogne was appointed business manager, a responsibility that included fund raising as well as general supervision of the plant and finances. The administration moved to fill other gaps in the institution's structure. It discovered, for example, that Arthur Nash, George Soberg, and Henry Opseth had served on the faculty for nearly 20 years without ever having been formally endorsed by a church conference, as the selection procedures then in force required. In response to a recommendation by Christensen the 1940 conference ratified the three appointments along with that of Martin Quanback, who had joined the faculty in 1938.[25]

With the approval of the LFC conference of 1942, the board of trustees took another step that might have been regarded as overdue: it officially proclaimed the demise of Augsburg as an integrated divinity school by revising the Articles of Incorporation. As formulated by Sven Oftedal 50 years earlier, Article 1 read: "The name of this corporation shall be Augsburg Seminary. The general purpose . . . shall be the training of young men in the ministry of the Lutheran Church . . . by . . . maintaining a theological seminary at Minneapolis, which shall include a preparatory school substantially as heretofore maintained."

The 1942 revision officially changed the institution's name to "Augsburg College and Theological Seminary," although the designation had been applied informally for more than 20 years. In redefining "general purpose," it employed the following language: "to educate and train young men for the ministry of the Lutheran Church by maintaining a theological seminary together with a preparatory college of liberal arts, which shall also have as its aim to offer both young men and women an education in general Christian culture as well as a training for Christian service in lay vocations."[26] The same corporation, board of trustees, and administration governed both branches of the school, but instead of being theoretically "within" Augsburg Seminary, the college was to operate "together with" the theological seminary, a change that formally invested Augsburg College with a separate identity.

Meanwhile, a more elaborate administrative structure slowly emerged. In January, 1941 Christensen believed the time had come to consider providing the college with a dean, a conviction fortified by the availability of Martin Quanbeck, a suitable candidate.[27] As registrar, chairman of the Education department, and director of teacher placement, Quanbeck already was involved in school administration, and he previously had gained experience in this area. Following graduation from the college in 1929 he had served as high school principal and later superintendent of schools at Mantorville, Minnesota, and on the faculty of Waldorf College, Forest City, Iowa. His professional training included graduate work in educational administration at the University of Minnesota, where he received his M.A. degree in 1933. He continued to study at Minnesota after his appointment to Augsburg, completing the requirements for his Ph.D. in 1952.

Although Quanbeck became dean in 1942–43, the potentialities of the new post did not develop immediately. The ancient tradition vesting Augsburg's president with authority in all areas of campus activity had a life of its own. Furthermore, Quanbeck's other roles restricted the time and energy available for the deanship. Nor was his tenure in the office continuous. Since supervision of the Education program was a demanding responsibility, he surrendered the post to Arthur Nash in 1946. Nash served until 1950, whereupon Quanbeck again was appointed dean.

Curriculum and faculty changes during the Christensen administration's first four years were relatively modest, conforming to the policy of gradualism announced by Christensen in 1939. Existing departments added a limited number of courses, but no new majors were established. A few of the new offerings foreshadowed later programs, notably the one in drama, taught for the first time in 1940–41, and three courses in home economics added the same year.

Consistent with the curricular pattern, most of the key faculty members of the Sverdrup era — Sveeggen, Hendrickson, Nash, Soberg, Ermisch, Melby, and Miss Mortensen — retained positions of influence. At the same time resignation, retirement, and death effected a few changes. James Pederson, director of athletics and physical education, was succeeded in 1938 by Richard Pautz, a graduate of the previous year who, as a student, had helped supervise the intramural athletic program. Agnes B. Tangjerd replaced Miss Storien as librarian in 1940. In the same year Andreas Helland retired, leaving the Norwegian department under the direction of Miss Marie Kjelaas, who had taught the beginning courses in Norse for a number of years. Carl Fosse died in April, 1942; his successor, Dr. Lawrence M. Jones, served until 1944 and again in 1946–47.

A number of new teachers, some of whom would serve for many years, also joined the faculty in the 1938–42 period. Norman C. Anderson, who had taught part-time in the early 1930s, returned in 1939 as student personnel director and instructor of journalism and religion. Joel Torstenson accepted a part-time assignment as instructor of history and social science in 1938, a position that became full-time two years later when Torstenson received his M.A. degree. In 1940 Leland Sateren assumed directorship of the band, and Philip Kildahl was appointed to teach courses in philosophy and history. A year later K. Berner Dahlen replaced Melby as Dean of Men, and also taught speech. Dr. Melvin A. Helland, son of Andreas, took up his duties as theological professor and member of the college religion faculty in 1941.

Like the academic realm, most facets of Augsburg life were marked by more continuity than change during the early Christensen years. A modest economic recovery was gradually banishing the austerity of depression, but most students were obliged to continue supporting themselves. Although completion of Memorial Hall expanded dormitory facilities, an upward enrollment trend (450 in 1939–40, 477 the following year) kept the campus overcrowded. For women, the situation was especially deplorable: Morton and West Hall were grossly inadequate and rapidly deteriorating.

Acquisition of the Sivertsen Clinic building partially alleviated the pressure. In the autumn of 1939 Dr. Ivar Sivertsen offered this property to Augsburg on condition that the school assume responsibility for an unpaid mortgage balance of $12,500. Since the building and the lot on which it stood originally had cost $72,000, and the expense of transforming the structure into a women's dormitory was estimated at a mere $10,000, the board of trustees gratefully accepted the gift. By September, 1940 Sivertsen Hall, equipped to house 39 women, was ready for occupancy.[28]

Inadequate facilities also continued to handicap sports. As in the past, every major activity took place off campus — football on the South High School field, basketball in the Minneapolis Armory, and baseball on a diamond owned by the Veterans' Hospital. Nevertheless, the athletic program expanded without establishing a spectacular record on the scoreboards. In 1939 the school resumed intercollegiate football, re-entered tennis competition after a lapse of several years, and introduced swimming as part of the physical education curriculum. Dan Elmer coached football in 1939; his successor, Robert C. Carlson, remained until entering military service in 1942. Carl Swanson, the basketball coach, joined the armed forces a year later.

The outbreak of World War II in September, 1939 fortified a student preoccupation with public affairs that had been growing for several years. An active International Relations Club sponsored frequent discussion sessions on world problems, sometimes with the assistance of an outside speaker, and convocation programs often featured lectures on topics related to the international crisis. The *Echo*, too, devoted more space to contemporary problems than in previous years.

In the early stages of World War II, Augsburg opinion apparently was even more neutralist and anti-war than the national average, student or adult. A poll taken by Student Surveys of America in October, 1939 revealed that four out of ten American college men felt disposed to volunteer for military service "If England and France were in danger of defeat and the United States declared war on their enemies. . . ." On this question, "Augsburg men voted unanimously No." Augsburg students also overwhelmingly opposed amending the Neutrality law so "that any country at war could buy supplies in the United States." [29]

German occupation of Denmark and Norway in April, 1940 brought the war closer to Augsburg without altering the college community's essentially neutralist position. An appearance on campus by a Norwegian-American spokesman who, while pleading for contributions to Norwegian relief called for a revival of ancient Viking militance and immediate American intervention in the war, aroused no visible enthusiasm. Norwegian relief, it was felt, deserved support, but entry of the United States into the conflict was another matter. [30] In May, 1940 students passed a resolution "individually and collectively" pledging "support to the maintenance of peace and freedom in our land and as far as possible in other lands, according to the ideals of our Christian faith." The same resolution authorized the student society president "to appoint ten or twenty men . . . to lead a movement for peace and promotion of humanitarian purposes in their respective communities." [31]

To what extent, if any, the student body president acted on this authorization is not clear. It is apparent, however, that the resolution reflected the influence of a student-faculty group whose spokesmen, notably Torstenson and Sateren, affiliated with a Twin City Lutheran chapter of the Fellowship of Reconciliation. Not all members of this circle were convinced pacifists, nor did they fully agree with one another on specific questions, but issues such as the morality of war and the degree to which American involvement abroad impeded the achievement of justice at home troubled all of them. These and related problems were explored in a number of campus settings, particularly Torstenson's classes, where animated discussions frequently developed.[32]

Although neither a member of FOR nor a declared pacifist, Christensen, too, worried about the militarization of American society, a concern that sustained sympathetic understanding between him and the Torstenson group. Even after the Japanese attack on Pearl Harbor, he declined to capitulate fully to the wartime spirit. "Already the signs of a rising tide of bitterness and hatred are clearly discernible in our country," he informed the LFC conference of 1942, adding:

We are called upon to fight and die for our country and for human ideals of justice and freedom. But if we are also summoned to assume attitudes of hatred and vengeance and inhumanity such as have long been openly inculcated among many of our enemies, then we must have courage to disobey men rather than God. Our institutions of Christian education must be willing to make every temporal and material sacrifice on behalf of our nation, but they must never become the instruments of un-Christian or anti-Christian attitude and propaganda.[33]

THE IMPACT OF World War II on campus life, which had been felt increasingly since enactment of the Selective Service act in September, 1940 was greatly intensified when the United States entered the conflict on December 7, 1941. College men subject to the draft wondered about the wisdom of immediate enlistment, and the possibility of a sudden decimation of the student body troubled the administration.[34] Enrollment statistics of 1941–42 registered a decline of 65 students from the previous year, a total that failed to indicate the number actually in school at the close of the second semester. More precipitous drops followed: 225 students did not return in 1943–44. A slight increase the following year was attributable to more women students.

The faculty also diminished. Nash, Dahlen, Kildahl, Jones, and Pautz joined the armed forces. As a conscientious objector, Sateren was assigned non-combatant duty. Several teachers temporarily accepted appointments elsewhere, or entered other lines of work. Torstenson left in 1943 to engage in farming, and later became involved in rural cooperative organization. Miss Pederson filled a high school position in 1945–46. Melby died unexpectedly in January, 1944 following a brief illness; John Stensvaag, who had taught in the seminary since 1942, succeeded him as chairman of the college religion department. In addition to Stensvaag, a number of other new teachers began their Augsburg ca-

195

reers during the war: Erling Urdahl, biology, in 1943; Alma Jensen, sociology, the same year; and Ruth Segolson, home economics, in 1944.

A smaller student body and reduced faculty precluded maintenance of a full program. As Christensen informed the LFC conference of 1943, "The courses offered have been limited for the coming year to what would seem to be a minimum if we are to continue functioning as a college." [35] Fortunately, financial repercussions were not as serious as the administration feared. Rental of Memorial Hall to house a military unit training at the University of Minnesota in 1943–44 partially compensated for loss of tuition income. More important, wartime prosperity made it possible for LFC congregations to carry a larger share of Augsburg's operating budget. In addition to averting deficits the school actually liquidated its outstanding debt in 1944, an achievement that led Houkom to comment: "Augsburg's fiscal situation was never more favorable than it is just at the present moment. . . ." [36]

Comparative prosperity encouraged post-war expansion discussion, as did a number of other circumstances. By the 1940s distrust of American higher education within the constituency was giving way to unqualified endorsement of Augsburg's aspiration to become a first-rate liberal arts college. In 1941 the LFC created a committee on educational policies. Its report, submitted to the conference of 1943, was very different in tone from the one submitted by the LFC board of education in 1923. Rather than belaboring the loss of Augsburg's original divinity school purity, the 1943 document lauded the institution for having "adjusted its plans and expanded its work to meet the demand and need of young people for college education." The report also implied that the school's mission transcended the LFC: "Augsburg . . . is the only Lutheran college in the Twin Cities . . . we should improve this opportunity and build up our college as a fully recognized Lutheran institution." Its most important recommendation called upon the trustees to "make every effort to secure accreditation of the College by the North Central Association." [37]

This action undoubtedly strengthened the administration's ability to face the increasing opportunities with more enthusiasm than it had in 1940. Christensen informed the LFC conference of 1944, "that now, during the time when our enrollment is reduced, the Faculty . . . is making special studies looking toward the enrichment and adjustment of the curricular offerings to meet the needs of the post-war period." He then proceeded to define the assumptions that were guiding administration and faculty thinking:

We believe that there is a great door . . . opened for a school like Augsburg, located as it is in a leading center of Midwestern Lutheranism. It is a door of service, too, that leads far beyond the circle of the young people in our own Lutheran Free Church. A large proportion of the students in our College has . . . for a number of years been from other Lutheran Church bodies. We do not regret this development whereby our field of service has been so greatly broadened, but that opportunity brings with it also a corresponding responsibility which we must prepare adequately to meet. These are times of transition, both in our country as a whole and in the Lutheran Church here. As the work of Augsburg is carried forward it will have to be increasingly related to this more inclusive setting. The colonial period of our existence is practically past. We must try to carry on true to our spirit and heritage in the larger environment into which we are being gradually led.[38]

Such a vision of the future necessitated plant expansion. In October, 1942 the trustees had appointed a Preliminary Building Plan Committee to study the next major step in Augsburg's building program. Together with the board of trustees, officials of the Alumni Association, and another committee set up to organize an appropriate commemoration of Augsburg's seventy-fifth year, the preliminary plan committee developed a proposal calling for "erection of a combined Library and Classroom building," and tying fund raising for this project to celebration of the school's diamond anniversary. Houkom presented the corporation resolution to the 1944 LFC conference together with an argument for its adoption.[39] After some discussion focusing chiefly on a reconciliation of Augsburg and Oak Grove claims, the assembly authorized a campaign to raise $200,000 for Augsburg's building, and $50,000 for a facility at the other school. This drive was soon set in motion under the direction of Rogne and Norman Anderson.[40]

Meanwhile, investigation of curriculum and other aspects of Augsburg's operation continued. In the spring of 1945 the faculty and board commissioned M. G. Neale, professor of Educational Administration at the University of Minnesota, to determine what innovations were essential for winning accreditation by the North Central Association. Neale submitted his report on July 5, 1945. Although his findings thoroughly endorsed Augsburg's goals and lauded several aspects of its program, the report as a whole was sobering. According to Neale:

. . . four critical areas [exist] where conditions at Augsburg College stand most in the way of approval of the Institution as a standard four year college. . . . The first . . . is in connection with conditions of faculty service [salary, tenure, retirement, and appointment], the second

197

on practically all items relating to the library, the third relating to a centralized and more effective business and financial administration, and the fourth in connection with . . . physical facilities. . . .[41]

To some extent Augsburg already was moving toward correction of these deficiencies. The building program marked a significant forward step. Several reforms in the school's administrative structure and practice also were in process prior to submission of the report, and others were soon initiated. The LFC conference of 1945 had given preliminary approval to a resolution abolishing the board of school directors, a change ratified by the next conference. In 1945–46 the board and administration substantially increased the library budget, formulated plans to build an addition to Sivertsen Hall, and appointed a "Future Campus Committee" to undertake a comprehensive study of physical facilities, including investigation of relocation in Augsburg Park.[42]

EARLY IN 1946 the effort to win accreditation became entangled with the challenge posed by expanding post-war enrollment. Initially the 1945–46 student body numbered 244; during the second semester that figure rose to 464. The next year marked a spectacular increase to 794, a total that included 399 demobilized veterans. Another substantial increase in 1947–48 raised college enrollment to 893; two years later it reached a high of 966.

Accommodating a student body of nearly 1,000 on a campus geared to less than half that number required several emergency measures. Memorial Hall was crowded to twice its normal capacity, and a section of Old Main was reserved for women's housing, "a most unsatisfactory arrangement," according to Christensen.[43] To ameliorate the classroom problem the administration rented space in Riverside Chapel, located about three blocks from campus. In addition it secured two barracks and a large military recreation hall from the War Surplus Administration. The latter, which was rebuilt on the future site of Melby Hall, served as Augsburg's physical education center for more than a decade, thereby permitting appropriation of the gymnasium area in the Main building for classrooms and temporary enlargement of the library. The board of trustees purchased a number of residences in the neighborhood that were adaptable to student and faculty housing. The former Tabernacle Baptist Church was converted into Augsburg's music building. Expansion beyond the original campus, a process that had begun with the acquisition of Sivertsen Hall, was advancing rapidly.

The influx of students dictated faculty as well as plant expansion. Nash, Dahlen, Kildahl, Jones, Sateren, Pautz, and Miss Pederson returned in 1946, and Torstenson a year later. The administration also employed many new instructors, some of whom achieved permanent tenure. Iver B. Olson became professor of Norwegian in the college, and of systematic theology in the seminary in 1945. Several appointments were made the next year: Ernest Anderson, director of physical education and basketball coach; Edor C. Nelson, football coach and physical education instructor; and Gerald Thorson, future chairman of the English department. In 1947 John and Vera Thut joined the music faculty, Bryce Shoemaker began teaching religion and philosophy, Mrs. Mimi Kingsley, Spanish, Bjarne E. Landa, Germanic languages, Stanley J. Remenski, chemistry, and Merton P. Strommen, religion. J. Vernon Jensen, history, and Manivald Aldre, chemistry, came in 1948; a year later, Raymond E. Anderson in speech, Paul G. Sonnack in religion, and John R. Milton in English accepted their appointments. Miss Mildred V. Joel became registrar in 1947, and Henry Bertness was made instructor in the Education department in 1950. The last two appointments released Martin Quanbeck for service as college dean on a full-time basis. Gertrude S. Lund assumed direction of the business education program in 1950.

While an overworked faculty and harassed administration struggled with problems created by an excess of students, long range development moved forward at an uncertain pace. Modest curricular expansion was accomplished during the 1946–50 period. Under the chairmanship of Howard M. Winholz a department of business administration, economics, and secretarial studies was established in 1946. A year later Torstenson began building a separate sociology department; political science, hitherto united with sociology and economics in the social science department, was combined with history in a joint department. The appointment of Raymond Anderson presaged a more complete speech and drama program, although a speech major was not offered until 1953. By 1949 enough home economics courses had been introduced to offer both a teaching and non-teaching major in that field. Meanwhile, the established departments were broadening their programs; history, for example, offered twice as many senior college courses in 1950 as ten years earlier.

To promote more curricular unity the faculty in 1947 reorganized itself along divisional lines. Previously the catalog had classified course offerings according to fields, but the departments had functioned as autonomous units under the detailed supervision of the president and, to a smaller extent, the dean. The new plan grouped all departments within three divisions—humanities, social science, and natural science—each operating under a chairman appointed by the president. Religion and philosophy were constituted as a separate division two years later, raising the total to four.[44] Despite this change the divisions failed to become significant units within Augsburg's academic structure. On the whole individual departments exerted more influence on the shaping of school policy, and their importance varied depending on the chairman's leadership.

The Neale recommendations relating to "conditions of faculty service" commanded immediate attention from the board and administration. Since 1902 permanent members of the college faculty had been elected by annual LFC conferences after being nominated by the general faculty and board of school directors. In accordance with a suggestion in the Neale report and an administration request, the LFC conference of 1946 surrendered this prerogative to the board of trustees, retaining, however, the authority to ratify appointment of seminary professors.[45]

On May 7, 1946, the trustees adopted the first retirement plan in Augsburg's history; it set the retirement age of faculty and staff at 68, and provided a modest schedule of benefits.[46] In 1947 the faculty recommended, and the board approved, a faculty ranking system. Traditional practice had divided the teaching force into so-called permanent professors and temporary instructors, but personnel in both categories had served under annual contracts with the former enjoying no formal protection. The new system established the conventional four-way classification of faculty members—instructors, assistant professors, associate professors, professors—and granted tenure following a probationary period of five years to teachers in the three upper ranks.[47]

Improving relations with the Minneapolis community was another goal of Augsburg's development program. In 1946 the administration appointed Pautz director of public relations, a new post within the institution's organizational structure. A few months later the board commissioned Elmer U. Berdahl, a former official of the Minneapolis Civic and Commerce Association, to conduct a fund-raising campaign among local firms and corporations—the first effort of its kind since Oftedal's attempt to enlist community support on behalf of New Main in 1901. Christensen's service on Mayor Hubert H. Humphrey's Council on Human Relations, created in 1946 to work against racial and religious discrimination in all areas of Minneapolis life, forged an indirect link between the college and community. As chairman of the council from 1948 to 1950, and an active member for two years thereafter, Christensen contributed substantially to its success in combating the more serious forms of discrimination, and in sensitizing public opinion to the civil rights issue.[48]

Unfortunately, Berdahl's campaign failed to produce "appreciable financial results"; by 1949 it had secured "two $5,000 gifts and a number of lesser" contributions. In discussing the outcome Clarence Carlsen, chairman of the board of trustees, refrained from blaming either the campaign manager or Minneapolis businessmen. "Our institution," Carlsen pointed out, "has made its own way modestly . . . and has not publicized itself a great deal. . . . It will take time to integrate ourselves more effectively with the Minneapolis community. . . . It will be remembered that Augsburg functioned for many decades as a Norwegian-American institution and . . . did not have much contact with . . . Minneapolis at large." [49]

Failure of the Minneapolis campaign further compromised building plans already disrupted by post-war inflation. The $250,000 fund drive launched in 1944 soon reached its original goal; by 1946 Rogne and Anderson had raised more than $260,000. However, a steep rise in costs forced a drastic revision of all construction estimates. As Houkom remarked in 1947, "it becomes ominously evident that a great deal of money will be needed in addition to what has been so generously given by our people recently." [50] Nevertheless, even with sufficient funds immediate construction would have been impossible, due to a shortage of building materials that persisted for many months after the war.

While the board and administration struggled with these problems the Augsburg Park project enjoyed a brief revival. With the backing of several faculty members Martin Quanbeck, who served on the Campus Plans Committee, developed an argument for relocation. According to his reasoning, the Richfield site was physically more desirable than the old location, and ultimately would be less costly since it did not involve expensive land acquisition—the college already owned, free from encumbrance, a plot eminently suited for campus use. Quanbeck's case attracted considerable support, particularly within the Augsburg faculty, but a board meeting held on July 18, 1946, unanimously committed the trustees "to a definite long-range program of campus expansion in [Augsburg's] present vicinity." [51]

After dealing the Augsburg Park dream a final blow, the board proceeded to adjust campus expansion to limits that appeared realistic and responsible. With the approbation of the LFC conference of 1947 it postponed indefinitely the planned addition to Sivertsen Hall, leaving the problem of housing for women unresolved. A year later it voted to defer building the library wing of the projected science-library facility in favor of a structure with space for science classrooms and administrative offices. After razing West Hall and Old Main's west wing to clear the site, construction began in the summer of 1948. Following dismissal of classes in June, 1949 the remainder of Old Main was demolished and the new building completed. Counting furnishing and fixtures it cost $575,000, leaving the school with a debt of approximately $100,000.[52]

Convinced that Science Hall would augment Augsburg's chances for accreditation, the administration in the autumn of 1949 decided to make a bid for North Central Association recognition. Early prospects appeared favorable. The institution survived scrutiny by NCA officials of its written application, an achievement opening the way for inspection of the school by a team of examiners who visited the school on January 16–17, 1950. Nine weeks later NCA voted against granting accreditation. In explaining this decision an association official called "particular attention to the need for improvement in faculty competence and conditions of service . . . the program of advanced education . . . library . . . certain phases of personnel services . . . business administration . . . financial support and . . . physical facilities." [53]

The Augsburg community responded to this blow with a creditable resilience. "While we are intensely disappointed," Christensen informed the 1950 LFC conference, "possibly the silver lining . . . is that we shall be challenged to move ahead more rapidly with . . . further steps of improvement than we otherwise might have done." [54] The question was not if, but when accreditation would be won.

THE OUTBREAK OF the war in Korea on June 25, 1950, created new problems for Augsburg as it did for all struggling private liberal arts colleges. A sharp decline in enrollment, due primarily to a waning of the post-World War II surge, seriously curtailed tuition income; in 1950–51 Augsburg's student body numbered 877 compared to 966 the previous year. At the same time price inflation, one of the war's accompaniments, increased pressures for higher faculty salaries, and raised the price of all goods and services needed to sustain a college. Surmounting this crisis while working to achieve accreditation — with its subsequent expense — required high educational statesmanship.

The financial reports for 1950–51 were nearly as discouraging as those issued during the Great Depression. "After many years of operating with a fairly well balanced budget," board chairman Carlsen reported, "we come to the Annual Conference this year [1951] with a deficit." [55] To restore balance the administration adopted several measures. It raised tutition from $150 to $165 per semester, reduced the teaching force by 18 per cent, and requested the Lutheran Free Church to contribute $80,000 to Augsburg's operating budget, an increase of $25,000 over the previous year.[56]

Although the congregations substantially met this quota, a further decline in enrollment, and a board decision to raise staff and faculty salaries contributed to another budgetary deficit in 1951–52. Augsburg's leadership again increased tuition, this time to $180 per semester, and requested $90,000 from the church. Unfortunately, the following year produced another unbalanced budget, chiefly because the LFC failed to meet its $90,000 quota. In 1954 the administration raised tuition to $200 per semester, and asked the church for $110,000. It also hopefully canvassed another possible source of support. Creation in 1951 of the Minnesota College Fund Association, an organization seeking corporate assistance for private institutions of higher learning in the state, provided token help: Augsburg's share in 1952 and 1953 accounted for about one per cent of its total current income, approximately the same amount as yielded by the school's small endowment fund.[57]

Notwithstanding a discouraging financial situation, the administration pushed the development program and accreditation effort forward. In response to a board recommendation the LFC conference of 1952 authorized a $400,000 campaign to liquidate the debt on Science Hall, and to finance construction of the library wing. After gaining conference approval the board initiated a two-stage drive: a preliminary phase under the leadership of Gilbert Berg, a Seattle businessman, and Sigvald V. Hjelmeland; and the campaign proper, directed by Pastor Clifford M. Johnson. By 1954 the Berg-Hjelmeland-Johnson team had raised more than $220,000, a sufficient sum to commence construction of the George Sverdrup Library.[58]

Meanwhile, the administration was endeavoring to remove deficiencies in Augsburg's internal structure standing in the way of accreditation. Assumption of the college deanship by Martin Quanbeck contributed substantially to this undertaking. Quanbeck's professional competence, capacity for work, careful attention to detail, understanding of Augsburg's past, and openness to change equipped him for leadership during a period of transition in the development of the school. His most cherished goal and most impressive accomplishment, broadening the faculty's role in the direction of academic affairs, corrected one of the more serious defects in Augsburg's structure.

It also encouraged the faculty to participate significantly in the accreditation effort. With the help of small subsidies younger faculty members accelerated their schedules for completion of graduate work, and in

1952–53 all teachers became involved in a comprehensive institutional self-survey, a project required of all colleges seeking NCA recognition. As might be expected, some faculty members found this assignment burdensome; most Augsburg teachers believed they already were overworked and underpaid. On the other hand, the self-study also strengthened a sense of community within the teaching force. It multiplied contacts among members of the group and promoted a feeling of identification with the school — no one who had served on a self-study committee could escape emotional concern while awaiting the final NCA verdict. In addition, greater familiarity with Augsburg's problems and potentialities heightened the effectiveness of most teachers, both in their own departments and as functioning members of the faculty as a corporate body.

The innovations resulting from the accreditation drive were relatively modest. No doubt the self-study stimulated ultimate curricular expansion by underscoring critical gaps in course offerings, but for the time being, no new departments were added. However, a few changes were immediately visible. The administration substantially increased appropriations for new library books and periodicals, faculty members became more conscious of "library-centered instruction," and plans for the new library received closer scrutiny than if they had been dealt with under other circumstances. The promotion of Dahlen from Dean of Men to Dean of Students concentrated responsibility for student personnel affairs to one office. The health service was expanded: instead of merely being on call, the college physician now maintained regular office hours at the health center in the west wing of Memorial Hall. Later the college established a shared health service with Fairview Hospital.[59]

Following Olaf Rogne's resignation in 1952, Burton P. Fosse accepted the post of business manager, taking office on February 1, 1953. Like Quanbeck, Fosse contributed substantially to the ultimate success of the accreditation effort. Neale's report had noted that Augsburg's "financial procedures" were "somewhat informal in comparison with those that would be reported high." [60] Fosse soon introduced a more sophisticated supervision of fiscal and business affairs, an innovation that corrected one of the institution's most serious shortcomings. A son of Carl Fosse, and a graduate of the University of Minnesota in engineering and business administration, he brought to Augsburg training and experience commensurate with his new responsibilities, as well as a deep personal loyalty to the school.

The accreditation campaign imposed additional burdens on the board of trustees, as well as the administration and faculty. Individual board members served on at least one of four working committees, all directly or indirectly concerned with bringing some aspect of the institution's operation in line with NCA standards. The expertise of R. E. Myhre, Minneapolis banker and treasurer of the board, was particularly important in establishing a systematic management of the school's investment policies.[61]

In the autumn of 1953 the administration was once more persuaded that improvements warranted a second bid for NCA membership. Application procedures were similar to those four years earlier: following approval of the required forms and documents, a team of examiners visited the campus, this time in December. Two months later the NCA Board of Review and Commission recommended Augsburg's admission, a decision ratified by the association on March 26, 1954. As might be expected, this action generated considerable satisfaction on the Augsburg campus. Christensen feared that it might also encourage complacency, thereby threatening the development program's momentum. In announcing the NCA action he commented: "We must continue to improve and strengthen many phases of our work; for admission to the North Central is not a 'completion' but a true 'commencement' affording both new responsibilities and many new opportunities for our college." [62]

THE MODERN
AMERICAN COLLEGE

 THE PERIOD FROM 1954 to 1962, when Christensen retired as president, was one of impressive growth in the history of Augsburg College. Enrollment expanded from 765 to 1,402; the faculty, counting both full and part-time, increased from 64 to 102; the operations budget tripled; "investment in plant" rose from approximately $1,500,000 to more than $3,700,000; and the library augmented its holdings by about 75 per cent. Even though substantial indebtedness partially offset the gain in plant investment, maintenance of such a rate of growth without a formal broadening of the supporting constituency reflected credit on the leadership of Christensen, Quanbeck, and Fosse.[1]

Academically, too, the school developed a momentum that extended into the post-Christensen years. In this area chemistry set a challenging pace. From Carl Fosse's death in 1942 until 1959 discontinuity had plagued the chemistry program. The basic laboratory arrangements in Science Hall were admirable and a number of competent instructors served, but most of them either remained for brief periods or divided their time between teaching at Augsburg and pursuing graduate work at the University of Minnesota. A change seemed imminent in 1956 when John R. Holum accepted the chairmanship, taking up his duties at the beginning of the second semester. However, disenchantment over the failure of an LFC referendum to approve church merger — a development that he feared restricted Augsburg's future — coupled with an attractive offer from Pacific Lutheran University at Tacoma, Washington, persuaded Holum to accept an appointment there in 1958–59.

A year later he returned to Augsburg as the second member of a three-man team headed by Courtland Agre, a capable scientist and thoroughly competent administrator who for several years had served as chairman of the chemistry department at St. Olaf College. Earl Alton, the team's junior man, joined the faculty in 1960, a delay permitting completion of his graduate study at the University of Michigan. Both Holum and Alton were St. Olaf alumni and former students of Agre.

The Agre team assumed its responsibilities "with the avowed purpose of 'starting from scratch' and building an outstanding chemistry department within five years." [2] This meant revising course offerings to meet the needs of students preparing for graduate work (on the assumption that such offerings also suited pre-medical and secondary education training); improving physical facilities; equipping the department for community service; and recruiting promising students. In addition, the department resolved to seek formal approval of its program by the American Chemical Society as soon as possible.

The aspiration to build an outstanding department was realized ahead of schedule. A more complete and balanced chemistry major soon replaced the minimal curriculum formerly offered. With considerable assistance from outside sources — including a $30,000 grant from the Hill Family Foundation, and several awards from the National Science Foundation — the department renovated its laboratories, acquired new equipment, expanded the chemistry library, conducted a summer institute for gifted high school students, launched a research program, and established a number of scholarships for chemistry majors. Tangible rewards were visible almost immediately. The number of chemisty majors grew steadily, and before long the department's objective of sending ten majors a year to graduate school was within sight. In April, 1962, less than three years after Agre became chairman, the American Chemical Society placed Augsburg on its approved list, a distinction held by approximately 15 per cent of all American colleges and universities. One recommendation accompanied ACS approval: expansion of the chemistry department to four full-time teachers, a goal that was achieved in 1963.[3]

Physics, too, progressed in the late 1950s. From the standpoint of personnel stability, offerings, and equipment, this discipline had not enjoyed exalted status within Augsburg's academic program. The appointment of Theodore J. Hanwick as professor of physics in 1956 decisively improved the situation. Hanwick had taught at a number of institutions, including Rutgers University, the State University of New Jersey, and the United States Naval Academy at Annapolis. After arriving at Augsburg he organized a physics major and became involved in research subsidized by grants as well as other professional activities.[4]

Since Arthur Nash's leadership had built a respectable program long before the 1950s, the development of biology was less noticeable than that of the other sciences. Nevertheless, the department advanced impressively, particularly after 1963. New offerings in cellular and developmental biology, plant morphology, and biochemistry, together with a seminar and an independent study program enriched the curriculum. Additional research laboratories, two for faculty and one for students, were provided. With the assistance of grants, both private and governmental, the department extended its research activity.[5]

It also recruited a larger faculty. Erling Urdahl, who had devoted part of his time to psychology, now served biology full-time. Erwin D. Mickelberg joined the department in 1956; Ralph L. Sulerud in 1964. Two years later Sulerud became biology chairman. Meanwhile, the number of full-time biology teachers increased from three and one-half in 1963 to seven in the centennial year.

Mathematics lagged behind chemistry, physics, and biology. George Soberg, who had chaired the department since 1933, commanded the respect and affection of students and colleagues, but the well-known explosion that was revolutionizing his field had opened a generation gap between young mathematicians and their elders. In addition, competition from government and industry for available Ph.Ds. impeded the recruitment of new talent. A number of able instructors served during the 1950s, but their effectiveness was hampered by brief tenure and preoccupation with graduate work. The appointment of Orval M. Haugsby in 1961 was a forward step, and as the decade advanced the department expanded. Henry G. Follingstad came in 1962, Beverly C. Durkee in 1965, and Dean B. Gulden a year later. Haugsby became chairman following Soberg's retirement in 1965, and when Haugsby resigned in 1967 Gulden accepted this post.

Augsburg's curricular structure placed the department of health and physical education within the natural science division. Anomalous as this may seem, the department achieved a stability that previously had been unattainable. Faculty turnover was remarkably low. Ernest Anderson, department chairman and basketball coach, and Edor Nelson, who coached football, completed 23 years of service in 1968–69. Other members of the department also had held their positions for extended periods. Mrs. LaVonne Peterson, director of physical education for women, arrived in 1950, Howard E. Pearson in 1956, and Edwin J. Saugestad in 1960.

Another characteristic of Anderson's department was its respect for the college's total educational effort. It placed on athletes rather than faculty the responsibility for maintaining academic eligibility. This regard for the proprieties apparently did not handicap intercollegiate sports; Anderson's basketball teams established a creditable record, winning the Minnesota Intercollegiate Athletic Conference title in 1963,

1964, and 1965. Performance in football was less impressive, although under Edor Nelson's coaching the baseball team captured several MIAC championships, a triumph recalling the glories of the late 1940s when Augsburg won two consecutive baseball titles.

Consistent with general development, the athletic-physical education program expanded. Course offerings were enriched and involvement in competitive sports widened — under Saugestad, for example, hockey emerged as a serious activity. Facilities, too, were improved. The basketball court in Si Melby Gymnasium was available by 1961–62 for intercollegiate contests, an advance terminating the era when home games were played in the Minneapolis Armory. Intercollegiate football and baseball meets continued to be scheduled off campus, but the college had acquired sufficient space near the gymnasium to provide practice fields.

WITHIN THE social science division sociology was the most innovative department. When Torstenson became chairman in 1947 a general sense of direction was evident, but the new department had formulated neither a detailed blueprint nor a precise timetable. An early statement of departmental objectives underscored several goals: "to help students attain a better understanding of society . . . to prepare students for social service . . . graduate training in social work, and . . . graduate work in Sociology . . . [and] to explore the relevance of Christianity to effective social service." [6]

The sociology program that evolved under Torstenson's leadership conformed to these goals. Early additions to the curriculum included "Intercultural Relations and Minority Problems," and "Introduction to Social Work," along with such standard offerings as social psychology and urban sociology. A course titled "Public Welfare" was introduced in 1952. Two years later the department established a third quasi-professional course, "Fields of Social Work" which, together with the existing courses in social work and public welfare, constituted a "Social Work Sequence" taught by Harold J. Belgum, a trained social worker and official of the Lutheran Welfare Society of Minnesota.[7]

Belgum, who served on a part-time appointment, also functioned as supervisor of a community experience program that sought to encourage contact between students in the sequence and welfare agencies throughout the metropolitan area. In 1957 the department broadened the scope of this program by requiring "field experience in a social agency as an integral part of the classroom course[s] in social work." [8] Students enrolling in one of the three courses received two semester credits for their regular class work and one credit for field experience. During the first six years of this experiment "at least two hundred students . . . participated," and "only four or five . . . failed to carry out their responsibilities." [9] Belgum remained in charge until 1960 when his wife, Merrilyn, was assigned to the post. She continued until 1965 when she was succeeded by Vernon M. Bloom.

Although sociology ranked as one of the most popular majors at Augsburg, Torstenson felt that notions of what his department was seeking to accomplish were often distorted. He frequently complained of a tendency both on and off campus to equate sociology with social work, the implication being that his department's sole preoccupation was to turn out well-meaning "do gooders" equipped with as much professional social work training as could be squeezed into an undergraduate college curriculum. The point was well taken. Many sociology majors did not become social workers, including some who enrolled in the social work sequence. Moreover, Torstenson and his associates regarded the sequence as essentially pre-professional, although a substantial number of students were recruited by social agencies after graduation. Equally important, the department did not understand "education for service" as being concerned only with charitable assistance to the disadvantaged. The primary objective of the sociology program was "to help students attain a better understanding of society . . . and [the] forces of social change," in the hope that departmental alumni would become effective agents of change. Torstenson argued that such an objective was consistent with the mission of a Christian liberal arts college.[10]

Building an adequate faculty was another problem facing the sociology chairman. Augsburg's location guaranteed the availability of talent to direct field experience, but a limited budget delayed expansion of the full-time teaching force. Following the resignation of Alma Jensen in 1954 the department included Torstenson and a succession of part-time or temporary instructors. The appointment of David M. Nordlie in 1961 was a gain, although his graduate work necessitated part-time service and leaves of absence. By 1968–69 the sociology faculty consisted of four full-time and five part-time teachers.

Despite frustrations, the sociology department contributed significantly to Augsburg's academic program. In the 1950s it turned out more majors than any other department. Within the Minnesota private college community its field experience venture became a pace setter, and on campus it sharpened awareness of the school's potentialities as an urban college.[11] Establishment in 1965 of the Augsburg College Social Science Research Center was a logical extension of Torstenson's pioneering efforts.[12]

Quiet evolution rather than bold innovation marked the development of Augsburg's history department in the 1950s and 1960s. Hendrickson had formally retired as department chairman and professor in 1946 after 46 years of service; actually he continued as a part-time teacher, chiefly in Latin, until 1952. Philip Kildahl, who had taught both history and philosophy, inherited the chairmanship and most of Hendrickson's courses. At the same time Bernhardt Kleven assumed responsibility for American history and the limited offerings in political science that were combined with history following creation of separate sociology and business administration-economics departments. During the post-war enrollment increase a number of part-time instructors were employed. However, the retrenchment of 1951 reduced the joint department to two men. Following Kildahl's resignation in 1952 Kleven became chairman, and Carl H. Chrislock joined the department.

It soon became apparent that two men could not manage a program ranging from surveys in western civilization, American history and government, to upper division offerings in Russian history, Renaissance and Reformation, history of England, and American diplomacy. The appointment of Orloue Gisselquist in 1956 allowed for more specialization. A fourth instructorship was established in 1960 which Donald R. Gustafson accepted a year later. Meanwhile, Mrs. Khin Khin Jensen, who had served on a part-time appointment in 1955–56, returned in 1959, dividing her time between the western civilization survey and courses in Asian history, her specialty.

Although it attracted a substantial number of majors, the department of business administration, economics, and business education faced a number of problems. In the early 1950s high faculty turnover hampered continuity of development. Under A. Robert Hemmingson, who arrived in 1957, the department achieved greater stability without resolving all difficulties. The claims of business administration and economics tended to work at cross purposes, and tight budgets inhibited a firm commitment to both. An economics major introduced in 1960 drew fewer students than anticipated, possibly because its offerings were limited. In addition, Hemmingson was frustrated by the shift of economics from the traditional "institutional" methodology of his earlier graduate training to an approach based on mathematical models. He left Augsburg in 1967 to begin a new career in library administration. A year later Bruce P. Budge, a capable accounting teacher who had served since 1960, resigned to accept an appointment at the University of Idaho. Meanwhile, the department's business education sector was faring better; it had operated under the efficient management of Miss Lund since 1950.

211

Martin Quanbeck continued as nominal chairman of the department of Education and psychology until 1954–55; actually Henry Bertness assumed direction of the program in 1950 when Quanbeck became college dean. Other members of the department included Marvin E. Trautwein (1950–59), and Carl R. Hammarberg, who arrived in 1953 and subsequently was appointed director of the Augsburg placement bureau. Bertness left in 1956 to accept an administrative position with the Tacoma, Washington, public school system; Einar O. Johnson succeeded him.

Under Johnson's chairmanship, Education made an effort to involve other departments in the secondary teacher training program. Specifically, faculty members from the subject-matter fields shared with Education the responsibility of supervising and evaluating the performance of student teachers and, wherever possible, taught the methods courses. According to Johnson this practice yielded two desirable results: it raised the quality of student teaching; and it built amicable understanding between Education and the other disciplines — tension between the teacher training and liberal arts sectors, so evident within some colleges and universities, was minimal at Augsburg.

The Education department also cultivated closer relations with Twin City public school systems. Previously an education candidate had performed his student teaching and secured his first position in small towns throughout Minnesota. By the early 1960s schools within the metropolitan area had opened their doors to Augsburg student teachers, and employed a considerable number of the college's graduates.[13]

On January 15, 1959, a faculty recommendation to the board of trustees that Augsburg institute an elementary education training program "for the Freshmen who enter in the fall of 1959" was approved. Miss Martha Mattson, an experienced and highly skilled administrator in the elementary education area who joined the faculty in 1960, organized the program. The first class of elementary teachers graduated in 1963.

Meanwhile, the Education department had expanded its staff and modified its structure. Mrs. Lyla Mae Anderegg was recruited in 1959, and Sheldon Fardig three years later. Psychology was constituted a separate department offering a major in 1961. In May of the following year the National Council for Accreditation of Teacher Education (NCATE) "granted full accreditation to Augsburg College for the preparation of secondary teachers with the Bachelor's degree as the highest . . . to be awarded." [14] Mrs. Ruth G. Ludeman, who succeeded Miss Mattson as director of elementary education, joined the faculty in 1967. Miss Mattson retired the following year.

A curriculum for the new department of psychology was developed by

Kenneth N. DeYoung, who joined the faculty in 1960, and Peter H. Armacost, Dean of Students, the plan being that DeYoung should head the program. However, his resignation in 1962 left the task of making the department fully operative to Mrs. Grace Hinrichs Dyrud. Mrs. Dyrud followed DeYoung's basic design with the addition of a few refinements. For example, she organized seminars in personnel management for business firms in the Twin City area as well as periodic institutes for high school teachers of psychology.[15]

WITHIN THE DIVISION of religion and philosophy the advance of religion was more impressive than that of its partner. A succession of competent instructors taught philosophy — Bryce W. Shoemaker, Robert E. Larsen, Albert B. Anderson, and Robert T. Sandin — but none of them remained at Augsburg long enough to give the department continuity. The appointment of William H. Halverson in 1959 stabilized the philosophy program for a few years. However, Halverson, an able scholar and outstanding teacher, shifted his commitment to administration; he left Augsburg in 1967 to accept an associate deanship at University College, Ohio State University.

Concomitant with the divisional reorganization of 1950, Augsburg's Christianity department changed its name to the Department of Religion. Whether this innovation had any particular significance is not clear. However, by the late 1950s the freshman course in Biblical studies sought "to introduce the students to the fact that the Bible is not only a religious . . . but also a historical document, and comes out of history." [16] As we know, Christensen had accepted the historico-critical approach to Biblical scholarship before 1930. Although this perspective profoundly influenced his teaching, Christensen hesitated to impose his views on the LFC. In addressing a 1944 pastor's institute held at Augsburg he commented: "it is not in harmony with our traditional position to attempt to define the exact manner in which the inspiration of the Scriptures is to be understood. . . . We have grave difficulty in thinking it possible to distinguish fully and finally between the human and divine elements in the mystery of inspiration." [17]

For many years the same circumspection guided religion instruction at Augsburg. While Melby directed the Christianity program, encouragement of Christian commitment rather than exposure to theological scholarship was the department's main concern. Stensvaag, Melby's successor as chairman of the Christianity department, introduced his Old Testament seminary classes to the historico-critical method — a departure establishing him as a pioneer among Midwest Scandinavian Lutheran theological professors — but maintained the Melby tradition in the college. The departmental statement in force during Stensvaag's chairmanship affirmed: "The fundamental aim in instruction is to lead as many as possible to personal faith in Christ, and to nurture the Christian life." [18]

When Stensvaag became dean of Augsburg Theological Seminary in 1953 Paul Sonnack assumed the religion chairmanship. Stensvaag's election as LFC president five years later occasioned another rearrangement of responsibilities: Sonnack became seminary dean, and Philip A. Quanbeck, who had joined the faculty in 1957 after completing his graduate work in New Testament studies at Princeton Theological Seminary, was appointed chairman of the religion department.

Although Sonnack and Quanbeck tended to insist that continuity with the past rather than drastic change marked the development of the religion program under their leadership, an impression that the department was becoming more "academic" and less "evangelistic" gained wide acceptance in the late 1950s.[19] Such a dichotomy oversimplified reality, but there was a shift in the program's emphasis. Entering freshmen discovered a striking difference between "Basic Bible" at Augsburg and their Sunday school classes at home — frequently the latter had implicitly if not explicitly accepted the Scriptures as "infallible" and "inerrant" both in a scientific and historical sense, while the former proceeded on the assumption that the Bible was, among other things, a human document with a history of its own. In Melby's day the transition from Sunday school to freshman religion had been considerably smoother. Subsequent courses in the religion curriculum often intensified the shock. Some students were startled to learn that the premises underlying the Christian faith and modern capitalism were not necessarily identical, that Christian obligation was social as well as personal, and that religious traditions other than Lutheran Christianity merited respect. Ultimately most students found these insights liberating, but a segment of the constituency believed the Augsburg religion department had become a nesting place for heretics, either of the "neo-Orthodox" or "modernist" variety.

Controversy reached a high point in the early 1960s, gradually abating thereafter. One of the by-products was a statement delivered by Philip Quanbeck to the closing session of the 1962 faculty workshop. According to Quanbeck, the courses in his department inquired:

into the basic documents of the Christian Faith . . . the history of the Church, and . . . the theology of the Church, which is the Church reflecting on the meaning . . . and content of the Christian Faith. Whatever else this is, it is at least an academic inquiry . . . while no person uses any sources without some pre-suppositions, we have the task of inquiring . . . into what the NT means to say when it speaks of Jesus, without insisting that we learn that he is just like . . . Heidi's Grandfather. Or we have the task to inquire into the history of the church, with all the tools that modern scholarship provides.

But [this] does not finally explain why biblical, historical and theological study is carried on . . . at Augsburg . . . the whole biblical tradition, is the object of study not simply as an artifact of the past . . . but rather because we believe we find there some clues as to the meaning of our existence. . . . The assumption is that in the biblical tradition which reaches some high point — the highest — in Jesus of Nazareth it is disclosed to us that the character of human life, its origin and destiny is somehow involved with God; that something happened in the life and work of Jesus which makes our situation a new situation.[20]

Catalog data leaves the impression that religion was Augsburg's largest academic department. However, since most of the religion instructors also taught in the seminary or other college departments, this impression is misleading. At one time or another, Merton P. Strommen, Karlis L. Ozolins, Iver Olson, Mario Colacci, Roger S. Jordahl, Melvin A. Helland, Terence E. Fretheim, Richard Husfloen, Harold Tollefson, and Orlin Mandsager served the religion department either on a part-time or temporary basis. Immediately following the merger of Augsburg and Luther seminaries in 1963 Stensvaag and Christensen, who had resigned as president of Augsburg a year earlier, joined the Luther faculty. Sonnack did so in 1967, and Fretheim in 1968. Meanwhile, John Benson (1963), Eugene Skibbe (1964), and Douglas J. Ollila (1966) became permanent members of the religion department.

UNDER GERALD H. THORSON, who succeeded Sveeggen as chairman in 1952, the department of English emerged as an influential force within the academic structure. With capable assistance from departmental colleagues — Anne Pederson in particular — the new chairman reorganized and expanded course offerings, especially in the area of modern literature; broadened Augsburg's participation in inter-collegiate English activities; worked for the raising of academic standards; and established the reputation of being an effective administrator. A 1943 Augsburg graduate and a specialist in Norwegian-American literature, Thorson opposed excessive academic specialization on the undergraduate level and advocated caution with respect to vocational programs. The report of a curriculum study conducted under his leadership argued that the humanities were "the cornerstone of a liberal education because it is in the humanities (religion, philosophy, literature, and history) that students are called upon to deal with the artistic, the moral, and the spiritual values which give vision and meaning to life." [21]

Like other academic departments English encountered difficulty in securing and retaining faculty, salaries and teaching loads being what they were. Nevertheless, a number of able people were recruited. Several who taught for relatively brief periods or on part-time appointments contributed notably to the English program — Mrs. Margaret Sateren Trautwein; John R. Milton, an expert on the literature and culture of the American West whose departure in 1957 was regretted by many colleagues; Mrs. Catherine Nicholl; Mrs. Gracia Christensen; and Ove J. H. Preus. K. Berner Dahlen taught part-time within the department during his tenure as dean of students and full-time thereafter. Miss Bertha Lillehei, who had taught in the late 1930s, returned in 1957. Mrs. Lorraine Livingston and Grier Nicholl joined the faculty in 1960.

The appointment of Thorson as chairman of the humanities division in 1958 reinforced a drive to broaden programs in foreign language, drama, and art. Language study had held a central position in the curriculum during Augsburg's first half-century. The modernization policy of the 1920s reduced its relative importance, but the faculty attempted to maintain academic majors in Norwegian, French, Greek, and Latin, an effort that collapsed during the Great Depression when austerity reduced these offerings to minors. Throughout the 1940s and early 1950s student demand for language offerings was not sufficiently urgent to warrant restoration of these majors.

A change became apparent by 1960. Anxiety to reaffirm Augsburg's commitment to the liberal arts — a viewpoint effectively articulated by Thorson — coupled with a heightened appreciation of foreign languages following the Soviet Union's successful Sputnik launch in October, 1957, generated a campaign to increase the language requirement from one to two years, and to re-establish language majors. Favorable public response to a Spanish conversation course taught in 1958–59 by Mrs. Mimi Kingsley on KTCA-TV, the Twin City educational channel, added impetus to the drive.

After a spirited debate extending through several sessions, the faculty on December 3, 1959, voted to raise the language requirement from eight to 14 semester credits for students whose high school preparation did not include at least two years of successful foreign language work. Soon thereafter language laboratories were installed in the space formerly occupied by the library on the first floor of Main; later these facilities were expanded and improved with the help of federal subsidies available under the National Defense Education act. Beginning in 1963 the college offered majors in French, German, and Spanish. Subsequently the Norse section of the modern language department organized a major in Scandinavian Studies, a combination including courses in general Nordic culture along with offerings in Norwegian. The department of classical languages also expanded its program, experimenting briefly with a Greek-Latin major that soon was abandoned in favor of a major in Greek and a strong minor in Latin.

In addition to Mrs. Kingsley, the permanent language faculty of 1959 included Bjarne Landa, German and Norwegian; Iver Olson, Norwegian; and Mario Colacci, Greek and Latin. Although these teachers constituted a nucleus for the expanding program, a considerable augmentation of faculty was necessary, particularly since Olson and Colacci taught in other departments. Ruth Aaskov was appointed to teach French in 1960, and Leif E. Hansen accepted a Norse instructorship in 1961. By the centennial year the department of modern languages consisted of ten and one-half faculty members.

Since the theatre was for many years suspect within the LFC, drama, unlike language study, lacked roots within the Augsburg tradition. By World War II the theatre had gained sufficient respectability to permit drama offerings in the curriculum, but a tight budget delayed organization of a full program.

The appointment of Lucy Mae Bergman in 1952 as speech and drama instructor marked a beginning. Together with John Thut of the music department Mrs. Bergman, a gifted teacher, directed a number of operettas and a performance of *The Mikado*. She also assumed responsibility for several plays, including a Christmas fantasy performed on the University of Minnesota campus in December, 1954 under the formal sponsorship of an Augsburg drama club.[22] Mrs. Bergman left in 1955; her successor, Roderick Robertson, who served for one year, directed the speech and drama department's first production, a performance of Arthur Miller's *All My Sons*, and two one-act plays.

Ailene H. Cole, who arrived in 1956, built on the foundations laid by Mrs. Bergman and Robertson. Her first venture was not reassuring: only one student responded to an announcement of tryouts for Thornton Wilder's *Skin of Our Teeth*. A recruiting campaign eventually yielded a cast, the performance was favorably received, and by the end of the year drama was moving into the mainstream of campus life.[23] In May, 1958 the National Collegiate Players (*Pi Epsilon Delta*), an honorary dramatic fraternity, admitted an Augsburg chapter to membership.[24] Meanwhile, another successful season highlighted by performances of Tennessee Williams' *Glass Menagerie* and Oscar Wilde's *The Importance of Being*

217

Earnest, had rewarded the efforts of Miss Cole and a growing student troupe.

The autumn of 1959 witnessed further advance: conversion of a church structure on Riverside Avenue recently acquired by the college into a speech and drama building. While far from ideal, the new facility was a distinct improvement over sharing the music building. Mrs. Esther Olson, whose experience included teaching drama at Luther College and the University of Minnesota, joined the department in 1960, raising its full-time faculty to three members. Raymond Anderson, the chairman, taught the upper division speech courses and supervised debate. In addition to their responsibilities in connection with drama, Miss Cole and Mrs. Olson taught beginning speech sections, as did Anderson.

Until the late 1950s Augsburg's neglect of the plastic arts — painting, drawing, architecture, and sculpture — was even more pronounced than its treatment of drama. Aside from a few offerings in the home economics curriculum, the academic program was bereft of courses in the area. This deficiency, long a source of concern on campus, was considered at the faculty workshop of September, 1954. Although no specific decision emerged the discussion encouraged two subsequent steps: establishment of a fine arts requirement for all students; and the recruitment in 1955 of Ivan Doseff, a retired member of the University of Minnesota faculty, to teach a course in painting. A year later Doseff introduced a course in modeling and sculpture that alternated with the one in painting on a two-year cycle. He continued at Augsburg until 1961.

Philip J. Thompson accepted an appointment as instructor of art in 1959. Soon after arriving on campus Thompson, a Concordia (Moorhead) graduate who had received his Master of Fine Arts degree at the University of Iowa a year earlier, organized an extra-curricular program, including an art and hobby club that encouraged avocational painting. Simultaneously, members of the college community were discussing the future of art as an academic discipline at Augsburg. On December 2, 1959, the faculty voted to establish an art department offering a minor, effective the following year.

The new department was soon on the road to success. As a teacher Thompson avoided imposing his own artistic tradition on students in favor of an effort to liberate their artistic talents, an approach that attracted gifted registrants to his classes. As department chairman he formulated goals that were both realistic and consonant with those of the college. On the delicate issue of liberal-arts elitism *vs.* vocationalism he steered a middle course. His first departmental statement stressed "experience in the disciplines of drawing, painting and sculpture . . . the

218

function of art in history and religion . . . [and] opportunities in teaching, graduate study, commercial designing, and avocational art." [25]

Thompson also cultivated every opportunity to integrate his department with other facets of Augsburg life. He responded positively to requests for artistic designs from planners of campus festivals. Frequent exhibitions of student productions, particularly paintings, diffused an awareness that the art department had come into existence. So, too, did the active participation of Thompson's students in Creative Arts week.[26]

For several years inadequate facilities hampered the art department. When Thompson arrived the program was housed on the first floor of Main in close proximity to the language laboratories — according to one rumor the sounds of a sculptor's hammer often flawed the language tapes being recorded during this period. Following the 1963 church merger the department moved into a building on Riverside Avenue formerly occupied by the LFC, where it remained until 1967.

By this time the department had expanded both program and faculty. In 1963 August Molder, a specialist in the fabrication of stained glass windows, accepted an appointment as Artist in Residence and part-time instructor. A year later a major in art was introduced and Norman Holen, whose chief interest was sculpture, joined the faculty. John Mosand, a graphic designer, was employed in 1967. Meanwhile, Thompson's growing reputation as a painter was enhancing the importance of his department.

Following Opseth's death on December 25, 1950, Leland Sateren was appointed chairman of the music department and director of the Augsburg College Choir. Since Sateren had served on the music faculty for several years, he knew the department's strengths and weaknesses. The preparation of music teachers for the public schools, he felt, had to be improved. Course offerings in theoretical music required enrichment. Extension of individual instruction, limited basically to piano and voice when Sateren became chairman, to organ and all the major instruments was imperative. In addition Sateren wanted to strengthen the performing groups. The choir came under his supervision, leaving a vacancy in the band directorship, a post he had held. Sateren also hoped the department would be able to maintain an orchestra of high quality.

These goals shaped the music department's evolution over the next two decades. A substantial expansion of faculty broadened the theoretical and applied music areas. Among the new teachers remaining for extended periods were Carl W. Landahl, who served until his death in 1961; Daryl Gibson; James D. Johnson, and Stephen Gabrielson. Of those whose tenure preceded the Sateren era, Jennie Skurdalsvold left in

1953, and Audrey Landquist a year later; John Thut retired in 1966; his wife, Vera, continued to instruct part-time for another year. The department also recruited a large corps of part-time teachers, including members of the Minnesota Symphony Orchestra and other Twin City musical organizations.

A. Mayo Savold, a musician with many years of successful experience in public school work, joined the faculty in 1952 as assistant professor of music and director of the band and choral club. Soon after he assumed its directorship the band attained a high level of excellence, an achievement placing instrumental music at Augsburg on a firm basis. Robert Karlén was appointed instructor of music in 1959, the intention being that he would direct an orchestra when sufficient talent became available. Karlén's group presented its first full concert on January 7, 1965, to a convocation audience in Melby Hall. The appointment of Eugene Vuicich, a specialist in stringed instruments, as assistant professor of music in 1967 improved the orchestra's long-range prospects.[27]

Under Sateren's leadership the choir added new dimensions to Augsburg's musical tradition. Both as director and composer he experimented with "new sounds in choral music," aspiring to make his vocal group as avant-garde as possible.[28] According to many critics, he succeeded. In reviewing the concert performed in Central Lutheran Church at Minneapolis on March 12, 1967, Paul McIntrye, pianist, composer, and member of the University of Minnesota music faculty, commented: "Avant-garde music by college students? Impossible. Yet there it was — tone clusters, glissandi, chance notation — and suddenly the traditional Gregorian intonation of the 'Gloria Patri.' " [29]

Like musical groups of earlier days, the choir and band organized annual tours, but with an important difference: the Sateren and Savold ensembles performed more often in civic auditoriums than church structures, and their itineraries were world-wide rather than Midwestern. In June and July, 1960 the band toured Alaska, participating as a featured attraction at the music festival in Anchorage; five years later the choir visited Europe. Service to the church remained vital, but contacts with the wider community multiplied. The department established close rapport with Upper Midwest public school music instructors — from time to time it organized clinics for directors. In the 1960s concerted performances with the Minnesota Symphony Orchestra became a regular feature of the musical year. Under the direction of Stanislaw Skrowaczewski of the symphony the two groups presented a special concert in the United Nations General Assembly on December 10, 1968, in commemoration of the 20th anniversary of the Universal Declaration of Human Rights.

THE PROGRESS OF Augsburg's academic program during the last eight years of Christensen's administration and beyond raised a number of important policy issues. By the late 1950s a wide gap separated admission standards and expectations within the classroom — too many students were failing courses or landing on academic probation. The faculty and administration responded with several measures. Student recruitment was strengthened and reorganized: Mark Johnson joined Donovan Lundeen as a member of the admissions staff in 1958; and later jurisdiction over recruitment was transferred from the development to the student personnel office. In two successive stages, one approved in 1959–60 and the second two years later, the faculty voted to raise entrance requirements. The impact of these steps was soon visible: beginning in 1960 the median high school rank of entering Freshmen rose significantly.[30]

Expansion of the faculty's role in policy making, a trend strongly encouraged by Dean Quanbeck, also needed formal clarification. At times it seemed that an inordinate amount of time was spent on drafting, discussing, and revising a succession of constitutions, particularly the provisions dealing with faculty prerogatives. Nor was full clarification achieved. Several faculty committees emerged as reasonably influential power centers — notably Educational Policies and Faculty Personnel Policies — and the authority of department chairmen increased, but a faculty senate theoretically representing the entire teaching force was not established until the mid-1960s. An Augsburg chapter of the American Association of University Professors was organized in 1966.

The comparative absence of any threat to academic freedom, rather than administration hostility to AAUP explains the tardiness of the latter's appearance. Except for one or two faculty members who in the 1950s were caught in a crossfire involving theological issues, Augsburg teachers believed that a free intellectual climate prevailed on campus. Even at the height of Joseph McCarthy's influence the faculty felt no pressure from the administration to conform to "acceptable" political and economic orthodoxies. On the contrary, the president and dean courageously defended both the freedom of Augsburg's classrooms and the right of professors to engage in political activity. In December, 1960 Christensen delivered a strong retort to a group of clergymen who had questioned the propriety of extensive faculty participation in the previous presidential campaign.[31]

In the theological realm the problem of academic freedom was more

221

sensitive than in such areas as politics and economics. However, a tolerance of diverse theological viewpoints was part of the Augsburg tradition, the "anti-humanist" crusade of the 1890s notwithstanding. Years earlier George Sverdrup had insisted that the confessions of the church bound him and the faculty "only as they vindicate themselves to our minds and heart as *truth*." [32]

Paradoxically, this tradition of openness generated less trauma while Augsburg was a relatively closed society than later when the contact with the outside world became more frequent. In reporting to the 1956 LFC convention Christensen alluded to the dilemma facing all church related colleges:

We find ourselves living in the midst of many conflicting theories of what higher education, including Christian higher education should be. It is not easy to chart and carry through a clear course which does full justice both to the ideals of educational freedom upon which Augsburg has in the past prided itself and to the principle of whole-hearted dedication to Christ and the Scriptures upon which alone, we are convinced, the edifices of true Christian freedom can be securely built. It requires at least a strong corps of teachers who are not only professionally competent . . . but who are also . . . well-grounded in 'theological principles', to meet the challenges of our time in a way that shall do justice, both to the enquiring minds of youth and to the searching questions advanced by sincere opponents of the Christian way of life or thought.[33]

Augsburg's administration failed to discover a formula that could assure an appropriate balance between professional competence on the one hand and Christian commitment and theological sensitivity on the other. To its credit, it never required subscription to a creedal statement or a formal profession of faith as a condition for appointment to the faculty. It did, however, weigh the religious orientation of applicants for teaching posts. A set of recommendations with respect to promotion of academic personnel formulated in 1949 by Christensen and the division chairmen and approved by the faculty listed "Christian character" as the first criterion followed in order by academic preparation, teaching ability, personality, experience, length of service at Augsburg, and general value to the institution.[34]

The next decade marked an important reordering of priorities. A statement adopted by the board of trustees in 1962 specified that promotion should be based on five criteria: preparation, classroom teaching, productive scholarship, experience, and "Other contributions of significance to the institution . . . including . . . service to the community and church." [35] The striking difference between these two sets of standards was one measure of Augsburg's transformation in the 1950s. Some friends of the college deplored the trend, fearing that it meant a steady drift toward "secularism" and irreligion. Others believed that, far from weakening the school's basic Christian commitment, the organization of a broader intellectual dialogue was strengthening it.

Augsburg's drive for academic excellence placed a burden on college services directly affiliated with the curricular program. Under Miss Joel's leadership the registrar's office adapted to heavier responsibilities with unobtrusive efficiency. The library also responded to broader challenges. Completion of the George Sverdrup wing in 1955 improved the physical setting, facilitating efforts to encourage library-centered instruction. The staff, too, was enlarged: in 1952 it consisted of Miss Tangjerd and two assistants; seven years later it had expanded to eight persons, including the librarian.

Karlis Ozolins was appointed associate librarian in 1959; he succeeded Miss Tangjerd as chief librarian the following year. At the same time Miss Tangjerd accepted a half-time appointment as archivist, a post she held until 1968. Meanwhile, Ozolins recruited several professionally trained librarians to serve on his staff. The library also appropriated additional space to house its operation. Following the 1963 merger it occupied the theological lecture room, located adjacent to the second floor collection, and in 1967 it pre-empted the room formerly serving as a faculty lounge on the ground floor of Science Hall.

The library's vital statistics reflect an ambitious effort to keep abreast of the times. From 1957 to 1962 its budget tripled — from about $21,000 to more than $60,000. After remaining on a plateau for the next year, expenditures again rose, exceeding $100,000 in 1966–67. A substantial augmentation of the book and periodical collection accompanied this budgetary pattern. When accreditation was achieved, holdings totaled less than 30,000 volumes; by the centennial year, 95,000. A collection of this size was scarcely adequate, but the trend of library development encouraged both faculty and students.[36]

STUDENT LIFE in the late 1950s and early 1960s was a mix of continuity and change. From the standpoint of church preference the student body changed very little. Geographical distribution shifted toward the Twin Cities: in 1953–54, 35 per cent resided there; eight years later that figure rose to 50 per cent.[37] While comprehensive statistics on socio-economic status are unavailable, it is clear that, as in the past, a preponderance of Augsburg students were non-affluent, with many wholly or partially dependent on their own earnings.

A number of complaints heard in former days also continued to be articulated. The campus was crowded, many facilities inadequate, much of the housing substandard, and the college lacked a student center. Equally important, the persistence of LFC norms with respect to "worldly pleasure" inhibited the development of a satisfactory social program. For more than 30 years an element within the student body had objected to Augsburg's conservative recreational standards. There was, however, an important difference between earlier student generations and that of the late 1950s: the former had rebelliously evaded rules which they regarded as unchangeable and the latter worked openly for a more liberal recreation policy.

Fortunately, the battle lines on such issues as dancing did not place the administration and faculty in one camp and the students in the other. The division was rather between liberal and conservatives within each group. It also is significant that a substantial number of religiously concerned students along with members of the religion faculty allied with the liberals, advancing a theological rationale for their stand. Fortunately, too, reasonable civility prevailed. The *Echo* remained free of faculty or administration censorship, and Dean Quanbeck maintained an open-door policy. Although the question of how permissive campus life should be remained unresolved in the centennial year, a restoration of the old order could not be anticipated. In 1958 the faculty reversed an administration effort to reinstate the all-encompassing ban on student drinking that had been in force earlier; and seven years later social dancing won official approval as a campus activity.[38]

Dismissing the dancing controversy as of less than cosmic significance, many students responded to broadening opportunities in art, drama, and music. With each passing year the Creative Arts Week program became more rich and diversified. Originating in 1953 as a "Creative Night" sponsored by the writer's club, this annual event expanded into a festival consisting of art exhibits, dramatic performances, concerts, and lectures by well-known critics or artists. Beginning in 1961 the Spring Antiphony — "An original concept blending art, music and the spoken word" — joined Creative Arts Week as a regular feature of the spring season.[39] It, too, became more impressive from year to year.

Political activity sporadically attracted a following. The college sponsored its first political action week in the spring of 1954, with Arthur Naftalin the featured convocation speaker.[40] Thereafter, both the Republican and Democratic-Farmer-Labor campus clubs became more vigorous and remained so until the early 1960s, when enthusiasm appeared to wane. The surge of interest in politics, while it lasted, helped lay the foundations of several political careers, notably that of Martin O. Sabo, class of 1959, who became leader of the minority caucus in the Minnesota House of Representatives in 1969.

The religious program continued to hold a central place in student life. Daily chapel, with the exception of one day set aside for convocations, remained part of campus routine, as did a Faith in Life week each semester, dormitory devotions, and an active Mission Society. The latter merged with the Student Christian Association in 1964–65, but since the two organizations had cooperated for some time, the significance of this move was minimal. Orlin Mandsager began his tenure as campus pastor in 1962, a position including responsibility for the chapel program, pastoral counseling, and part-time teaching in the religion department.

If the religious program's structure suggests continuity with the past, there were pronounced shifts in emphasis. Perhaps the changing style of Faith in Life week most sensitively registered the trend. An *Echo* story of October 13, 1950, defined the week "as a time of crisis at Augsburg. . . . Other things are put aside . . . and students and faculty alike seek what the Lord has to give. Some find salvation, a new life for the first time; some learn of a deeper and richer life with God; others perhaps are called to missions or . . . [the] ministry." Fourteen years later Loren Halvorson, the chief Faith in Life week speaker, faulted the church for isolating "itself from the needs of the community." After establishing identity with God, Halvorson added, "man must go into the city" where "he puts his Faith into action"; he "must live in a secular world and yet not become a part of that world." [41]

Change rather than continuity marked the development of student government. From Weenaas' time through the golden era of student power under Georg Sverdrup and until 1945, this facet of Augsburg life had operated on the town meeting principle. The student president and other officials were directly accountable to the student society, whose membership included all academy, college, and seminary registrants. The entire group met periodically to decide broad policy questions. In 1945 the student society delegated its authority to a representative council elected annually by the various classes, including the seminarians, who were assigned one seat on the 25-man council. At the same time the president continued to be chosen by the student body. A later change established the student president as an independent executive, analogous to a governor or the president of the United States.

The steep rise in enrollment following World War II created problems for student government. Many of the veterans manifested only slight interest, and the large commuting element lacked close identification with campus life. To some extent the latter problem persisted, but by the late 1950s unmistakable signs of revival were visible. Among other things, student leaders launched a campaign to secure representation on faculty committees. Although this campaign failed to win a decisive triumph, a joint student-faculty judicial council possessing substantial authority was established, and a number of committees admitted student observers.

Peter H. Armacost succeeded K. Berner Dahlen as Dean of Students in 1959, a shift that did not alter the student personnel program's basic direction, particularly since Miss Mortensen continued as Dean of Women for five more years. Armacost's "main concern was that . . . Student Personnel Services . . . remain in the mainstream of the educational effort." He assigned high priority to personal adjustment of students, but sought to avoid the danger that pursuit of this goal might "really contribute pressure toward conformity. . . ." A student personnel committee consisting of Armacost, the Dean of Women, and three faculty members formulated broad policy, an arrangement that maintained an important link between personnel policy and the educational program.[42]

Armacost left Augsburg in 1965 to accept a position with the Association of American Colleges in Washington, D.C. Glen W. Johnson, Armacost's successor who had served as assistant dean since 1961, carried on in the same tradition. Miss Mortensen retired in 1964; she was replaced by Miss Fern Martinson, formerly Dean of Women at Augustana College, Sioux Falls. Two years later the appointment of Thomas R. Holman as college psychologist strengthened the personnel department's counseling effort.

In the early 1960s a drive to create a "society system" on campus gained momentum — the designation "fraternity-sorority" was scrupulously avoided. Proponents argued that such a system would enrich social life, build rapport between campus and off-campus students, bridge the gap separating other interest groups within the college community, and promote the sponsorship of socially useful projects. On April 15, 1964, the student council adopted the report of a special committee appointed earlier to investigate the question. The report recommended a society system operating under the jurisdiction of a council and in strict accordance with procedures designed to prevent discrimination of any kind.[43]

Following student council acceptance an all-school referendum registered a vote of 270 in favor of and 213 against the scheme. Thereupon, the issue was referred to the student personnel committee and ultimately the faculty; the latter voted for the proposal by an overwhelming majority. Formation of the societies began early in 1965; a year later ten of them were operative.[44] As the centennial year approached the society system's long-range impact could not be determined. No one claimed that it was completely fulfilling the goals promised by its original advocates or that it was transforming student life for better or worse. At the same time the societies apparently had become an established institution within Augsburg's structure.

WHILE AUGSBURG'S educational program was responding to change, one somber continuity persisted: an inadequate economic base both from the standpoint of operating income and development. Although this difficulty plagued most private liberal arts colleges, a number of circumstances intensified Augsburg's problem. Clearly a church constituency of less than 100,000 members could not support an educational enterprise of such size and scope. Additional space for buildings and facilities was imperative: unlike institutions located in smaller population centers, Augsburg could extend its campus only through purchase of expensive urban real estate on a rising market. Furthermore, a poverty-stricken past had precluded the accumulation of capital reserves. On June 30, 1954, "Total Endowment and Other Non-Expendable Funds" equalled only $100,698.82.[45]

Among the steps that seemed to promise an amelioration of the school's financial plight, a broadening of the constituency through merger of the LFC with other Lutheran groups appealed to the leaders of Augsburg — which is not to say that economic privation was the only motive impelling them to support church union. In May, 1950 Christensen informed the board of trustees: "After long and careful thought, I have come to believe that the Lutheran Free Church might well at this time, without . . . being untrue to its heritage, begin to explore the possibilities of union with other Lutheran bodies closely related to it in spirit and background."[46] Thereafter, he and George S. Michaelsen, a key member of the board of trustees, emerged as effective proponents of merger.[47]

Church union, whatever its merits and long-range impact, fell short of being the financial panacea that some friends of the school had hoped. For one thing, its achievement required time. When the American Lutheran Church was constituted in 1960 the LFC was not one of its components; two congregational referenda, one taken in 1955 and the second in 1957, had registered insufficient majorities, a circumstance delaying merger until 1963. Nor did affiliation with the ALC substantially augment Augsburg's income, at least not immediately. In 1961 the LFC contributed $136,255 to Augsburg College and Seminary; two years later the ALC appropriated $126,750 for Augsburg College's current operations and $13,255 for its capital funds.[48]

A campaign to place the Cedar-Riverside area under the federal urban renewal program created another illusory hope: that Augsburg might be permitted to acquire land for campus use at non-speculative prices set by redevelopment authorities. However, early in 1961 the Minneapolis City Council defeated a renewal proposal, an action obliging private institutions in the area to manage their own redevelopment programs without benefit of eminent domain. Moreover, these programs had to operate within a context that included two projects armed with that prerogative: Interstate Freeway 94, and the University of Minnesota west bank campus.

By this time the college was responding to its development challenge on a broad front. When federal loan funds became available in 1955, it constructed the long-deferred women's dormitory, appropriately named Gerda Mortensen Hall. Reluctantly, it raised tuition (from $200 per semester in 1956 to $400 in 1962), and other fees. Under the competent direction of Burton Fosse it negotiated the purchase of real estate to provide space for campus expansion. By degrees it organized a more serious effort to forge a closer relationship with the Minneapolis community. A director of public relations had been appointed in 1946; a year later the board of trustees was enlarged from five to nine members. The size of the board was again increased in 1958, this time to twelve members, and to fifteen in 1960.

Norman L. Nielsen assumed office as vice-president in charge of development on July 1, 1958. Assisted by a board committee and two consultants Nielsen's office formulated a 20-year master campus plan that won board approval and was unveiled during homecoming festivities in October of the same year. The plan projected four 5-year stages of growth culminating in 1978 and entailing an expenditure of nearly $8,000,000. Phase one included construction of a gymnasium-auditorium, student union, and housing to accommodate 125 men and the same number of women. It also envisaged raising $500,000 for "educational development." The date for beginning construction of the gymnasium was set at January 1, 1960.[49]

Nielsen's development program got off to an auspicious start. Attention in 1959 was focused on the projected gymnasium, already named for John Sigurd Melby. On April 5, 1960, ground-breaking ceremonies heralded the start of construction; a year later the Spring Antiphony was "the first big event" held within its walls.[50] Meanwhile, Leonard F.

228

Ramberg, a Minneapolis banker and prominent civic leader, consented to serve as general chairman of the Augsburg Development Council, an appointment hailed by Christensen as "a major forward step in the present program of building and strengthening the college." [51] George Michaelsen, president of the board of trustees, informed the LFC conference of 1961 that development was "being pursued aggressively," adding that its efforts had yielded "increased financial gifts to Augsburg." [52]

Financial reports were less encouraging. While the new gymnasium added $1,000,000 to investment in plant, a debt of $750,000 encumbered the facility.[53] Instead of moving ahead with further plans, the board of trustees weighed the desirability of engaging Booz, Allen and Hamilton, a management consultant firm, "to conduct a survey and develop a comprehensive plan for Augsburg." [54] On October 26, after receiving a preliminary report from the firm, the trustees engaged its services. A month later Nielsen resigned, effective January 1, 1962, to accept a position with Lutheran Brotherhood Insurance Company.[55]

On December 6 Christensen stunned the faculty by announcing that he, too, was resigning, effective September 1, 1962. At times some of the teachers had disagreed with details of his policy — his reluctance to liberalize the social program, for example — but nearly all of them admired and appreciated his strong commitment to honest intellectual inquiry. They also recognized that his leadership had moved Augsburg from its "colonial period" into the mainstream of American higher education. By 1961 the school's educational program had achieved a high level of excellence in several areas.

Inevitably, conjecture about why the two resignations were tendered as well as their possible relationship to one another produced a number of theories. Nielsen issued no clarifying statements. Christensen's letter of resignation advanced two basic reasons for his wish to be relieved of presidential responsibility. "First and foremost," he was convinced that Augsburg needed "a more vigorous and effective leadership, both on campus and in the community, than I seem able to give at my present stage of life and strength." Second, he desired "to devote [his] remaining years of service . . . to study, teaching and direct religious work, more fully than would be possible while continuing to bear major administrative responsibilities." His decision "in this matter . . . was made about a year ago. . . ." [56] On December 8, after engaging in "a full and open discussion of all the implications," the trustees accepted Christensen's resignation. George Michaelsen informed the 1962 LFC conference: "Out of consideration for the man and in the sincere hope that it might also prove to be in the best interests of Augsburg the Board acceded to his wishes. . . ." [57]

THE NIELSEN AND CHRISTENSEN resignations, coming at a time when the college faced crucial issues with respect to its future, created an atmosphere of crisis at Augsburg. The board filled the Nielsen vacancy by naming Herbert W. Knopp, who for several years had served as a development consultant, as acting director of development, an arrangement that left the new president free to participate in the appointment of a permanent Nielsen successor. With the help of an elected faculty committee the board also instituted a search for presidential candidates. Unfortunately, the selection process failed to choose a new president before the effective date of Christensen's retirement. To fill this gap the board elected Leif S. Harbo, an Augsburg alumnus who was completing a distinguished career in public school administration, as interim president. The 1962 LFC conference ratified the board's action.

Although only one year in duration, the Harbo interregnum was a noteworthy period in Augsburg's history. Final approval of merger by the LFC necessitated several steps affecting Augsburg, including transfer of the seminary to the Luther campus in St. Paul, and of the college to ALC control. Ironically, the latter was basically effected through application of the Pattee-Bacon plan, with one important practical difference: the church was expected to provide a considerably smaller proportion of the school's total income than in the 1890s.

Before Harbo's administration ended the Booz-Allen-Hamilton report also spurred important decisions of long-range significance. Unlike the 1958 development plan, its recommendations realistically balanced means and ends, and assigned higher priority to the educational program than to brick and mortar. It laid particular stress on a substantial increase of faculty salaries, especially on the associate and full professor level; higher appropriations for the library; clarification of admission and student recruitment procedures; and a planned expansion of the student body, with due regard to an appropriate balance between men and women (55 per cent of the former), as well as an equal number of commuters and campus dwellers. In the area of new construction it proposed a college center and additional dormitory space by the autumn of 1965, providing capital funds were available. On October 25, 1962, the board adopted the report's basic recommendations, thereby establishing it as a guideline for the new administration.

230

THE SEARCH FOR a president ended on February 24, 1963, when Oscar A. Anderson accepted an offer extended to him by the board ten days earlier. Born in Minneapolis on April 19, 1916, Anderson was educated at Minnehaha Academy, Augsburg College, and St. Olaf College, where he received his B.A. *magna cum laude* in 1938. After graduation from Luther Theological Seminary in 1942 he entered the parish ministry, a calling he followed until 1948 when he became executive director of the International Young Peoples Luther League of the Evangelical Lutheran Church. Six years later he resigned this post to accept the pastorate of Trinity Lutheran Church at Moorhead, Minnesota, which he held until his appointment to Augsburg. Although a churchman rather than an educator, Anderson had established close ties with the academic community, particularly at Moorhead, the home of Concordia College and Moorhead State College. In addition he had recently studied at Union Theological Seminary, an experience that heightened his awareness of contemporary trends in theological scholarship.

Anderson assumed his responsibilities at Augsburg on July 1. He soon infused the office with a new style without fundamentally altering the course set by his predecessors. Faculty meetings were conducted with greater dispatch, and Anderson moved more easily in the Rotary-Kiwanis circuit than Christensen; many members of the Augsburg community found it more appropriate to call the new president "Oscar" than to address Christensen as "Bernhard." John D. Sorenson, an assistant in the office of public relations during the summer of 1962, was impressed with Anderson's "directness . . . conviction . . . energy . . . confidence in the direction which he is taking [and] good humor that creeps into even the most passionate discourse." [58] As the campus turmoil of the late 1960s gathered force, college presidents needed an ample reserve of such qualities.

Changes in structure and personnel accompanied the transition from the old administration to the new. The board of trustees became the board of regents — a designation favored within the ALC — and by stages was enlarged, a move permitting broader representation of the professional and business communities. Leonard Ramberg became a member of the board in 1962, succeeding Michaelsen as chairman two years later. On December 10, 1964, Anderson announced the appointment of a board of advisors headed by Walter H. Judd; its main function was to help augment financial support for the college. Clifford M. Johnson, vice-president in charge of development since 1962, resigned in 1964; he was succeeded by Kenneth P. Fagerlie. Harold Kambak, director of public relations, and Abner Batalden, director of alumni relations, had left the previous year to accept other posts. They were replaced by Donald Sorlien and Jeroy Carlson, respectively. Richard Holy became director of church relations in 1964. Sigvald Hjelmeland continued as associate director of development.

Turnover in the academic area was less sweeping but nonetheless important. Gerald Thorson resigned as English chairman in 1964 to accept a similar post at St. Olaf College; the vacancy created by his departure was not permanently filled until 1968 when F. Mark Davis was assigned to that position. On March 2, 1965, Martin Quanbeck resigned as Dean of the College effective at the close of the academic year, but continued as a member of the Education faculty. Kenneth C. Bailey, chairman of the philosophy department at Concordia (Moorhead), replaced Quanbeck as dean, taking office in the summer of 1965.

Shortly before resigning Quanbeck prepared a report based on a thorough study of the academic program and approved by the Educational Policies Committee. This document proposed no basic shift in emphasis, but advanced two controversial recommendations: adoption of a three-term system in place of the semester arrangement; and a phased liquidation of the home economics program. Both were adopted, the former more overwhelmingly than the latter.[59]

The decision to drop home economics was in no sense a reflection on Miss Segolson and her colleagues, Mrs. Katherine Peterson and Miss Ruth Songsteng, whose efforts had established a program fully accredited by state and federal authorities. The problem was rather an economic one. Operating a program that could meet constantly rising standards in terms of faculty size and equipment required a considerable expenditure per student. If home economics had been regarded as indispensable to Augsburg's liberal arts commitment, the faculty undoubtedly would have voted to retain it despite the cost factor. As it was, many faculty members agreed with the guideline defined by a faculty curriculum committee in 1956: "Vocational majors should be kept in the curriculum, but not at the expense of the liberal arts. If there is to be a choice between a vocational course and a stronger liberal arts program, the wise decision will always be made in favor of the latter." [60]

On December 2, 1964, the faculty approved a recommendation by the social science division calling for establishment of a political science department and major. The following year Myles C. Stenshoel, formerly political science professor at Augustana College (Sioux Falls), was appointed chairman and assigned responsibility for developing a program that became operative in 1966–67. In that year Mrs. Norma C. Noonan, a specialist in Soviet foreign policy, joined the department, and in

1967–68 a third member was added. As Augsburg's centennial approached, the department of business and economics was undergoing a similar reorganization and expansion, including a strengthening of course offerings, the addition of a combined business-economics major, and augmentation of the department's teaching force.

The creation of a separate political science department necessitated a restructuring of the history program now headed by Chrislock, who had succeeded Kleven as department chairman in 1963 — two years later Kleven retired as a member of the faculty. The new history program introduced several changes. It reduced emphasis on Europe in favor of heavier stress on the non-Western world. It also sought to provide students majoring in history with a variety of seminar opportunities; each of the five faculty members offered one seminar every year in his specialty.

These innovations were extensions of the drive to augment the academic program that began in earnest during Christensen's administration. At the same time consciousness of Augsburg's role as an urban institution became sharper. Anderson frequently coupled the "city college" theme with affirmations that Augsburg also was committed to the liberal arts and affiliated with the church. By stages a stronger urban emphasis became evident. Under the directorship of Robert W. Clyde the Social Science Research Center accepted assignments on specific urban problems, not only as a service to the community, but also in the belief that such research was adding to the total *corpus* of social science knowledge. In 1968–69 a grant from the ALC helped establish an urban programs office coordinated by William L. Youngdahl.

The campus community also responded to demands that minority history and culture be given more stress. Many faculty members and students felt that this need could be met most effectively by restructuring existing courses rather than launching ambitious programs in minority studies. Surveys of what was being done within the prevailing program were reassuring — the history faculty, for example, included two non-Western specialists — and potentialities for further improvements within established courses were discernible. Nevertheless, new curricular patterns were explored. A significant experiment known as the "Crisis Colony," an interdisciplinary class aiming to provide "a 'feeling' knowledge of communities and social conditions . . . known only intellectually before," was undertaken in 1968.[61] The college also endeavored to recruit more minority students, and negotiated an arrangement with the Way community center permitting Augsburg students to earn academic credit by taking a course in Afro-American culture taught by Milton D. Williams, educational director of the Way. In addition, discussions looking

233

toward a "consortium of collegiate effort" by several Upper Midwest institutions were conducted in 1968–69.

Meanwhile, the development program, which appeared to be stalled after the completion of Melby Hall, had resumed its advance. The ultimate pattern of redevelopment in the Cedar-Riverside area was slow to crystallize, but through land purchase the college acquired sufficient space for a viable campus — roughly a triangular tract bounded by Interstate 94, Riverside Avenue, 20th Avenue, and 25th Avenue South. The goal of a college center by 1965 was not achieved. Instead, the board authorized construction of the Studio Building in 1964–65, a facility designed as an art center, but pressed into service as a temporary student union until the college center was built. With the help of federal loan funds construction of the latter and Urness Tower, a dormitory for women named in honor of Mr. and Mrs. Andrew Urness, who had contributed generously to the college, began in the autumn of 1966. Both were ready for occupancy in the autumn of 1967.

Urness Tower restored a degree of physical visibility to the campus, recalling the days when Old Main dominated the landscape. As Willmar Thorkelson noted in June, 1969: "Stand on the Nicollet Mall in the heart of Minneapolis, look east on Sixth St., and 20 blocks distant you can see the tower building of America's 'most urban' Lutheran college." In 1969 it was uncertain when available resources would permit building the men's tower dormitory originally scheduled for construction along with the Urness facility. Nevertheless, response to the Centennial Building Fund campaign encouraged development officials; many Twin City firms and individuals participated for the first time in an Augsburg capital fund drive. Rapport between the school and its metropolitan neighbors needed improvement, but the town-gown relationship was more amicable and mutually rewarding than it had been a decade earlier.

TWO ACADEMIC REVOLUTIONS, one dating from the 19th century and the other barely emerging as Augsburg prepared to commemorate its centennial, profoundly affected American higher education in the 20th century. The nation's graduate schools and large universities generated the first. For denominational schools it involved escape from sectarian ghettos and the development of sufficient academic competence to meet accreditation norms established by the larger institutions. The proportion of its students gaining admission to graduate school and entree into the professions became the most reliable measure of a small college's success in coping with the first revolution.

The second proceeded beyond concern with academic competence to a search for "new ways of learning . . . new formulations of the world," and "new concepts of man and society." [62] Although far from "confessional" in a theological sense, it appeared to take the religious dimension of human existence seriously. In 1969 no one could perceive what curricular shape it would assume. Henry D. Aiken, professor of philosophy and the history of ideas at Brandeis University, suggests that it might include:

. . . new forms of extra-curricular activity that would replace Big Ten football with education programs conducted by college students and faculty in ghetto high schools; unconventional do-it-yourself courses by concerned teachers on problems of race relations and on the deadly imperialist politics of the technetronic societies; experimental work not only in creative writing, but in all forms of artistic and intellectual activity that do not fit established conceptions of the 'higher learning'; offbeat interpretations of recent and contemporary history that are not afraid to acknowledge the 'revolutionary' assumptions from which they proceed; and, not least, efforts toward cross-generational dialogue in which it is not assumed in advance that the only teachers have professorial rank.[63]

By 1910 Augsburg began to move haltingly toward the first revolution; in the next 30 years the school took additional forward steps and in the late 1950s was advancing significantly. By 1969 the first revolution had scarcely run its course, but the college's claim to academic excellence was credible.

Meanwhile, members of the Augsburg community were developing an awareness of the second revolution. A statement issued by President Anderson in April, 1969 characterized the city as an "unlimited laboratory" where "students and their teachers, through work-study programs, now have the opportunity to observe first-hand what textbooks have implied from afar." Anderson recognized that "some respected educators . . . would have the college or university retreat once more behind the ivied wall in the face of the giant tasks of making urban civilization livable. But Augsburg chooses to be of the city." [64] The emergence on campus of experimental programs such as the Crisis Colony suggested that this language was more than rhetorical.

On the other hand it was by no means certain that Augsburg would become a creative center of the second academic revolution. Whether the college community possessed sufficient wisdom to translate noble aspirations into effective action remained to be determined. So, too, did Augsburg's capacity to withstand whatever "law and order" backlash might be gaining strength within American society. The financial problem also was critical; many potential donors, whether taxpayers, church-goers, or businessmen, tended to prefer schools that supported continuity rather than change. Finally, the process of communicating and interpreting Augsburg's educational effort to the outside world required a high degree of skill.

Some advocates of experimental innovation believed their course to be consistent with Augsburg's earliest traditions, the school's retreat into isolation during its middle period notwithstanding. Sven Oftedal and Georg Sverdrup were sensitive to the plight of disadvantaged groups within American society and keenly conscious of the psychological lift provided by ethnic self-esteem. They were profoundly critical of the Norwegian and Norwegian-American establishments of their day. The two young professors also tried new teaching methodologies — the early examination system, for example — in an effort to help the student discover his own identity. Both emphatically rejected ivory tower concepts of education, believing that institutions of learning should relate organically to the communities (or congregations) that they ostensibly served. Augsburg could adopt a bold stance toward change without rejecting its 100-year heritage.

NOTES

CHAPTER 1 — IN THE BEGINNING

[1] *Catalog and Announcements of Augsburg Seminary*, 1907–08, 8, 9. Copies of all catalogs may be found in Augsburg College Archives.

[2] *Catalogue of Augsburg Seminary*, 1892–93, 7–8.

[3] In 1917–18 seminary enrollment was 26, the college, 25, and the academy, 63. Ten years later the count was 23, 248, and 42, respectively.

[4] E. Clifford Nelson and Eugene L. Fevold, *The Lutheran Church Among Norwegian-Americans: A History of the Evangelical Lutheran Church*, 1:126–150 (Minneapolis, 1960).

[5] Nelson-Fevold, 151–190.

[6] Nelson-Fevold, 191–198; G. Everett Arden, *The School of the Prophets: The Background and History of Augustana Theological Seminary, 1860–1960*, 69–173 (Rock Island, 1960).

[7] Christian Saugstad, *Augsburgs Historie*, 3 (Minneapolis, 1893).

[8] August Weenaas, *Mindeblade, Eller Otte Aar i Amerika*, 1–21 (Volden, 1890); Arden, 158; Nelson-Fevold, 198–200; Andreas Helland, *Augsburg Seminar Gjennum Femti Aar, 1869–1919*, 25–26 (Minneapolis, 1920).

[9] Helland, *Augsburg Seminar*, 35–39; Weenaas, *Mindeblade*, 26–27.

[10] Helland, *Augsburg Seminar*, 47.

[11] Saugstad, 4–5.

[12] Helland, *Augsburg Seminar*, 40–45.

[13] Weenaas, *Mindeblade*, 28.

[14] Weenaas, *Mindeblade*, 29.

[15] Helland, *Augsburg Seminar*, 49.

[16] Arden, 167–168; Helland, *Augsburg Seminar*, 27–28, 58–68; Nelson-Fevold, 1:200–218.

[17] Weenaas, *Mindeblade*, 46–47.

[18] Weenaas, *Mindeblade*, 48; Helland, *Augsburg Seminar*, 70–71.

[19] Saugstad, 6. See remarks of Pastor I. Tharaldsen to 1890 Convention of the United Church in *Beretning om Det 1ste Aarsmøde for Den forenede norsk-lutherske Kirke i Amerika*, 45 (Minneapolis, 1890). See also address of J. A. Bergh to Augsburg's 50th anniversary festivities quoted in *The Lutheran Free Church Messenger*, January 15, 1920, 3–4.

[20] Helland, *Augsburg Seminar*, 63.

[21] Helland, *Augsburg Seminar*, 113–118, 133–134; Helland, *Georg Sverdrup, The Man and His Message*, 49–50, 63–64 (Minneapolis, 1947).

[22] Weenaas, *Mindeblade*, 54.

[23] For an account of this episode, see J. A. Bergh address quoted in *The Lutheran Free Church Messenger*, January 15, 1920, 4.

[24] *Beretning om 2det aarlige Konferentsemøde af Konferentsen for den norsk-dansk ev. Lutherske Kirke i Amerika*, 34–36 (Hartland, Wisconsin, 1871).

[25] *In the District Court of the State of Minnesota In and For the Fourth Judicial District and County of Hennepin . . . March, 1897 . . . Affidavits of Sven Oftedal, et al*, 64 (Minneapolis); Ole Paulson, *Erindringer*, 225–226 (Minneapolis, 1907).

[26] Paulson, *Erindringer*, 229–230.

[27] *District Court . . . Minnesota . . . Sven Oftedal, et al,* 64–65.
[28] *Beretning . . . Konf . . . 1872,* 31–32.
[29] Paulson, *Erindringer,* 232–233.
[30] *Beretning . . . Konf . . . 1872,* 33.
[31] Weenaas, *Mindeblade,* 63.
[32] Lucile M. Kane, *The Falls That Built A City* (St. Paul, 1966).
[33] *Minneapolis Tribune,* November 1, 1872.
[34] John H. Blegen, *"Biografiske optegnelser for mine Barn,"* 108. The original handwritten manuscript is in the Manuscripts Division of the Minnesota Historical Society, St. Paul.
[35] *Beretning . . . Konf . . . 1873,* 53.
[36] *Beretning . . . Konf . . . 1873,* 57.
[37] Weenaas, *Mindeblade,* 74–75. The letter of call inviting Oftedal to join the Augsburg Seminary faculty is in the Oftedal Papers, Augsburg College Archives. See A. Weenaas and M. Falk Gjertsen to Oftedal, August 29, 1873.
[38] Lars Lillehei, "Sven Oftedal," in *Augsburg Seminary and The Lutheran Free Church,* 16–21 (Minneapolis, 1928).
[39] *Skandinaven,* January 30, 1874. Also the full text of *"Aapen Erklaering"* is carried in Helland, *Augsburg Seminar,* 440–442. On impact of the Declaration, see Nelson-Fevold, 224–226.
[40] *Skandinaven,* March 10, 1874; Lloyd Hustvedt, *Rasmus Bjørn Anderson, Pioneer Scholar,* 153–154 (Northfield, 1966).
[41] Helland, *Augsburg Seminar,* 91.
[42] Helland, *Augsburg Seminar,* 92–94; *Beretning . . . Konf . . . 1874,* 62–66.
[43] Helland, *Augsburg Seminar,* 119.
[44] Helland, *Georg Sverdrup,* 50.
[45] Helland, *Georg Sverdrup,* 71.
[46] Helland, *Georg Sverdrup,* 235. For a balanced biographical sketch of Georg Sverdrup, see John O. Evjen (trans.), "Georg Sverdrup," in *Augsburg Seminary and the Lutheran Free Church,* 5–15.
[47] Helland, *Georg Sverdrup,* 12–22.
[48] Udgivne i Udvalg, *Johan Sverdrup: Taler Holdte i Storthinget, 1851–1881,* 1, 616–617 (Kjøbenhavn, 1882).
[49] See, for example, his address of June 14, 1875, delivered at the dedication of the Augsburg Main Building. The complete text is in Professor Georg Sverdrup's *Samlede Skrifter i Udvalg,* 3:93–97 (Minneapolis, 1910).

CHAPTER 2 — THE SEARCH FOR A COLLEGE PROGRAM

[1] David T. Nelson, *Luther College: 1861–1961,* 90–91 (Decorah, 1961).
[2] Nelson, 183–185.
[3] Theodore C. Blegen, *Norwegian Migration to America: The American Transition,* 274 (Northfield, 1940).
[4] Theodore Blegen, 244.
[5] Nelson-Fevold, 1:143.
[6] Arden, 157–160.
[7] Weenaas, *Mindeblade,* 23–24.
[8] For a statement of Weenaas' pragmatism, see his report in *Beretning . . . Konf . . . 1875,* 38.
[9] Weenaas, *Mindebladet,* Appendix 1, *"Hvad vi Ville,"* 8–9.
[10] Weenaas, *Mindebladet,* 24.
[11] Helland, *Augsburg Seminar,* 438–439.
[12] For an account of the Racine meeting, see Helland, *Augsburg Seminar,* 47–53.

[13] Helland, *Augsburg Seminar*, 51.
[14] Weenaas, *Mindebladet*, 29.
[15] *Beretning . . . Konf . . . 1871*, 42; Helland, *Augsburg Seminar*, 346–347.
[16] Helland, *Augsburg Seminar*, 55.
[17] Weenaas, *Mindebladet*, 33–34; Weenaas, *Livserindringer: Fra Norge Og Amerika*, 130 (Bergen, 1935).
[18] *Beretning . . . Konf . . . 1871*, 42.
[19] *Beretning . . . Konf . . . 1871*, 14.
[20] *Beretning . . . Konf . . . 1871*, 36.
[21] *Beretning . . . Konf . . . 1872*, 72.
[22] *Beretning . . . Konf . . . 1873*, 54.
[23] James Gray, *The University of Minnesota: 1851–1951*, 49–50, 63 (Minneapolis, London, 1951); Frederick Rudolph, *The American College and University*, 283–284 (New York, 1962).
[24] *Beretning . . . Konf . . . 1873*, 53.
[25] *Beretning . . . Konf . . . 1874*, 62–65; Helland, *Augsburg Seminar*, 442–452.
[26] Helland, *Augsburg Seminar*, 121.
[27] Weenaas, *Mindebladet*, 83.
[28] *District Court . . . Minnesota . . . Sven Oftedal, et al*, 73.
[29] Weenaas, *Mindebladet*, 87.
[30] *District Court . . . Minnesota . . . Sven Oftedal, et al*, 74.
[31] *Beretning . . . Konf . . . 1874*, 63.
[32] Helland, *Augsburg Seminar*, 450. See 442–452 for full text of the *Interpretative Statement*.
[33] Helland, *Augsburg Seminar*, 443.
[34] Helland, *Augsburg Seminar*, 347–349.
[35] Helland, *Augsburg Seminar*, 350–351.
[36] Helland, *Augsburg Seminar*, 349–350.
[37] Helland, *Augsburg Seminar*, 450–451.
[38] Helland, *Augsburg Seminar*, 442.
[39] Gisle Bothne, *Det Norske Luther College, 1861–1897*, 127 (Decorah, 1897).
[40] Bothne, 128–129.
[41] Helland, *Augsburg Seminar*, 443–444.
[42] Helland, *Augsburg Seminar*, 444–445.
[43] Helland, *Augsburg Seminar*, 452.
[44] Helland, *Augsburg Seminar*, 445.

CHAPTER 3 — "EXCLUSIVELY . . . A DIVINITY SCHOOL"

[1] *Beretning . . . Konf . . . 1875*, 58–62.
[2] Helland, *Augsburg Seminar*, 378, includes a summary of student enrollment by departments from 1869 through 1919.
[3] *Beretning . . . Konf . . . 1876*, 36–39.
[4] John Blegen, 102–105, 113–114, 115.
[5] *Beretning . . . Konf . . . 1884*, 38.
[6] *Beretning . . . Konf . . . 1876*, 39; *1879*, 32, 34–35.
[7] Weenaas, *Livserindringer*, 162–163.
[8] *Beretning . . . Konf . . . 1875*, 63–66.
[9] Weenaas, *Mindebladet*, 92.
[10] Johan Olsen to The Theological Faculty of Augsburg Seminary, April 10, 1876, in Augsburg College Archives.
[11] *Beretning . . . Konf . . . 1876*, 27–31, 36–43.
[12] Nelson-Fevold, 1:225–226; Helland, *Augsburg Seminar*, 115.

[13] *Beretning . . . Konf . . . 1876*, 58.

[14] Helland, *Augsburg Seminar*, 145–146; 455–459.

[15] *Beretning . . . Konf . . . 1877*, 42–45, 50–51.

[16] Isaac Atwater, ed., *History of The City of Minneapolis*, 153–154 (New York, 1893).

[17] *Beretning . . . Konf . . . 1878*, 39–41.

[18] *Beretning . . . Konf . . . 1878*, 82–83; *1879*, 52; *1880*, 70–73; *1882*, 52–54, 90–91; Helland, *Georg Sverdrup*, 81–83.

[19] *Beretning . . . Konf . . . 1880*, 70; *1881*, 38.

[20] Nelson-Fevold, 1:235–237. For a classic statement of the Old School position, see *"De 30's Erklaering,"* in *Folkebladet*, August 10, 1882. Georg Sverdrup's reply defines the New School position in Helland, ed., *Samlede Skrifter i Udvalg*, 2:120–143 (Minneapolis, 1910). A complete file of *Folkebladet* from the first copy in August, 1877, to the last date of publication on July 30, 1952, may be seen in Augsburg College Archives.

[21] *Folkebladet*, December 21, 1882.

[22] Helland, *Georg Sverdrup*, 100.

[23] *Folkebladet*, December 28, 1882, February 8, 1883; Helland, *Augsburg Seminar*, 197.

[24] *Folkebladet*, April 19, 1883; *Beretning . . . Konf . . . 1883*, 34–39.

[25] *Beretning . . . Konf . . . 1883*, 67–71; Helland, *Augsburg Seminar*, 200–204; *Georg Sverdrup*, 100–111. A summary of the proceedings and debates of the 1883 Convention appears in *Folkebladet* for June 7, 14, 21, 1883.

[26] Nelson-Fevold, 1:234, 302–335.

[27] *Beretning . . . Konf . . . 1885*, 22; *1889*, 27–28.

[28] John J. Skørdalsvold, in a *Folkebladet* editorial on May 24, 1883, urged Augsburg's leaders to provide more educational opportunity for non-clergy, and also suggested the introduction of science courses into the curriculum.

[29] *Beretning . . . Konf . . . 1884*, 40, 77.

[30] *Beretning . . . Konf . . . 1885*, 11.

[31] Data on Augsburg's instructors and part-time teachers is included in Helland, *Augsburg Seminar*, 372–377.

[32] Helland, *Georg Sverdrup*, 117–118.

[33] Quoted in John M. Blum, et al, *The National Experience: A History of the United States*, 456 (New York, 1963).

[34] *Beretning . . . Konf . . . 1881*, 73–74.

[35] *Beretning . . . Konf . . . 1885*, 28–29.

[36] *Beretning . . . Konf . . . 1885*, 59.

[37] *Beretning . . . Konf . . . 1883*, 33, 73–74; Helland, *Augsburg Seminar*, 368.

[38] John Blegen, 172.

[39] *Beretning . . . Konf . . . 1886*, 64; *1889*, 33, 83; Helland, *Augsburg Seminar*, 367, 369.

[40] *Beretning . . . Konf . . . 1888*, 53, 95.

[41] Helland, *Augsburg Seminar*, 379–381.

[42] *Catalogue of Augsburg Seminary, 1892–1893*, 7; *Folkebladet*, August 22, 1890.

[43] Helland, *Augsburg Seminar*, 443.

[44] For development of these themes by Sverdrup, see Helland, ed., *Samlede Skrifter i Udvalg*, 1:358–384; 3:131–135. See also Oftedal letter to *Skandinaven*, March 10, 1874.

[45] In 1869, when he was only twenty years old, Georg Sverdrup wrote an essay setting forth his opinion concerning the proper organization of the Lutheran Church. See Helland, ed., *Samlede Skrifter i Udvalg*, 2:39–53, 4:171. According to Weenaas, Sverdrup and Oftedal envisaged a broad reform of American Lutheranism

that would serve as a model for the reform of the Norwegian State Church. See Weenaas, *Livserindringer*, 150.

46 Helland, ed., *Samlede Skrifter i Udvalg*, 3:6.

47 *Beretning* . . . *Konf* . . . *1877*, 55.

48 *Beretning* . . . *Konf* . . . *1877*, 80–81.

49 Nelson-Fevold, 1:318–321; Helland, ed., *Samlede Skrifter i Udvalg*, 2:133.

50 Helland, ed., *Samlede Skrifter i Udvalg*, 2:137.

51 Ivar Welle, *Kirkens Historie*, 3:264–266 (Oslo, 1948).

52 Johs. Lavik, *Spenningen I Norsk Kirkeliv*, 39–40 (Oslo, 1946).

53 For an account of Bjørnson's American tour, see Lloyd Hustvedt, 163–172.

54 Nina Draxten, "Kristofer Janson's Beginning Ministry," in *Norwegian-American Studies*, 23:126–174 (Northfield, 1967); O. N. Nelson, ed., *History of the Scandinavians and Successful Scandinavians in the United States*, 1:418–419 (Minneapolis, 1901).

55 *Folkebladet*, December 22, 1881.

56 *Folkebladet*, January 5, 1882.

57 Elias Aas, "The Pioneer Pastor," 43, unpublished manuscript in Augsburg College Archives.

58 J. E. Sars, *Norges Historie*, 6:14–15 (Kristiania, 1909).

59 Sars, 6:8–10.

60 Helland, ed., *Samlede Skrifter i Udvalg*, 1:209–210.

CHAPTER 4 — WHAT IS A DIVINITY SCHOOL?

1 For a full discussion of the 1890 merger, see Nelson-Fevold, 1:302–335; 2:3–37.

2 For an English translation of the Articles of Union, see Nelson-Fevold, 2:338–341.

3 Nelson-Fevold, 2:43.

4 *Beretning* . . . *Den f. Kirke* . . . *1890*, 117.

5 Nelson-Fevold, 2:29–30.

6 *Beretning* . . . *Den f. Kirke* . . . *1890*, 117.

7 Nelson-Fevold, 2:31.

8 *Folkebladet*, June 18, 1890; Nelson-Fevold, 2:32.

9 For several versions of the conspiracy theory, see Lars Lillehei, ed., *Augsburg Seminary and the Lutheran Free Church*, 99 (Minneapolis, 1928); Georg Sverdrup, "Hvorledes St. Olaf College Kom ind i Den forenede Kirke," in *Folkebladet*, November 18, 1891; Helland, *Augsburg Seminar*, 222–223.

10 Nelson-Fevold, 2:40.

11 *Folkebladet*, July 30, 1890.

12 *Catalog, 1890–91*, 23–25.

13 Nelson-Fevold, 2:44; Helland, *Augsburg Seminar*, 378.

14 *Folkebladet* reprinted the letter on August 5, 1891.

15 For examples of exchanges, see *Folkebladet*, September 30, November 11, 1891.

16 Helland, *Georg Sverdrup*, 151; Nelson-Fevold, 2:44fn; *Folkebladet*, August 19, 1891.

17 *Folkebladet*, March 11, 1891.

18 *Folkebladet* carried the original letter on April 15, and the retraction on May 27, 1891.

19 *Beretning* . . . *Den f. Kirke* . . . *1891*, 20–21.

20 *Beretning* . . . *Den f. Kirke* . . . *1891*, 92.

21 *Beretning* . . . *Den f. Kirke* . . . *1891*, 19.

22 *Beretning* . . . *Den f. Kirke* . . . *1891*, 140.

[23] *Folkebladet*, September 30, 1891.

[24] *Beretning . . . Den f. Kirke . . . 1891*, 147.

[25] For Mohn's report, see *Beretning . . . Den f. Kirke . . . 1891*, 98–101.

[26] *Beretning . . . Den f. Kirke . . . 1891*, 133.

[27] *Luthersk Kirkeblad*, 1:426 (July 4, 1891).

[28] *Folkebladet*, July 1, 1891.

[29] *Folkebladet*, September 9, 1891; Peer Strømme, *Erindringer*, 303–304 (Minneapolis, 1923).

[30] *Folkebladet*, September 2, 1891.

[31] *Folkebladet*, September 23, 1891.

[32] William C. Benson, *High on Manitou: A History of St. Olaf College, 1874–1949*, 81–95 (Northfield, 1949).

[33] Kenneth Bjork, ed., "Thorstein Veblen and St. Olaf College: A Group of Letters by Thorbjørn N. Mohn," in *Norwegian-American Studies and Records*, 15:122–130 (Northfield, 1949).

[34] *Catalog, 1900–1901*, 3.

[35] Helland, ed., *Samlede Skrifter i Udvalg*, 3:214.

[36] Helland, ed., *Samlede Skrifter i Udvalg*, 3:217–218.

[37] Helland, ed., *Samlede Skrifter i Udvalg*, 3:223.

[38] Helland, ed., *Samlede Skrifter i Udvalg*, 3:221.

[39] Helland, ed., *Samlede Skrifter i Udvalg*, 3:216.

[40] Helland, ed., *Samlede Skrifter i Udvalg*, 3:232.

[41] Helland, ed., *Samlede Skrifter i Udvalg*, 3:228.

[42] Helland, ed., *Samlede Skrifter i Udvalg*, 3:230.

[43] *District Court . . . Minnesota . . . Sven Oftedal, et al*, 74.

[44] See, for example, comment of J. A. Bergh, a Sverdrup adversary, in his volume, *Den norsk lutherske Kirkes Historie i Amerika*, 241 (Minneapolis, 1914).

CHAPTER 5 — SCHISM

[1] *Beretning . . . Konf . . . 1877*, 45–47.

[2] For full text of Ueland letter, see *District Court . . . Minnesota . . . Sven Oftedal, et al*, 104–110.

[3] See Nelson-Fevold, 2:52, for comment on Hoyme's course.

[4] *Forhandlingerne ved Den forenede Kirkes tredie Aarsmøde i Dawson, Minnesota, fra 15de til 23de Juni 1892*, 78 (Chicago, 1892).

[5] *Forhandlingerne . . . Den f. Kirke . . . 1892*, 64–67.

[6] *Folkebladet*, July 15, 1891.

[7] The original Board of Trustees Minutes are in Augsburg College Archives. See also *Folkebladet*, January 13, 1892.

[8] *Folkebladet*, March 23, 1892.

[9] *Beretning . . . Den f. Kirke . . . 1892*, 182–184.

[10] *Beretning . . . Den f. Kirke . . . 1892*, 185–188.

[11] *Forhandlingerne . . . Den f. Kirke . . . 1892*, 70.

[12] Peer Strømme, 304.

[13] Peer Strømme, 305. For Sverdrup's reply, see *Forhandlingerne . . . Den f. Kirke . . . 1892*, 155–156.

[14] *Forhandlingerne . . . Den f. Kirke . . . 1892*, 7.

[15] *Beretning . . . Den f. Kirke . . . 1892*, 156–158.

[16] For high point of debate, see *Forhandlingerne . . . Den f. Kirke . . . 1892*, 113–130. See also *Folkebladet*, June 29, 1892, for extended comment.

[17] *Beretning . . . Den f. Kirke . . . 1892*, 168.

[18] *Beretning . . . Den f. Kirke . . . 1892*, 158.

[19] *Beretning . . . Den f. Kirke . . . 1892*, 162.
[20] *Forhandlingerne . . . Den f. Kirke . . . 1892*, 130–132.
[21] *Forhandlingerne . . . Den f. Kirke . . . 1892*, 129–130, 135, 139.
[22] The original minutes are in Augsburg College Archives. See also *Folkebladet*, August 10, 1892; Nelson-Fevold, 2:62.
[23] *Folkebladet*, August 10, 1892.
[24] *District Court . . . Minnesota . . . Sven Oftedal, et al*, 117–119.
[25] *Beretning . . . Den f. Kirke . . . 1893*, 103–104.
[26] *Beretning . . . Den f. Kirke . . . 1893*, 184–185.
[27] *Luthersk Kirkeblad*, 3:170 (March 11, 1893). The final tally is printed in *Beretning . . . Den f. Kirke . . . 1893*, 190.
[28] *Beretning . . . Den f. Kirke . . . 1893*, 23–30.
[29] *Beretning . . . Den f. Kirke . . . 1893*, 192–203.
[30] *Beretning . . . Den f. Kirke . . . 1893*, 194. For Schmidt's remarks, see *Forhandlingerne . . . Den f. Kirke . . . 1893*, 151–152. On Mohn's attitude, see Nelson-Fevold, 2:64–65.
[31] *Forhandlingerne . . . Den f. Kirke . . . 1893*, 99–102.
[32] *Referat fra Mødet af Augsburgs Venner, afholdt i Minneapolis, Minn., fra 21de til 23de November, 1893*, 33–34 (Minneapolis, 1894).
[33] *Forhandlingerne . . . Den f. Kirke . . . 1893*, 189.
[34] In the contest for treasurer of the United Church, Lars Swenson, the "majority candidate," polled 500 votes to 153 for Halvor Engemoen, the "minority candidate." See *Beretning . . . Den f. Kirke . . . 1893*, 174.
[35] *Beretning . . . Den f. Kirke . . . 1893*, 202; *Forhandlingerne . . . Den f. Kirke . . . 1893*, 177–182.
[36] *Forhandlingerne . . . Den f. Kirke . . . 1893*, 209.
[37] *Forhandlingerne . . . Den f. Kirke . . . 1893*, 192–193.
[38] *Folkebladet*, June 21, 1893. A full text of the resolutions is printed in *Folkebladet*, July 12, 1893.
[39] *Beretning om Frikirkens Møde i Minneapolis, Minn., fra 9de til 13de Juni, 1897*, 47–50 (Minneapolis, n.d.).
[40] For differing versions of the publishing house confrontation, see *Folkebladet*, June 21, 1893; Nils C. Brun, ed., *Fra Ungdomsaar: en oversigt over Den Forenede Norske Lutherske Kirkes Historie og fremskridt i de svundne femogtyve aar*, 58–63 (Minneapolis, 1915).
[41] *Luthersk Kirkeblad*, 3:504–507 (August 5, 1893).
[42] *Luthersk Kirkeblad*, 3:507–508 (August 5, 1893); *Beretning . . . Den f. Kirke . . . 1894*, 116–117.
[43] Brun, 135, 157–158; *Beretning . . . Den f. Kirke . . . 1899*, 223–229.

CHAPTER 6 — RALLY AND SLUMP — 1893–1911

[1] *Beretning . . . Den f. Kirke . . . 1894*, 193.
[2] *District Court . . . Minnesota . . . Sven Oftedal, et al*, 42.
[3] *Beretning . . . Den f. Kirke . . . 1894*, 200–203.
[4] *Beretning . . . Den f. Kirke . . . 1895*, 22.
[5] *Beretning . . . Den f. Kirke . . . 1895*, 180–181, 188, 191.
[6] *Beretning . . . Frikirkens Møde . . . 1897*, 47–48.
[7] *Beretning . . . Den f. Kirke . . . 1896*, 185.
[8] *Beretning . . . Den f. Kirke . . . 1897*, 215–216; *Folkebladet*, December 9, 1896.
[9] *Supreme Court, State of Minnesota, Nils C. Brun, et al v. Sven Oftedal, et al, April Term, 1898*, 1038, 1040, 1041.

[10] Helland, *Augsburg Seminar*, 255; *Beretning . . . Frikirkens Møde . . . 1898*, 55. A copy of the decision is appended to the Board of Trustees Minutes for June 21, 1898.

[11] *Beretning . . . Den f. Kirke . . . 1898*, 231–232.

[12] *Beretning . . . Den f. Kirke . . . 1899*, 261–263.

[13] *Beretning om Den Lutherske Frikirkes 3 die Aarsmøde afholdt i Dalton, Otter Tail Co., Minn., fra 7de til 11te Juni 1899*, 30–33 (Minneapolis, 1899).

[14] *Beretning . . . Augsburgs Venner . . . 1894*, 35.

[15] Helland, *Augsburg Seminar*, 378.

[16] *Beretning . . . Frikirkens Møde . . . 1897*, 35.

[17] Board of Trustees Minutes, September 26, 1895; *Beretning . . . Augsburgs Venner . . . 1896*, 30.

[18] Helland, *Augsburg Seminar*, 252.

[19] *Beretning . . . Augsburgs Venner . . . 1896*, 40; *Beretning . . . Frikirkes . . . 1899*, 30.

[20] *Beretning . . . Frikirkes . . . 1899*, 72–73.

[21] *Beretning . . . Frikirkes . . . 1900*, 16–17.

[22] *Mindeblade om Indvielsen af Augsburg Seminariums nye Bygning*, 9–18 (Minneapolis, 1902).

[23] He had, for example, preached the festival sermon on the occasion of Augsburg's 25th anniversary. See *Beretning . . . Augsburgs Venner . . . 1894*, 15–23.

[24] Carl G. O. Hansen, *My Minneapolis*, 181–183 (Minneapolis, 1956).

[25] Carsten Hansteen and Laur Larsen to Georg Sverdrup, November 27, 1901, in untitled bound volume of documents concerning M. Falk Gjertsen case in the Georg Sverdrup Papers, Augsburg College Archives.

[26] *Minneapolis Times*, December 30, 1900.

[27] Kristiania Politikamer to Georg Sverdrup, June 14, 1901, in untitled documents.

[28] *Minneapolis Times*, June 30, 1901. An earlier statement by Gjertsen to *Folkebladet* (May 1, 1901), gave a different version of his departure.

[29] *Folkebladet*, May 1, 1901. Hansen comments on page 181 that the Gjertsen affair "surely was the talk of the town for some time."

[30] Report of a Trinity Congregation investigating committee in untitled documents 26–27; *Folkebladet*, September 4, 1901.

[31] Report of investigating committee, 2, 28–29; *Minneapolis Times*, January 16, 1902; *Minneapolis Tribune*, January 16, 1902.

[32] M. Falk Gjertsen to Sven Oftedal, March 1, 11, 1901, in Sven Oftedal Papers, Augsburg College Archives.

[33] Report of investigating committee, 12, 18, 20–21.

[34] *Skandinaven*, May 4, 1901.

[35] Helland, *Augsburg Seminar*, 262; *Beretning . . . Frikirkes . . . 1901*, 30.

[36] A. C. Paul to Otto Hanson, June 2, 1902, in Oftedal Papers.

[37] Helland, *Augsburg Seminar*, 261; *Beretning . . . Frikirkes . . . 1901*, 30.

[38] *Beretning . . . Frikirkes . . . 1901*, 61.

[39] *Beretning . . . Frikirkes . . . 1901*, 63; *1902*, 90.

[40] *Beretning . . . Frikirkes . . . 1901*, 62–63.

[41] *Mindeblade*, 77–78.

[42] Oftedal report to Augsburg Corporation, June 5, 1903, in Oftedal Papers.

[43] Helland, *Augsburg Seminar*, 378; Brun, ed., *Fra Ungdomsaar*, 150.

[44] Benson, 133–134, 141–143.

[45] David T. Nelson, *Luther College, 1861–1961*, 145, 147, 180–181, 185 (Decorah, 1961).

[46] See *Catalog, 1910–11*, 44, for synopsis of academy program after addition of fourth year.

[47] Helland, *Augsburg Seminar*, 270–276, 362, 365, 367–370.

48 Helland, ed., *Samlede Skrifter i Udvalg,* 3:65–97.

49 Helland, *Augsburg Seminar,* 278–285, 467–470; *Georg Sverdrup,* 273–277.

50 *Beretning . . . Frikirkes . . . 1906,* 31–32.

51 Helland, *Augsburg Seminar,* 286–290; *Georg Sverdrup,* 278–282.

52 Helland, "Twenty Letters to Lars," a confidential Augsburg memoir, 17, in the Andreas Helland Papers, Augsburg College Archives.

53 *Beretning . . . Frikirkes . . . 1907,* 72.

54 Board of Trustees Minutes, July 9, 1907; *Folkebladet,* July 17, 1907.

55 Helland, *Augsburg Seminar,* 293.

56 Interview with Gerda Mortensen, March 31, 1967.

57 Helland, *Augsburg Seminar,* 294–298.

58 *Beretning . . . Frikirkes . . . 1909,* 28–29.

59 *Beretning . . . Frikirkes . . . 1909,* 113.

60 *Beretning . . . Frikirkes . . . 1909,* 105; *Folkebladet,* June 23. 1909.

61 *Beretning . . . Frikirkes . . . 1909,* 106, 112.

62 *Folkebladet,* September 29, 1909. Interview with Paul G. Sonnack, Sr., March 31, 1967.

63 *Beretning . . . Frikirkes . . . 1908,* 107; Board of Trustees Minutes, June 15, 1908, June 15, 1909.

64 *Beretning . . . Frikirkes . . . 1910,* 40–47; *Folkebladet,* June 29, 1910.

65 *Beretning . . . Frikirkes . . . 1910,* 35, 39–40.

66 *Folkebladet,* April 5, 1911.

CHAPTER 7 — PATTERNS OF STUDENT LIFE

1 Helland, ed., *Samlede Skrifter i Udvalg,* 3:111–112.

2 *Beretning . . . Konf . . . 1883,* 34.

3 Helland, ed., *Samlede Skrifter i Udvalg,* 3:113.

4 Interview with Peder Konsterlie, March 31, 1967.

5 John Blegen, 138–149; H. N. Hendrickson to Edward S. Jones, February 8, 1932, in Hendrickson Papers, Augsburg College Archives; *Beretning . . . Konf . . . 1889,* 32.

6 John Blegen, 118.

7 For early Constitution of Boarding Club, see "*Boarding Klubben Protocol,*" 32–36. These and other minute books are in Augsburg College Archives.

8 See Minute Book for Medical Aid Society Constitution, 1–4; Helland, *Augsburg Seminar,* 331.

9 "Rules Governing Baths and Lavatories," Medical Aid Society Minutes, 9–11.

10 Agnes B. Tangjerd, "The George Sverdrup Library: A Story," 1–2, in Augsburg College Archives; *Beretning . . . Konf . . . 1872,* 76–77.

11 *Beretning . . . Konf . . . 1872,* 77–78.

12 Tangjerd, 4.

13 *Folkebladet,* March 3, 1881.

14 *Katalog for "Idun" og Augsburg Seminariums Bibliothek* (Minneapolis, 1892) lists all the holdings of the Augsburg libraries.

15 "Minutes of the Students' Historical Association of Augsburg Seminary," November 9, 1898.

16 The minutes include an inventory of the volumes purchased.

17 Tangjerd, 4.

18 Tangjerd, 6.

19 Students, pleading that they were heavily burdened with other concerns, submitted a petition to the faculty requesting teachers to assume full responsibility for the library. See Faculty Minutes, November 1, 1909.

[20] *Beretning . . . Den f. Kirke . . . 1908*, 49; *Augsburg Echo*, March, 1908. A complete file of the school's newspapers is in the Augsburg College Archives.
[21] Tangjerd, 7.
[22] Tangjerd, 5; *Augsburg Echo*, January, 1904, September–October, 1907.
[23] Interview with Gerda Mortensen, April 8, 1967.
[24] *Beretning . . . Den f. Kirke . . . 1925*, 35; *Augsburg Echo*, May 27, 1926.
[25] "Register of Demosthean Society," September 25, 1872 to May 3, 1876.
[26] See Athenaeum and Norønna Minutes; *Catalog, 1908–09*, 49.
[27] "*Referat Bok for den Nationale Øvelsesforening og Norønna fra 4de Okt. 1878 . . . til 17de Febr. 1899.*"
[28] *Beretning . . . Konf . . . 1873*, 56.
[29] H. N. Hendrickson, "Music at Augsburg," 1, a typewritten manuscript in the Hendrickson Papers.
[30] *Beretning . . . Konf . . . 1879*, 53.
[31] *Beretning . . . Konf . . . 1880*, 48.
[32] *Beretning . . . Konf . . . 1883*, 32–33, *1884*, 38.
[33] Johannes L. Nydahl, *Afholdssagens Historie*, 267 (Minneapolis, 1896).
[34] Quoted in Nydahl, 265.
[35] Nydahl, 295–298; Hendrickson, 2.
[36] Leola Nelson Bergmann, *Music Master of the Middle West: The Story of F. Melius Christiansen and the St. Olaf Choir*, 60 (Minneapolis, 1944).
[37] Hendrickson, 2–3.
[38] Bergmann, 44.
[39] Bergmann, 52.
[40] Bergmann, 51.
[41] Unless otherwise indicated, all information concerning prohibition activity on the Augsburg campus has been taken from "*Referater, Augsburg Seminarium Prohibitionsklub*," Augsburg College Archives.
[42] "*Forhandlinger, Skoledirectionen*," 64, Augsburg College Archives.
[43] "*Forhandlinger, Skoledirectionen*," 68.
[44] *Katalog, 1890–91*, 11.
[45] "*Referater af Missionsforenings Forhandlinger.*"
[46] Bergmann, 41.
[47] Interview with Bernhard Helland, April 8, 1967.
[48] Hendrickson, 3–4.
[49] *Augsburg Echo*, March, April, 1905; March, April, 1907.
[50] *Augsburg Echo*, November, December, 1905; January, 1907.
[51] *Augsburg Echo*, April, May–June, September–October, November, December, 1906.
[52] See Hans Urseth's remarks on this problem in *Mindeblade*, 63–64.
[53] *Beretning . . . Den f. Kirke . . . 1927*, 216.
[54] *Augsburg Echo*, May–June, 1905; May, 1907; May–June, 1909.
[55] Interview with Peder Konsterlie, March 31, 1967.
[56] A copy of the petition is in the Board of Trustees File, Augsburg College Archives. See also Board of Trustees Minutes, January 18, 1906; *Augsburg Echo*, February, 1906.
[57] Helland, "Twenty Letters to Lars," 14–15.
[58] *Catalog, 1907–08*, 8, 9.
[59] *Catalog, 1908–09*, 8, 13.
[60] *Augsburg Echo*, September–October, 1907.
[61] *Augsburg Echo*, April, 1908.
[62] For an anti-athletic polemic, see "*En samtale med Onkel*," in *Augsburg Echo*, March, 1908.

CHAPTER 8 — TOWN AND GOWN

[1] John Blegen, 100.

[2] John Blegen, 141–142.

[3] Quoted in Martin Shirley, *Historiske Smuler samlede ved Augsburg Seminarium og Konferentsens Aarsmøder*, 9 (Minneapolis, 1879).

[4] Helland, ed., *Samlede Skrifter i Udvalg*, 1:358–384.

[5] Helland, ed., *Samlede Skrifter i Udvalg*, 1:361.

[6] Helland, ed., *Samlede Skrifter i Udvalg*, 1:381–382.

[7] Helland, ed., *Samlede Skrifter i Udvalg*, 1:383.

[8] Lillehei, ed., *Augsburg Seminary and the Lutheran Free Church*, 20.

[9] Minneapolis Board of Education Minutes, April 11, 1878; April 20, 1880; April 18, 1882; April 25, 1883; April 15, 1884; April 21, 1885.

[10] Weenaas, *Livserindringer*, 195.

[11] Bergh, 228–229.

[12] Hustvedt, 157.

[13] Lillehei, ed., *Augsburg Seminary and the Lutheran Free Church*, 20–21.

[14] *District Court . . . Minnesota . . . Sven Oftedal, et al*, 7.

[15] A copy of the Commercial Club resolution, dated June 3, 1901, is in the Oftedal Papers.

[16] *Beretning . . . Frikirkes . . . 1902*, 41–44, 57–58.

[17] A. C. Paul to S. S. Glartun (Willmar, Minnesota businessman), June 3, 1902, in Oftedal Papers. See also Wallace G. Nye to H. A. Urseth, February 4, 1903, in Urseth Papers. Augsburg leaders attempted to influence the Commercial Club through Norse-American businessmen. See Halvor Shipstead to Andreas Helland, May 27, 1902, in Helland Papers.

[18] *Folkebladet*, April 6, 1882.

[19] Helland, ed., *Samlede Skrifter i Udvalg*, 1:177, 188.

[20] Faculty Minutes for December 3, 1907, note with apprehension that Augsburg was "located in an area where young men are threatened with grave dangers and temptations."

[21] *Beretning . . . Den f. Kirke . . . 1891*, 78.

[22] *Folkebladet*, July 27, 1892.

[23] On Washburn-Nelson senatorial contest, see William W. Folwell, *A History of Minnesota*, 3:489–499 (St. Paul, 1926); George M. Stephenson, *John Lind of Minnesota*, 97–101 (Minneapolis, 1935).

[24] *Folkebladet*, January 23, 1895.

[25] See, for example, *Minneapolis Journal*, January 23, 1895.

[26] *Folkebladet*, January 30, 1895.

[27] *Fortune Magazine*, 13:116 (April, 1936).

[28] Hanson, 133–137.

[29] *Folkebladet*, October 1, 1913.

[30] Nydahl, 262–263; *Folkebladet*, April 19, 1883.

[31] Nydahl, 264–265.

[32] L. G. Almen to Knute Nelson, July 17, July 25, 1892, in the Knute Nelson Papers, Minnesota Historical Society, St. Paul.

[33] Nydahl, 272–274.

[34] Nydahl, 294, 298; *Folkebladet*, October 21, 1896.

[35] *Minneapolis Tribune*, November 2, 1892.

[36] *The Progressive Age*, November 5, 1892.

[37] *Folkebladet*, September 30, 1896.

[38] *Beretning . . . Frikirkes . . . 1908*, 60; *1913*, 281.

[39] Augsburg Alumni Association Minutes, May 24, 1912.

[40] *Lutheran Free Church Messenger*, April 15, 1922; *Folkebladet*, October 25, 1922.

CHAPTER 9 — THE EMERGENCE OF AUGSBURG COLLEGE

[1] See T. O. Burntvedt, "Memorial Address," in *George Sverdrup: 1879–1937*, 8 (Minneapolis, 1938); N. N. Rønning, *Fifty Years in America*, 187–188 (Minneapolis, 1938).

[2] Georg Sverdrup to George Sverdrup, July 8, 1902; Charles C. Torrey to George Sverdrup, February 1, 1903, in the Sverdrup Papers.

[3] Georg Sverdrup to George Sverdrup, January 8, 1907.

[4] See *Folkebladet*, September 29, 1909, for a full account of George Sverdrup's early life. On his plans to complete the doctorate degree, see Charles Torrey to George Sverdrup, October 12, 1907.

[5] Rønning, 188.

[6] Helland, *Augsburg Seminar*, 429.

[7] See *Folkebladet*, December 16, 1925, January 13, 1926, for biographical data on Birkeland.

[8] Helland, *Augsburg Seminar*, 312–313; *Beretning . . . Frikirkes . . . 1919*, 41, 53–54.

[9] Faculty Minutes, March 7, 1910.

[10] Faculty Minutes for March 6, 1911, carry the full text of the Haynes report.

[11] *Beretning . . . Frikirkes . . . 1911*, 54, 124; Helland, *Augsburg Seminar*, 315.

[12] Faculty Minutes, May 25, 1911; Board of Trustees Minutes, July 11, 1911.

[13] E. B. Pierce to the President, Augsburg Seminary, May 8, June 4, 1915, in the Sverdrup Papers.

[14] A communication from Royal R. Shumway to George Sverdrup, March 23, 1916, enclosed the reports of individual inspectors. In the Sverdrup Papers.

[15] E. B. Pierce to George Sverdrup, May 17, 1916, in the Sverdrup Papers.

[16] Royal Shumway to George Sverdrup, February 20, 1917.

[17] *Beretning . . . Frikirkes . . . 1916*, 39–40; *1917*, 35; *1918*, 30–31.

[18] *Augsburg Echo, May*, 1919.

[19] *Beretning . . . Frikirkes . . . 1919*, 50–51, 161.

[20] Board of Trustees Minutes, July 15, 1919; Faculty Minutes, August 6, September 3, 1919.

[21] On Evjen controversy, see Helland, *Augsburg Seminar*, 321–323; *Beretning . . . Frikirkes . . . 1919*, 44–45.

[22] Helland, *Augsburg Seminar*, 413–425.

[23] Augsburg Alumni Association Minutes, November 28, 1919.

[24] *Lutheran Free Church Messenger*, April 15, 1920.

[25] Augsburg Alumni Association Minutes, March 30, 1920.

[26] *Lutheran Free Church Messenger*, June 15, 1920.

[27] *Beretning . . . Frikirkes . . . 1920*, 110, 151–154, 222.

[28] *Lutheran Free Church Messenger*, June 15, 1920.

[29] See exchange between *"En gammel Augsburger"* and Elias P. Harbo, in *Folkebladet*, July 31, August 4, September 8, 1920.

[30] *Folkebladet*, January 26, 1921.

[31] *Folkebladet*, March 2, 1921.

[32] *Folkebladet*, May 4, 1921.

[33] See *Folkebladet*, April 27, 1921, for article by Birkeland summarizing varied opinions.

[34] *Beretning . . . Frikirkes . . . 1921*, 34–35.

[35] *Beretning . . . Frikirkes . . . 1921*, 32–33.

[36] *Beretning . . . Frikirkes . . . 1921*, 43–46.

[37] *Folkebladet*, June 29, 1921; *Beretning . . . Frikirkes . . . 1921*, 236–243.

[38] *Lutheran Free Church Messenger*, November 15, 1921.

NOTES — CHAPTER TEN

[39] *Folkebladet,* June 21, 28, 1922; *Beretning . . . Frikirkes . . . 1922,* 232.

[40] Board of Trustees Minutes, July 15, 1922, July 31, 1923; *Beretning . . . Frikirkes . . . 1923,* 35.

[41] *Beretning . . . Frikirkes . . . 1921,* 36–37, 164.

[42] *Folkebladet,* September 14, 1921.

[43] Theresa G. Haynes, "Augsburg Park, A Forgotten Dream," *Minnesota History,* 40:378 (Winter, 1967).

[44] *Beretning . . . Frikirkes . . . 1922,* 173.

[45] *Beretning . . . Frikirkes . . . 1926,* 149–150.

[46] Haynes, 379.

[47] *Folkebladet,* December 7, 1921.

[48] Data concerning curricular expansion and change is gathered from Augsburg College catalogs.

[49] See *Lutheran Messenger,* February 1, 1955, for biographical sketch of Melby. See also Bernhard Christensen, "Si Melby of Augsburg," in *The Lutheran Ambassador,* December 10, 1968.

[50] J. S. Melby to George Sverdrup (1930?), in the Sverdrup Papers.

[51] *Augsburgian,* 1922, 97–100; 1924, 94–97, 100–101.

[52] *Augsburg Echo,* December, 1924.

[53] *Augsburgian,* 1926 (n.p.); 1928, 82–85.

[54] *Augsburgian,* 1928, 86–89.

[55] Governor Theodore Christianson to General Douglas MacArthur, January 18, 20, 1928; Walter H. Newton to J. S. Melby, January 19, 23, 1928; Douglas MacArthur to William S. Haddock, January 19, 1928; Douglas MacArthur to Walter H. Newton, January 19, 1928; Ludwig I. Roe to J. S. Melby, January 23, 27, 1928; *Wall Street Journal,* January 23, 1928, all in Melby Papers.

[56] See *Folkebladet,* September 15, 1920, for Professor Lillehei's comments on social refinement as an educational goal.

[57] *Augsburgian,* 1922, 30–40; 1924, 72–80; 1926 (n.p.).

[58] *Augsburgian,* 1926 (n.p.).

[59] See, for example, Henry P. Opseth, "The Appreciation of Music," in *Augsburgian,* 1924, 79.

[60] Leland B. Sateren, "Opsethiana," *Christmas Echoes,* 24ff (Minneapolis, 1951).

[61] Carl Fosse, "Christianity in Science," *Lutheran Messenger,* October 15, 1936. See *Lutheran Messenger,* April 28, 1942, for biographical sketch of Fosse.

[62] "Distinguished Alumni Citations, Friday, October 20, 1967," Arthur B. Nash Biographical File, Augsburg College Archives.

[63] Interview with Mrs. Marion Lindemann, February 9, 1967.

[64] *Augsburg Echo,* November 7, 1945; *Lutheran Messenger,* July 21, 1953.

[65] *Augsburgian,* 1928, 9, 68.

CHAPTER 10 — DEPRESSION DECADE

[1] *Beretning . . . Frikirkes . . . 1928,* 23–27.

[2] *Beretning . . . Frikirkes . . . 1923,* 15–16.

[3] *Beretning . . . Frikirkes . . . 1923,* 42–44.

[4] *Beretning . . . Frikirkes . . . 1923,* 101–104.

[5] *Beretning . . . Frikirkes . . . 1923,* 134–135, 137–139.

[6] *Folkebladet,* April 2, 9, 16, 23, 30, May 14, 1924.

[7] *Folkebladet,* May 7, 21, 28, 1924.

[8] *Beretning . . . Frikirkes . . . 1924,* 159.

[9] *Beretning . . . Frikirkes . . . 1924,* 140–141.

[10] *Beretning . . . Frikirkes . . . 1925,* 130, 161–162; *Folkebladet,* June 24, 1925; Board of Trustees Minutes, July 1, 14, 1925.

[11] *Beretning . . . Frikirkes . . . 1925,* 135–136.

[12] *Folkebladet,* March 31, 1926, carried the report in full. See also *Beretning . . . Frikirkes . . . 1926,* 134–142.

[13] Augsburg Alumni Association Minutes, June 10, 1926; *Beretning . . . Frikirkes . . . 1926,* 144.

[14] *Beretning . . . Frikirkes . . . 1926,* 148–150, 173–174; *1927,* 28–29, 127; *Folkebladet,* June 30, 1926.

[15] *Beretning . . . Frikirkes . . . 1927,* 35–37; *1928,* 33–35.

[16] *Beretning . . . Frikirkes . . . 1928,* 124–125. The report is in English.

[17] *Beretning . . . Frikirkes . . . 1927,* 34, 128.

[18] *Folkebladet,* June 6, 13, 1928.

[19] Lars P. Qualben and Claus Morgan, *Norsk Luthersk Kirkelig Forening,* 34 (Minneapolis, 1928).

[20] J. S. Melby, *The Chief Fallacies of Dr. Qualben's "Bluebook,"* 15–16 (n.d.).

[21] Lars Qualben, "Augsburg and Lutheran Church Unity," 6, a mimeographed manuscript in the Qualben Papers.

[22] *Beretning . . . Frikirkes . . . 1928,* 29–33.

[23] Claus Morgan to George Sverdrup, September 21, 1928; O. H. Sletten to George Sverdrup, October 24, 1928, in the Sverdrup Papers.

[24] *Folkebladet,* June 20, 1928.

[25] *Beretning . . . Frikirkes . . . 1928,* 180–181.

[26] Board of Trustees Minutes, June 16, July 10, 11, 24, 1928. For Sverdrup's version of negotiations, see George Sverdrup to A. S. Berg, September 19, 1928, in the Sverdrup Papers. For Qualben's version, see "Augsburg and Lutheran Church Unity," 9–13.

[27] *Beretning . . . Frikirkes . . . 1929,* 31–32.

[28] *Beretning . . . Frikirkes . . . 1929,* 57–58.

[29] *Beretning . . . Frikirkes . . . 1930,* 45–46, 57–60.

[30] Hammer's 1930 report commented: "It is conservative to say that Augsburg . . . needs $50,000 from the Lutheran Free Church annually." *Beretning . . . Frikirkes . . . 1930,* 36.

[31] *Beretning . . . Frikirkes . . . 1931,* 31.

[32] Board of Trustees Minutes, June 4, 1931.

[33] *Beretning . . . Frikirkes . . . 1931,* 33–34.

[34] *Beretning . . . Frikirkes . . . 1931,* 52.

[35] *Beretning . . . Frikirkes . . . 1932,* 39.

[36] *Beretning . . . Frikirkes . . . 1932,* 47–49.

[37] *Annual Report of the Lutheran Free Church 37th Annual Conference, June 13th to 18th, 1933,* 22, 28–30 (Minneapolis).

[38] Board of Trustees Minutes, April 19, 20, 1933; *Annual Report . . . LFC . . . 1933,* 39.

[39] *Annual Report . . . LFC . . . 1934,* 28–30, 33–36.

[40] Board of Trustees Minutes, May 16, July 10, 1934.

[41] *Annual Report . . . LFC . . . 1935,* 29–32.

[42] *Annual Report . . . LFC . . . 1935,* 28.

[43] *Annual Report . . . LFC . . . 1936,* 35; *1937,* 38.

[44] *Beretning . . . Frikirkes . . . 1931,* 39; *Annual Report . . . LFC . . . 1941,* 29.

[45] Board of Trustees Minutes, April 29, 1931; *Beretning . . . Frikirkes . . . 1931,* 32–33, 53.

[46] *Annual Report . . . LFC . . . 1934,* 87–90.

[47] *Annual Report . . . LFC . . . 1937,* 39.

48 *Beretning . . . Frikirkes . . . 1931*, 40; *1932*, 48.

49 *Augsburg Echo*, October 28, 1935.

50 *Augsburg Echo*, November 24, 1933.

51 *Augsburg Echo*, March 29, 1934.

52 *Beretning . . . Frikirkes . . . 1931*, 32–33; *Catalog, 1931–32*, 33.

53 Tangjerd, 8–9; *Augsburg Echo*, January 19, 1929; January 26, 1934; Lindemann interview, February 23, 1967.

54 Bernhard M. Christensen to George Sverdrup, February 22, 1927, in the Sverdrup Papers.

55 Christensen to Sverdrup, August 13, 1927.

56 Christensen to Sverdrup, December 3, 1927.

57 Christensen to Sverdrup, January 25, 1928.

58 Christensen to Sverdrup, May 18, 1928.

59 Christensen to Sverdrup, October 17, 1928.

60 Christensen to Sverdrup, November 29, 1928.

61 Christensen to Sverdrup, November 21, 1928.

62 Christensen to Sverdrup, November 29, 1928.

63 A copy of the theological faculty's resolution is in the Sverdrup Papers, December, 1928.

64 Christensen to Sverdrup, April 1, October 9, 1929; January 24, 1930.

65 C. Lloyd Bjornlie to Martin Quanbeck, August 2, 1966, in Dean of the College Collection, Augsburg College Archives.

66 George Sverdrup to Theodore Blegen, March 29, 1930, in the Sverdrup Papers; *Beretning . . . Frikirkes . . . 1930*, 43.

67 Martin Quanbeck to C. Lloyd Bjornlie, August 5, 1966, in Dean of the College Collection.

68 *Beretning . . . Frikirkes . . . 1920*, 47–48.

69 In requesting Dean Shumway of the University of Minnesota to intervene on behalf of an Augsburg graduate seeking admission to the University of Wisconsin, Sverdrup commented: "I am sorry to be compelled to bother you so frequently . . . but these matters are of first importance to Augsburg College." See George Sverdrup to R. R. Shumway, May 18, 1932, in the Sverdrup Papers.

70 *Beretning . . . Frikirkes . . . 1931*, 36.

71 Board of Trustees Minutes, September 21, 1932.

72 Interview with Abner B. Batalden, January 2, 1967; *Annual Report . . . LFC . . . 1936*, 39.

73 *Augsburg Student Hand-Book and Directory, 1933–34*, 9 (Minneapolis, 1933).

74 *Student Hand-Book, 1934–35*, 9.

75 *Annual Report . . . LFC . . . 1937*, 44.

76 George Sverdrup to John A. Houkom, February 6, 1937, Sverre Norborg to Clergy of the Lutheran Free Church, February 20, 1937, in Board of Trustees Collection.

77 Minutes of Augsburg Corporation, May 11, 1937; George Sverdrup to Corporation members, April 5, 1937, in Augsburg College Corporation Collection.

78 *Annual Report . . . LFC . . . 1937*, 44.

79 *Annual Report . . . LFC . . . 1937*, 40.

80 *Annual Report . . . LFC . . . 1937*, 57–58.

81 *Augsburg Echo*, October 8, 1937.

82 *Augsburg Echo*, January 21, 1938.

83 *Annual Report . . . LFC . . . 1938*, 38–40.

84 Bernhard Christensen, "George Sverdrup, Teacher," in *George Sverdrup: 1879–1937*, 23.

85 Christensen, "George Sverdrup, Teacher," 17.

NOTES — CHAPTER ELEVEN

CHAPTER 11 — "THE COLONIAL PERIOD IS . . . PRACTICALLY PAST"

[1] John Houkom to Andreas Helland, January 5, 1938; Houkom to P. A. Sveeggen, February 22, 1938, in Board of Trustees Collection; *Annual Report . . . LFC . . . 1938*, 35.

[2] *The Lutheran Messenger*, March 1, 1938. See also Norborg article in *Folkebladet*, April 27, 1938.

[3] Board of Trustees Minutes, March 9–10, 1938; Augsburg Corporation Minutes, March 9, 1938.

[4] Houkom to Burntvedt, April 25, 1938. This and the following related correspondence may be found in the Board of Trustees Collection.

[5] Houkom to Andreas Helland, March 23, 1938.

[6] Christensen to Houkom, March 19, 1938.

[7] Norborg to Houkom, March 14, 1938.

[8] Houkom to Norborg, March 22, 1938; Houkom to Christensen, March 23, 1938; Houkom to Burntvedt, March 23, 1938; Burntvedt to Houkom, March 26, 1938; Andreas Helland to Houkom, April 2, 1938.

[9] *The Lutheran Messenger*, May 1, 1938.

[10] *Folkebladet*, May 11, 1938; *The Lutheran Messenger*, May 15, 1938.

[11] *Folkebladet*, May 18, 25, 1938. One *Folkebladet* correspondent asserted that for the Board of Trustees to submit only one candidate to the Annual Conference resembled "Hitlerism." (*det ser ut som en slags "hitlerisme."*) June 8, 1938.

[12] Interview with K. Berner Dahlen, December 31, 1968.

[13] *Folkebladet*, June 15, 22, 1938, carried a full account of the proceedings interspersed with critical comment. Interview with Gerda Mortensen, December 31, 1968; Dahlen interview, same date.

[14] *Annual Report . . . LFC . . . 1938*, 128–129; *Folkebladet*, June 22, 1938.

[15] Board of Trustees Minutes, June 13, 1938. The board also confirmed the nomination of Norborg as theological professor, but he declined the appointment. See Board of Trustees Minutes, July 28, 1938.

[16] *The Lutheran Messenger*, July 1, 1938.

[17] *The Lutheran Messenger*, November 1, 1938; *Folkebladet*, November 9, 1938; *Augsburg Echo*, November 17, 1938.

[18] *Annual Report . . . LFC . . . 1939*, 25, 27.

[19] *Annual Report . . . LFC . . . 1939*, 33–34.

[20] *The Lutheran Messenger*, July 1, 1938.

[21] *Annual Report . . . LFC . . . 1940*, 34.

[22] *Annual Report . . . LFC . . . 1940*, 35.

[23] *Annual Report . . . LFC . . . 1940*, 31.

[24] *Annual Report . . . LFC . . . 1940*, 39.

[25] *Annual Report . . . LFC . . . 1940*, 60.

[26] *Annual Report . . . LFC . . . 1942*, 40, 49–50.

[27] Christensen to Houkom, January 7, 1941, in the Board of Trustees Collection.

[28] *Annual Report . . . LFC . . . 1940*, 26–27; *1941*, 22.

[29] *Augsburg Echo*, November 16, 1939.

[30] Interview with Joel S. Torstenson, February 21, 1969.

[31] *Augsburg Echo*, May 29, 1940.

[32] Torstenson interview, February 29, 1969.

[33] *Annual Report . . . LFC . . . 1942*, 35.

[34] *Augsburg Echo*, December 17, 1941.

[35] *Annual Report . . . LFC . . . 1943*, 34.

[36] *Annual Report . . . LFC . . . 1944*, 30–31.

[37] *Annual Report . . . LFC . . . 1943*, 104–105.

[38] *Annual Report . . . LFC . . . 1944*, 40.

[39] Board of Trustees Minutes, October 13, 1942; *The Lutheran Messenger*, May 9, 1944; *Annual Report . . . LFC . . . 1944*, 33–35.

[40] *Annual Report . . . LFC . . . 1944*, 54–55, 130–133; Board of Trustees Minutes, July 11, 1944.

[41] M. G. Neale, "A Survey of Augsburg College," 51, in Dean of the College Collection.

[42] *Annual Report . . . LFC . . . 1945*, 33, 36–37, 44; *1946*, 39, 49; Board of Trustees Minutes, October 31, 1945.

[43] *Annual Report . . . LFC . . . 1947*, 38.

[44] Faculty Minutes, September 30, 1947; Minutes of Faculty Conference (Fall Workshop), September 8–9, 1949.

[45] *Annual Report . . . LFC . . . 1946*, 49.

[46] Board of Trustees Minutes, October 31, 1945; March 19, May 7, 1946.

[47] Board of Trustees Minutes, January 21, May 6, 1947; *Annual Report . . . LFC . . . 1947*, 42.

[48] The Christensen Papers include considerable correspondence relating to the council.

[49] *Annual Report . . . LFC . . . 1949*, 33.

[50] *Annual Report . . . LFC . . . 1947*, 34.

[51] See memorandum to the Campus Plans Committee Minutes, July 2, 1946; Board of Trustees Minutes, July 18, 1946.

[52] *Annual Report . . . LFC . . . 1951*, 38.

[53] Norman Burns to Bernhard Christensen, April 3, 1950.

[54] *Annual Report . . . LFC . . . 1950*, 37.

[55] *Annual Report . . . LFC . . . 1951*, 37.

[56] *Annual Report . . . LFC . . . 1951*, 45.

[57] *Annual Report . . . LFC . . . 1952*, 38, 45; *1953*, 30, 44–45; *1954*, 37, 50.

[58] *Annual Report . . . LFC . . . 1952*, 64; *1953*, 31–33; *1954*, 36, 143–144.

[59] *Annual Report . . . LFC . . . 1952*, 37–38.

[60] Neale, 23.

[61] *Annual Report . . . LFC . . . 1954*, 35.

[62] Christensen to members of faculty and staff, March 27, 1954, in the Christensen Papers.

CHAPTER 12 — THE MODERN AMERICAN COLLEGE

[1] *Annual Report . . . LFC . . . 1954*, 40; *1955*, 43; *1962*, 60–61, 70–71; Tangjerd, 20.

[2] "Chemistry Department Data, American Chemical Society Committee of Professional Training," 6 (March 21, 1961), in Chemistry Department files, Augsburg College Archives.

[3] Interview with Earl Alton, April 2, 1969. See also J. H. Howard to Bernhard M. Christensen, April 5, 1962, Chemistry Department files.

[4] "A Proposal to Research Corporation," 4–5 (February 6, 1962), Chemistry Department files.

[5] Interview with Ralph L. Sulerud, May 2, 1969.

[6] *Catalog, 1956*, 75.

[7] Annual Report of Sociology Department, 1954–55 (typewritten), Sociology Department files.

[8] Merrilyn Belgum, "A Report on Undergraduate Social Work Training at Augsburg College," 1963, 2, Sociology Department files.

[9] Belgum, 1.

[10] Interview with Joel Torstenson, April 4, 1969.

[11] Data on undergraduate programs in social work, 1966–67, is in Sociology Department files.

[12] See "A Proposal for an Augsburg College Research and Resource Center," 1965, Sociology Department files.

[13] Interview with Einar O. Johnson, April 8, 1969.

[14] Einar Johnson to faculty, June 1, 1962, Dean of the College files, Augsburg College Archives.

[15] Interview with Mrs. Grace H. Dyrud, December 28, 1968.

[16] Philip Quanbeck, "When Faith Goes to a Church College," in *Lutheran Standard*, 3 (March 18, 1969).

[17] Bernhard Christensen, "The Idea of the Lutheran Free Church," in *Freedom and Christian Education*, 37 (Minneapolis, 1945). According to Evjen, Georg Sverdrup's "conception of inspiration . . . was conservative, although he cast aside verbal inspiration." See *Augsburg Seminary and The Lutheran Free Church*, 11.

[18] *Catalog, 1953*, 61; interview with John Stensvaag, November 14, 1968.

[19] Interview with Paul Sonnack and Philip Quanbeck, November 14, 1968.

[20] Philip Quanbeck, "The Purpose and Program of the Department of Religion," 4–5, Department of Religion files.

[21] "Report of the Faculty Study Committee on the Educational Program," 4, 1956, Dean of the College Collection.

[22] *Augsburg Echo*, December 8, 1954.

[23] "Theatre at Augsburg," in Drama Department Scrapbook, 1, 1957–58.

[24] Howard C. Morgan to Ailene Cole, May 29, 1958, in Drama Department Scrapbook, 1957–58.

[25] *Catalog, 1960*, 58–59.

[26] Interview with Philip Thompson, April 12, 1969.

[27] Interview with Leland Sateren, April 21, 1969.

[28] Sateren interview.

[29] *Minneapolis Star*, March 13, 1967.

[30] Faculty Minutes, January 7, 1960, November 16, 1961; Peter H. Armacost, "Student Personnel Highlights," 5, August 1, 1965, in Dean of Students' files.

[31] Faculty Minutes, December 8, 1960.

[32] Christensen, "George Sverdrup, Teacher," 20.

[33] *Annual Report . . . LFC . . . 1956*, 35.

[34] Faculty Minutes, June 6, 1949.

[35] Board of Trustees Minutes, October 25, 1962.

[36] Interview with Karlis Ozolins, April 30, 1969.

[37] In 1953–54 the distribution was: 29 per cent LFC, 56 per cent other Lutheran, 15 per cent non-Lutheran. Eight years later, 26 per cent were LFC, 60 per cent were other Lutheran, 14 per cent were non-Lutheran. See *Annual Report . . . LFC . . . 1954*, 40; *1962*, 61.

[38] Faculty Minutes, February 27, 1958, May 19, 1965.

[39] *Augsburg Echo*, April 20, 1961.

[40] *Augsburg Echo*, March 25, 1954.

[41] *Augsburgian*, 1964, 28–29.

[42] Armacost, 1, 3.

[43] *Augsburg Echo*, April 22, 1964.

[44] *Augsburg Echo*, November 11, December 9, 1964; Faculty Minutes, December 2, 1964; *Augsburgian*, 1966, 166–175.

[45] *Annual Report . . . LFC . . . 1955*, 41.

[46] Board of Trustees Minutes, May 9, 1950. Christensen's statement was dated May 4, 1950.

[47] For an account of merger, see Eugene L. Fevold, *The Lutheran Free Church*, 272–302 (Minneapolis, 1969).

[48] *Annual Report . . . LFC . . . 1962*, 31; *Reports and Actions of the Second General Convention of the American Lutheran Church*, 286 (Minneapolis, 1964).

[49] Board of Trustees Minutes, October 13, 1958.

[50] *Augsburgian*, 1961, 100.

[51] *Augsburg Echo*, September 16, 1960.

[52] *Annual Report . . . LFC . . . 1961*, 40–41.

[53] *Annual Report . . . LFC . . . 1962*, 71.

[54] Board of Trustees Minutes, August 22, 1961.

[55] Board of Trustees, Executive Committee Minutes, November 20, 1961. The *Minneapolis Star* of November 24 carried the story of Nielsen's resignation.

[56] Board of Trustees Minutes, December 8, 1961.

[57] *Annual Report . . . LFC . . . 1962*, 58.

[58] *Augsburg Echo*, October 11, 1963.

[59] Faculty Minutes, February 3, March 3, 1965.

[60] "Report of the Faculty Study Committee on the Educational Program," 1956, 25.

[61] *Augsburg College Now*, April, 1969.

[62] See Kenneth Keniston, *Young Radicals: Notes on Committed Youth* (New York, 1968).

[63] Henry D. Aiken, "The Revolting Academy," *The New York Review of Books*, 35 (July 11, 1968).

[64] *Augsburg College Now*, April, 1969.

INDEX

INDEX